W9-DEC-125

WITHDRAWN

WITHDRAWN

ESSAYS ON VALUE AND DISTRIBUTION

By the same Author

    *ESSAY ON VALUE AND DISTRIBUTION

  **ESSAYS ON ECONOMIC STABILITY AND GROWTH

***ESSAYS ON ECONOMIC POLICY (*In Preparation*)

330.16
K12e

72831

HB
771
K2

BiP99

ESSAYS ON VALUE
AND DISTRIBUTION

by

NICHOLAS KALDOR

THE FREE PRESS OF GLENCOE, ILLINOIS

GOSHEN COLLEGE LIBRARY
GOSHEN, INDIANA

BCL

First published 1960
All rights reserved

© NICHOLAS KALDOR, 1960

Printed in the United States of America

CONTENTS

INTRODUCTION

THE essays collected in this volume belong to that general field of economic theory which is traditionally known as the "theory of value and distribution". They were written at scattered intervals extending well over twenty years, though the majority of them date from the 1930s and reflect the intellectual approach of economics in that period. The main characteristic of that approach, as was stated at the very beginning of the earliest of the papers reprinted here (written in 1933), is to seek insight into economic phenomena through "a more rigorous formulation of the conditions under which it is possible to make generalisations about the factors determining economic equilibrium", i.e., by exploring more thoroughly "the economics of that abstract world in which it is possible to give an exact account of the course of events solely by the aid of scientific generalisations", the latter being derived from "a few self-evident postulates alone". In the course of years I have become increasingly sceptical of the usefulness of the "static" approach of neo-classical economics, and if I were writing today, I would certainly not be so confident in asserting that in advancing along the path of increasing purity and generality, the micro-economics of the neo-classical school has *not* "lost its 'relevance to facts'," or has *not* "come increasingly to neglect the operation of those forces which 'really matter'." Though the implications of these particular essays are largely critical of that theory—since they concentrate on clarifying the rigid framework of assumptions necessary for validating its basic assertions—they do show an insufficient awareness of the fact that meaningful generalisations about the real world can only be reached as a result of empirical hypotheses, and not by *a priori* reasoning.

The essays are grouped according to their particular subject-matter—an arrangement which, with one or two exceptions, proved compatible with preserving the chronological order in which they were written. Except in a few instances in which subsequent work has shown the particular conclusions to have been erroneous or incomplete, the papers are printed (except for occasional improvements in grammar) without alteration; but wherever definite errors were found in the original presentation, an indication of this is given in a footnote or (in one instance) by giving a revised version in the text. All such additions or alterations are clearly shown by putting square brackets around the added or revised text.

The first essay is largely devoted to an analysis of the various meanings, or types of meanings, of the term "indeterminateness"—the range of problems which are nowadays discussed, at a more sophisticated mathematical level, under the terms of existence, uniqueness and stability of equilibrium—and it may continue to prove useful to students who require a guide to the different senses in which this term was employed by Walras, Edgeworth or Marshall, or the authors of the Austrian School. It is notable also for an early exposition of the "cobweb theorem", and for promoting the future popularity of that theorem by giving it its felicitous name (which occurred to me in the course of an oral exposition of that theorem at the L.S.E. seminar).

The second essay (written almost simultaneously with the first) poses an important question—i.e., what determines the *size* of the individual firm in long-run equilibrium? Orthodox theory postulates a U-shaped cost curve, which asserts that each firm has an "optimum size" beyond which it becomes progressively less efficient. But whereas the assumption of falling costs can be adequately supported on account of indivisibilities and economies of scale, to explain the upward-sloping part of the curve, reliance must be placed on the existence of diseconomies of large-scale organisation: a rather shadowy factor, which may be important in creating obstacles to fast rates of growth, but not to size as such. The very fact that the simultaneous existence of firms of vastly different sizes has become such a common feature of industry shows that diseconomies of large scale mangement cannot be an important limiting factor on *size*. Despite the considerable literature on this subject in the last twenty-five years, I cannot say that much of an advance has been made in understanding what determines the size-distribution of firms in any particular industry, or even that the implications of this question have yet been fully grasped.

The next group of essays is devoted to the subject of imperfect (or monopolistic) competition, brought into sudden prominence in the early 1930s by the appearance of two books on the subject by Joan Robinson and E. H. Chamberlin. The first three of these papers form a connected set of ideas which ought to be considered together: they express my protest against the excessive formalism of these theories built on notions of questionable validity (such as the notion of a "demand curve" confronting each particular firm) and using a technique that is apt to conceal the true complexity of the problems presented by competition in imperfect markets. The fourth essay on advertising (written considerably later) is of a somewhat different character: it was written as a preliminary memorandum for an enquiry (not subsequently carried out) into the effects of advertising on the organisation and efficiency of industry. One particular section of that paper (A Digression on Selling Costs, on pp. 130-135), belongs however to the general theory of monopolistic competition, and completes my criticism of Professor Chamberlin's theories. In the field covered by these four papers my views have changed very little; and though, if I were writing afresh, I would put some of the points rather differently and shift the emphasis given to some others, I would, on the whole, take up much the same position.

The two short notes on the subject of welfare economics are reproduced here mainly because each of them became the progenitor of an extensive literature. The note on welfare propositions and inter-personal comparisons of utility (originally published in the *Economic Journal* of September, 1939), introduced the idea of "compensation tests" as a means of differentiating policy measures which bring about an increase in aggregate real income from those which do not. This idea was subsequently taken up and developed by Professor Hicks and, following him, the proposition was subjected to a searching examination by a whole host of economists (including Scitovsky, Baumol, Little, Samuelson, Arrow, Graaf, Reder, Dobb and many others), until it became a veritable *cause célèbre* under the flattering title of the "New Welfare Economics". On re-reading the original note in the light of all this subsequent work (some of which, I must confess, I found too tedious to read and some of which was plainly beyond my comprehension), I still feel unrepentant in rejecting Professor Robbins' proposition that the impossibility of making inter-personal comparisons of utility puts an effective bar to "economics as a science saying anything by way of prescription". In the light of this subsequent work I feel, however, that it would have been wiser to have protected the "scientific status" of Ricardo, Cobden and the many other opponents of the Corn Laws by suggesting that in their capacity as "economists *qua* economists" they should have recommended that actual compensation be paid to the landlords (instead of sticking my neck out by suggesting, as it turned out somewhat unwisely, that the question whether compensation be actually paid or not could safely be left to the politicians). For none of the strictures of Scitovsky, Samuelson, Arrow, Little *et al.* against the validity or sufficiency of compensation tests alters the fact that repealing the Corn Laws *and* compensating the landlords was in every way a preferable alternative to leaving the Corn Laws "in being".

The second note on the "optimum tariff" was less deserving of fame since it was merely intended to rescue from oblivion a proposition originally put forward by Edgeworth and Bickerdike some thirty years earlier. In this purpose it proved remarkably successful, as the extensive post-war literature on the "optimum tariff" (by Scitovsky, Kahn, Johnson, Gorman, Graaf, Polak and others) testifies. No doubt (as so often happens in economics) the revival of interest in this question was greatly aided by the balance of payments problem of post-war Europe, and the need to demonstrate that any non-discriminatory method of dealing with this problem (by means of currency devaluations, for example) might have imposed additional losses through an (avoidable) deterioration in the terms of trade.

The long essay on the theory of capital is devoted to an examination of how much of the neo-classical theory of capital and interest survives the criticisms brought against it by Professor Knight and others. It is in this field that my position has shifted most since these papers were written. Though I was conscious of the numerous difficulties raised by the notion of capital as a factor of production (in particular the insoluble problem of how the *quantity* of capital is to be measured), I was still a firm believer in the view that the possibilities of substituting capital for labour through the use of different techniques of production had a critical rôle to play in the pricing process—that without it, we could not explain what determined the rate of profit (i.e., the rate of return on capital, as distinct from the rate of interest on money loans) or the division of the product between wages and profits. (This comes out more clearly, I think, from the subsequent "rejoinder" to Knight, reprinted as an Appendix to that essay, than from the essay itself.) It would be impossible within the context of this Introduction to set out the reasons which now lead me to reject the whole notion of a production function and the marginal productivity theory of distribution which is based on it—to do so would require a thorough exposition of my present views on technical progress and economic growth, and this I hope to do in a future work.[1] The critical point on which my present views differ radically from the views of my 1937 article is to be found in the sentence (printed on pp. 184-85 below) that "so long as the quantity of annual labour service remains constant with variations in

---

[1] Though an indication is given in the paper on economic growth in the *Economic Journal*, 1957, which is reprinted in the companion volume [*Essays on Economic Stability and Growth*, on pp. 264-270].

the quantity of capital, and so long as the quantity of no other type of services remains constant, *there will be a unique correlation between the rate of interest and the amount of labour input per unit of final output*" (italics added), i.e. between the rate of return on capital and the productivity of labour. I do *not* now believe that there is any such "unique correlation" and would assert, on the contrary, that knowing the output per head and the capital per head does not tell us anything about the rate of return (or of distributive shares) until we also know how productivity is rising over time, and in addition, we take *either* the level of wages in terms of output as given *or* the propensities to consume out of profits and wages respectively, as given. (I would still maintain, however, that acceptance or rejection of the proposition in the passage italicised is the critical dividing line between those who in some form or another adhere to the neo-classical theory, and those who reject it altogether.)

It should be noted, however, that in a final section of that article on the economics of a slave state (pp. 185-88), which was added more or less as an afterthought, I stumbled upon an alternative theory which I now regard as of far greater relevance—i.e. the proposition that the rate of return on capital is "the system's 'maximum rate of growth', the rate of which the stock of resources would increase, per unit of time, if consumption were reduced to zero and the services of all productive resources were devoted exclusively to their own production". (The maintenance cost of slaves was excluded from "consumption" in this context.) The theory put forward in these pages was, as I afterwards discovered, very analogous to the general equilibrium theory of von Neumann which was published in the following year[1] (though worked out considerably earlier). But in the context of my article it served only the purpose of demonstrating that, starting from an economy where all goods are capital goods and where the rate of interest reflects simply the net productivity of the whole system (its maximum potential rate of growth—which is the same thing as the Marxian notion of the excess of the goods produced in a period over the goods consumed in their production) it is still possible to arrive at the Böhm-Bawerk-Wicksellian theory by postulating that the slaves are "liberated" and the quantity of labour is treated as an independent variable. It is the latter derivation which I now think was erroneous if applied (as it was clearly intended to be applied ultimately, even if not as the first step)

[1] In a volume entitled *Ergebnisse eines mathematischen Seminars*, ed. K. Menger, Vienna, 1938; reprinted in English in the *Review of Economic Studies*, vol. XIII, 1945-46, p. 1.

to a growing (non-stationary) economy with technical progress.[1]

The last of the papers reprinted here on "Alternative Theories of Distribution" is separated from the preceding one on capital theory by an interval of eighteen years and fully reflects the change in my outlook (or, as I would prefer to regard it, my increased maturity) during that period. It presents a bird's eye comparison of the various approaches to the problem of distribution (in fact, I could equally well have said value-and-distribution) by the classical, neo-classical and neo-neo-classical theorists (if the latter term could justifiably be applied to the "degree of monopoly" and "full cost" theories which followed upon the new doctrines of imperfect competition). Its main defect, I think, lies in its extreme compression. It puts forward views that had been gradually evolved through the lecturing experience of many years, and telescopes them into a few pages—this is particularly true of the section on marginal productivity—whereas a convincing treatment would have required an exposition of many times that length. But its real aim was something even more ambitious: an attempt to integrate Keynesian macro-economics with value and distribution theory, and to show that the "classical" approach of Ricardo and Marx could in turn be regarded as a special case of the latter. I cannot claim that up to the present time I have succeeded in gaining many adherents to these rather radical views. (Most of the references in papers since published have been sceptical if not contemptuous.) Yet in the five years that have elapsed since it was written, I have become increasingly confident of the fruitfulness of this approach, which provides the basis of all my subsequent ideas on the economics of non-stationary states. But unfortunately, not only economic states, but also ideas, are non-stationary; and a final systematic presentation of them must be left to some future occasion when I can feel confident that the growth of "growth models" itself approaches a state of stable equilibrium.

One of the problems besetting an author who wishes to reprint essays published over a long run of years is to decide how to deal with appellations that are no longer appropriate. Economists seem peculiarily prone to undergo a bewildering change of titles: plain Misters become Professors (or sometimes in reverse), or else become knighted, and finally (the most distinguished of them) become Lords. Some, alas, are no longer referred to by any kind of title. It would have been useless

---

[1] For all these reasons my present views on capital theory are far closer, I suppose, to Knight's 1935 views than would appear from these papers; but I hesitate to say this, since I do not suppose that Professor Knight would find my present views any more to his liking than those of Böhm-Bawerk and the Austrians.

to revise all these appellations in the light of what is appropriate at the present moment, since these, in turn, might become out of date, possibly before the present volume was out in print. The best course appeared to be to stick to the original appellations of the essays, thus preserving a period flavour.

It remains to express my thanks for permission to reprint to the various journals in which the papers originally appeared, the names of which are given in a footnote at the beginning of each essay. Finally I should also like to express my very great debt to Mr. Hugh R. Hudson, formerly of King's College, Cambridge, and now of the University of Adelaide, who undertook the arduous task of preparing these papers for publication and seeing the book, in its various stages, through the press. He has helped me considerably in the selection of passages that needed to be revised, as well as in their actual revision, and also in detecting numerous typographical or grammatical errors or inconsistencies which appeared in their original form. He is also responsible for the preparation of the authors' index, at the end of the volume. I am, however, to be held solely responsible for any errors, major or minor, which remain.

NICHOLAS KALDOR

KING'S COLLEGE, CAMBRIDGE
January 1960

Part I

THE THEORY OF EQUILIBRIUM

THE DETERMINATENESS OF STATIC EQUILIBRIUM[1]

A MORE rigorous formulation of the conditions under which it is possible to make generalisations about the factors determining economic equilibrium may be regarded as one of the main achievements of theoretical development during the last fifty years. The growing realisation both of the difficulties confronting the use of the analytical method and of the usefulness of its application have led to a gradual "purification" of theory; to a more and more precise statement of the conditions under which its generalisations can be applied.

Hence the evolution of "static" theory: the economics of that abstract world in which it is possible to give an exact account of the course of events solely by the aid of scientific generalisations. Hence, also, the concept of a "determinate" equilibrium: an equilibrium whose nature can be rigorously determined from a few self-evident postulates alone. All this has helped, of course, to make economics more technical and incomprehensible to the layman; but no one who studies it seriously would maintain that in advancing along this path economics has gradually lost its "relevance to facts"; or that economists, in their anxiety to preserve the validity of their "laws" have come increasingly to neglect the operation of those forces which "really matter". For in any analytical study, forces whose laws of operation are known must clearly be separated from others in whose behaviour no such "uniform principles" have yet been detected; and the only satisfactory way to detect and account for the influence of the latter in the real world is by assuming them away and examining what events would be like in their absence. It is, moreover, only by employing this "method of difference" that we can hope gradually to extend the range of phenomena over which we can make generalisations.

The assumptions of static theory are, therefore, nothing else than the conditions necessary to make equilibrium "determinate":

[1] Originally published in *Review of Economic Studies*, February, 1934.

the conditions under which we can give a scientifically precise description of the actual course of economic phenomena. Once these assumptions have been specified and have gained general acceptance as the limits within which deductive speculation must proceed, any new elements subsequently discovered which play a rôle in shaping the course of events are likely to be put down as "causes of indeterminateness", since the human mind finds it easier to alter the conclusions arrived at within an accepted framework, than to alter the framework itself. Whenever, therefore, new causes of "indeterminateness" are said to be detected this is merely another way of saying that a new set of determining forces has been found: forces whose behaviour and manner had not hitherto been reducible to uniformities and whose influence must therefore also be assumed absent if the existing body of generalisations is to be regarded as valid. Once the existence of these additional forces has been incorporated in the main body of assumptions, the "indeterminateness" disappears (it has been buried in the assumptions) and the "abstractness" of pure theory has advanced one stage farther.

All this is clearly in accord with the main canons of scientific analysis; it is the only possible procedure to adopt if we aim at a clarification of the intricate inter-relationship of events by investigating the causal sequence of phenomena.

The assumptions under which modern economics has found it possible to determine the position of equilibrium from the "system of data" (a set of independent variables whose behaviour can be described by a "law", i.e. by a uniform principle) namely, the utility functions of individuals and the production functions of goods, are the following:

1. A closed economy (either an isolated individual or a completely self-sufficient community, with a given volume of human and natural resources).
2. "Perfect knowledge": all the relevant prices quoted in all markets are known to all individuals.
3. "Perfect competition": all exchanges are carried out in markets so large that no individual can influence any of the prices with which he is confronted.

4. "Direct exchange": all goods, services, etc., are exchanged directly for one another, while all prices are expressed in one of the goods serving as a unit of account.

Finally, if account is taken of the time-dimension, i.e. of the fact that all economic phenomena take place in time, some additional assumptions have to be introduced, regarding (i) the behaviour of the independent variables, the data, in time; (ii) people's expectation of this behaviour or, more precisely, people's expectation of the future course of prices. The simplest assumptions in these respects and those which have been implicit in static analysis are the following:

5. All independent variables remain constant through time.
6. All individuals expect the prices actually ruling to remain in force permanently: no price-changes are anticipated.[1]

These assumptions we may thus regard as the "accepted framework" of static theory:[2] and it is the sufficiency of this framework which is, in fact, contested when the "determinateness" of equilibrium is called into question. Investigations of such "causes" of indeterminateness have become only too frequent in recent theoretical literature; though in many cases no clear formulation has been given of the conditions which would cover them, i.e. the precise change of framework which they necessitate. The following note attempts to remedy for this deficiency and, by classifying the various "causes", at the same time to clear up the confusion which has arisen over the concept of indeterminateness itself. We shall make the above enumerated assumptions as the

[1] Just because the dependence of equilibrium on anticipations is not always clearly realised, this assumption is hardly ever expressly stated although it is inherent in any type of static analysis which aims at demonstrating the tendency towards equilibrium independently of the degree of foresight. The only alternative assumption consistent with the degree of abstractness necessary for the generalisations of pure theory would be the assumption of *complete foresight*: that everybody foresees correctly the future course of prices. In this latter case, however, there is no need to assume constancy of the independent variables in order to show the determinateness of equilibrium: and consequently this latter assumption can be more conveniently adopted as the basis of "dynamic" as distinct from a "static" type of analysis. Cf. Hicks, "Gleichgewicht und Konjunktur," *Zeitschrift für Nationalökonomie*, Vol. IV, No. 4.

[2] Or rather a rough summary of them; a precise enumeration would have to include assumptions in regard to the legal system (e.g. the institution of private property, the freedom and sanctity of contract) and a number of other things which, though essential for other purposes, are irrelevant to the following analysis.

"accepted framework" of static theory, our starting-point, ignoring consequently all those complications (such as indeterminacy due to the use of money or the absence of perfect competition) which were eliminated by them and with which static theory in general is not directly concerned.

I

The objections which have been raised concerning the sufficiency of static analysis can be summarised under three main headings:

(i) It has been pointed out that static analysis only succeeds in deriving the *conditions of equilibrium* from its "system of data", but not the *position of equilibrium*; i.e. it can point to a system of prices which, *if established*, would secure equilibrium, but it cannot determine the system of prices which will actually be in operation once equilibrium has been established. For the mere fact that there is, in any given situation, at least one system of prices which, if established, would secure equilibrium, does not imply that this particular set of prices will also be put into operation immediately; and if any other set of prices is established, not only will further price-changes become necessary, but the equilibrium system of prices (i.e. that particular set of prices which does *not* necessitate further changes in prices) will itself be a different one. It is not possible, therefore, to determine the position of equilibrium from a given system of data, since every successive step taken in order to reach equilibrium will alter the conditions of equilibrium (the set of prices capable of bringing it about) and thus change the final position—unless the conditions are such that either (1) an equilibrium system of prices *will* be established immediately, or (2) the set of prices actually established leaves the conditions of equilibrium unaffected (in which case the final position will be independent of the route followed).

(ii) An altogether different type of objection is that the system of data may itself be of such a nature as to admit of *more than one* position of determinate equilibrium from a given situation, i.e. that there may be more than one system of prices capable of securing equilibrium. This objection refers to the problem whether the *conditions* of equilibrium (as already defined) are unequivocally determined by the data or not; and arises, therefore, also in those cases—moreover, it only becomes important in those cases—where the position of equilibrium is otherwise determinate (*i.e.* where from the conditions of equilibrium we can derive the equilibrium position).

(iii) Finally, it has been pointed out that not only may equilibrium be "indeterminate" (in the sense that the process of adjustment itself alters the conditions of equilibrium), but that furthermore, if the various forces do not react instantaneously on the incentive of price changes, the economic system need not tend towards a position of equilibrium at all. The successive alterations of prices will then merely represent a constant or an expanding range of fluctuations.

We shall examine these objections in turn by enumerating, in each case, the conditions which are necessary to make them inoperative (or in the absence of which they would be operative). We shall call an equilibrium "determinate" or "indeterminate" according as the final position is independent of the route followed, or not;[1] we shall call equilibrium "unique" or "multiple" according as there is one, or more than one, system of equilibrium-prices, corresponding to a given set of data; and, finally, we shall speak of "definite" or "indefinite"[2, 3] equilibria, according as the actual situation tends to approximate a position of equilibrium or not.[4]

[1] In using the word "indeterminateness" in this sense we are merely following traditional terminology, since this is the sense in which both Marshall and Edgeworth have employed the term. Since, however, both had demonstrated it in the example of a barter-exchange, this type of indeterminateness is often associated with the absence of perfect competition though, as we shall see below, it is not really eliminated by any of the customary definitions of a "perfect market".

[2] It is questionable how far the term "equilibrium" is justified in connection with "indefiniteness", i.e. divergent fluctuations which do not lead to a position of equilibrium at all. The main reason for employing the term "indefinite" in the present paper—as will be apparent to the reader—is to preserve the symmetry of the classification.

[3] We shall use the terms "indefiniteness" and "instability" interchangeably in the last section of this paper, just because neither of these expressions conveys with sufficient precision the meaning desired. The word "unstable" would really be more suitable than "indefinite", but for the fact that it is generally used in a different sense—to denote a "passing equality of supply and demand" which does not represent equilibrium (when, for example, a "forward falling" supply curve cuts the demand curve from above—this is the sense in which Walras and Marshall use the term) or a "minimum" rather than a "maximum" position (see p. 25 below).

[4] The relations between determinate and indeterminate (definite and indefinite) equilibria can be illustrated on the diagram on next page. Let us assume there are only two price system; then the price system will consist of only one price (one exchange-ratio). Let us measure this price on the vertical axis and let us measure time on the horizontal axis, t_0 being the "base period", the starting-point of the investigation. Then the

B

Since the problem of "multiple equilibria" only becomes of interest, if the position of equilibrium is otherwise determinate, while the problem of "indefiniteness" only arises in cases where equilibrium is indeterminate, we shall first examine the conditions necessary to make equilibrium determinate; then the conditions under which this determinate equilibrium will also be "unique"; and finally the conditions under which an indeterminate equilibrium will be definite.

II

(*a*) Since the "indeterminateness" of equilibrium[1] on the above definition can only arise through the disturbing influence of intermediary situations, equilibrium will always be determinate, if the position of equilibrium is *immediately* reached. This implies the presence of certain conditions which will vary according to the nature of the general situation contemplated:

line A will represent the condition of equilibrium at t_0; it will also represent the conditions of equilibrium at any other point of time, if equilibrium is determinate; and it will represent the position of equilibrium from t_0 onwards, if the equilibrium is "established immediately". Curve B represents the actual course of prices in case

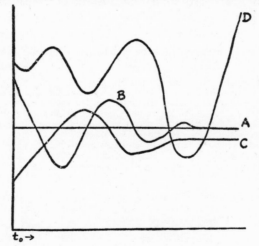

FIG. 1

equilibrium is determinate, but "not immediately reached"; curve C the case of an indeterminate but definite equilibrium; while curve D the case of an indefinite equilibrium. The case of "multiple equilibria" (not shown in the diagram) could be represented by the presence of several A lines.

[1] The word "equilibrium" is always used in this article in the sense of a "full equilibrium", as meaning the "long-period equilibrium" of Marshall.

α. In the case of the isolated individual we must assume either that Robinson Crusoe possesses "full experience" before he undertakes any economic activity and thus starts his activities with an equilibrium system of dispositions; or else that he accidentally places himself at the very beginning in such a situation that every successive acquisition of experience merely serves to confirm him in his existing dispositions, but does not induce him to change these dispositions. (The word experience merely relates to Crusoe's knowledge of his own tastes and preferences and his knowledge of environmental conditions. It excludes any accumulation of knowledge which represents a change in the technical terms at which he can obtain various things.)

β. In the case of the closed community we must have in addition to full experience on everybody's part (i.e. full knowledge of all individuals in regard to their own tastes and abilities)[1] the condition that *all* exchange transactions will be undertaken at the *same* system of prices.[2, 3] This will be the case if either:

(i) Buyers and sellers, meeting simultaneously in the market, go on "crying" prices, revising and re-revising their list of offers, but not entering into any actual exchange, until they hit upon a system of prices which secures equilibrium for everybody and in all parts of the market (Walras' assumption)[4]; or

(ii) buyers and sellers, knowing that all sellers can re-contract with all the buyers, and vice versa, make only *provisional* contracts until a system of prices is reached where no re-contracts could be made with advantage to all the re-contracting parties. (Edgeworth's assumption.[5])

[1] Which is something more than what we already assumed under "perfect knowledge": namely that all individuals know all the relevant prices quoted in the market.

[2] Since under a given "constellation" of data, there will be one system of prices only at which *all* transactions can be concluded (as any other price system will necessitate further transactions at *different* prices) this is merely another way of saying that the process of exchange should *start* at equilibrium prices.

[3] This was first explicitly stated by Jevons. He erroneously assumed, however, that the realisation of this condition follows from his own "Law of Indifference": namely that there can be only one price in one market at the same time. Cf. *Theory of Political Economy*, 4th ed., p. 94.

[4] *Elements*, 6th ed., pp. 129-30.

[5] *Mathematical Psychics*, pp. 17, 35 ff., Appendix IV. Also *Papers*, Vol. II, pp. 311-12.

Both these assumptions come to much the same thing; they should both be considered as attempts to formulate the conditions under which buyers and sellers are able to find out the true "equilibrium price" *before* they undertake any exchange activity—but Edgeworth also thought that this state of affairs followed from the "principle of re-contract" and is thus a property of "perfect competition". Whether it is so considered or not is irrelevant, so long as it is made clear that this is *not* the same thing as either the condition (*a*) that prices should be given to all individuals (that no individual should be able to influence, by his own actions, the prices of the market), or (*b*) that there should be "perfect intercommunication" and thus only one price for the same good *at the same time*—both of which are used as definitions of a "perfect market". While Edgeworth's analysis may be slightly obscure and Walras' assumption slightly ridiculous, the main idea stands clear: in a really perfect market (in a market which is sufficiently perfect to make equilibrium determinate) it is not by trial and error that prices are established; in so far as there is any initial higgling and bargaining this should be done by playing with chips and not with hard cash (by making only provisional and not final or irrevocable contracts). The formation of prices must *precede* the process of exchange and not be the result of it.[1]

(*b*) Equilibrium will be determinate, however, even if it is only gradually established, so long as the position of equilibrium is independent of the actual path followed:

α. This will be true for Robinson Crusoe, if his system of data (his tastes and obstacles), in any one period of time is not affected by his actions in the previous period. It must either be assumed that there is no carry-over of goods from one period to the next, or that there is a constant carry-over; and that his effective scale of preferences in any one period of time is unaffected by his want-satisfying activities in the previous period.[2] Then at the beginning of every period Crusoe is confronted with the same initial situation; his only inheritance from the past is his gradually accumulated

---

[1] The only (otherwise imperfect) market in the real world where this condition is fulfilled is the auction-sale.

[2] The actual length of time chosen as the time unit is irrelevant so long as there is a *definite period of time* for which the above conditions are satisfied and we are only interested in the total of his activities for that period.

experience. We can assume that he has no experience at the beginning; his initial actions will then be accidental or "irrational"; but the gradual accumulation of experience will lead him, through a process of relative valuation, to a gradual change of his daily dispositions until he reaches a situation where no further accumulation of experience will induce him to change his dispositions any further—so long as the initial data (the independent variables) remain unchanged. It can then be shown that this final position will be the same as the one he might have reached at the beginning if, by some accident, he placed himself in equilibrium straight away; in other words, that corresponding to a given set of data, there is always at least one system of dispositions which would merely be confirmed, not altered, by the gradual accumulation of experience.

It seems to be this problem of the effects of experience with which the "causal-genetic approach" of the Austrian School has been mainly concerned.[1] The aim of the latter is to exhibit, not so much the conditions of equilibrium under a given situation (the task assumed by the "functional" theories), but to show how, in a given situation, a position of equilibrium is reached—the problem of how prices come into being rather than what system of prices will secure equilibrium. It is, however, only under our present very rigid assumptions that a causal-genetic theory can reach the same conclusions concerning the nature of equilibrium as are evolved, by using a different method, by the "functional" theories. In the absence of these conditions it is only by means of a "theory of the path" (a theory showing what determines the actual path followed) that a causal-genetic approach can arrive at generalisations concerning the nature of equilibrium—and such a theory has not hitherto been forthcoming, although the necessity for it has frequently been emphasised by writers of the Austrian School.

β. For the closed community, substantially the same conditions will be required as in the case of Crusoe: that tastes and obstacles, on each day, for everybody, should be unaffected by the events of the previous day. It is here, however, that Marshall's famous

---

[1] Cf. especially, Hans Mayer, *Der Erkenntniswert der funktionellen Preistheorien, Wirtschaftstheorie der Gegenwart*, Vol. II, *passim*.

assumption[1] of the constancy in all exchanges of the marginal utility of one of the goods exchanged, must be introduced. Unless the "marginal utility of money" is constant, the condition of "no-carry-over" is insufficient in itself to secure determinateness *within any one period*, if exchanges do not begin at equilibrium prices. For the mere fact that with the gradual accumulation of experience everybody moves towards an equilibrium system of *individual* dispositions will not necessarily bring about a tendency towards a "continuous equilibrium" in the *market* situation: i.e. the market will not necessarily acquire an ability to hit upon the equilibrium prices at the beginning of each period. If it does not, it is only under Marshall's assumption that the final rates of exchange will be independent of the terms on which the first exchanges were made.[2]

Further reflection shows, however, that the necessity for introducing this condition depends on the interpretation of the words "gradual accumulation of experience". If we assume that individuals accumulate experience relating not only to their own system of data but also to the tastes and obstacles of others, they will gradually acquire an ability to judge the equilibrium prices of a given market;[3] and, therefore, the proportion of the total amount exchanged, within any period, which will be exchanged at the "final rates of exchange" will continuously grow until it equals the whole—since it will then be in the long-run interest of

[1] *Principles*, esp. Appendix F. Marshall's assumption is generally classed as an alternative to Walras' and Edgeworth's; which in a sense it is. From our point of view, however, the one tries to formulate the circumstances in which all exchanges will be concluded at the *same* price; while the other tries to demonstrate how equilibrium can be determinate *without* this condition being fulfilled. (The value of Marshall's analysis consists in showing that in a large number of cases—where only a small part of an individual's resources are spent on the commodity in question—the indeterminacy introduced by this case is not likely to be very important.)

[2] There is, of course, no inconsistency between our initial assumption of "direct exchange" (absence of money as a medium of exchange) and the assumption of a constant marginal utility of "money". For the validity of Marshall's assumption is not dependent upon the use of money, as is often mistakenly assumed (an error for which Marshall himself is partly responsible) but upon the question whether the single commodity does or does not "use up" a considerable proportion of our total resources. Nor is there any need to assume either the "measurability" or the "independence" of utilities in order to attach a precise meaning to Marshall's notion. (Cf. Hicks, "A Reconsideration of the Theory of Value", *Economica*, February, 1934, p. 64, for the expression of this condition in terms of the modern, "relative-utility" analysis.)

[3] In our view, it is the absence of any need for this sort of knowledge, and not the absence of inter-personal exchange as such, which explains why the sort of difficulty which Marshall's fiction attempts to eliminate does not arise in the case of Crusoe.

every individual that he should make as many exchanges as possible at equilibrium prices.[1]

It may be objected, however, that this alternative assumption—that individuals will be able to judge equilibrium prices before any transactions are made—is inconsistent with one of our initial assumptions since it means that they are influenced by expected future prices rather than by prices already ruling. It all depends on how rigidly this assumption is interpreted, and it can easily be shown that under our present assumption of a "constant carry-over" a *very rigid* interpretation would lead, by a different route, to the same result. For a rigid interpretation in this case would imply that the final rate of exchange on any day is generally expected to be the ruling price of the following day—which means that it would *become* the initial rate of that day. Now, it follows from Marshall's analysis (in the Appendix on Barter), that though the final rate will always deviate from the true equilibrium price, if the latter is not hit upon at the beginning, it *can never deviate so much* as the initial rate;[2] i.e. prices must move *towards* the true equilibrium price during the day. Consequently, if the final rate of Day One always becomes the initial rate of Day Two, then the final rate of Day Two will show less deviation from the true equilibrium rate than the final rate on Day One. On successive days, therefore, the deviation will become less and less until it finally disappears (or as we stated it above, the proportion of the total transactions made at the final rate of exchange on any day will become greater and greater on successive days). This leaves the condition of a "constant carry-over" (which implies that the conditions of supply and demand on any day should be the same as those on every other day) as the sole condition of determinateness, under our static assumptions.

III

This closes our investigation of the conditions under which the position of equilibrium is determinate. We must next enquire under

---

[1] On this point cf. Wicksteed's analysis in *Common Sense of Political Economy*, Vol. I, Chapter VI, pp. 219-26.

[2] Except in the case where one of the goods has no "marginal utility" at all to one of the parties, and thus the market-supply of that good, as distinct from the volume available, is "fixed".

what conditions this position will be "unique", i.e. what are the possibilities of *multiple* positions of determinate equilibrium?

(i) Hitherto we have tacitly assumed that the nature of the initial data is such that they yield what might be called "normal-shaped" basic curves.[1] The principle of an "increasing marginal rate of substitution"[2] being applicable to both utility and production functions, psychological indifference curves will be convex downwards throughout, while the production indifference curve will be concave downwards throughout. Under these conditions there is only one equilibrium position possible for Robinson Crusoe, and normally there will be only one position of equilibrium for the community as a whole. In the case of the community, however, the possibility of multiple equilibria is never completely eliminated thereby. For if the owners of resources have *any* demand for the use of their own resources (if these resources represent a "good" in their own utility functions), the supply curve for such resources (which is the owners' aggregate demand curve for all other resources) must turn backwards at a certain price; and then there is always a possibility that this "backward-rising" supply curve should cut the demand curve in more than one, and so at least in three, points.[3] This is Walras' well-known case of multiple equilibria,[4] and the assumption necessary to eliminate it as a possibility is that the owners should have no *immediate* use for their own resources, i.e. that not only the volume of resources available but also the market supply of those resources should be a given quantity.

A similar case of multiple equilibria which is compatible with the assumption of normal-shaped utility and production functions, is the case of a "backward-falling" demand curve—when the elasticity of the demand curve becomes zero, and then negative, *before* the price reaches zero. It then also becomes possible for this

---

[1] We use the expression "basic curves" for curves denoting the properties of the basic utility and production functions; as distinct from the "derived curves" (such as the supply and demand curves) which are derived from those functions and from the actual quantitative magnitudes in each individual's initial possession.

[2] Cf. Hicks, "A Reconsideration of the Theory of Value", *Economica*, February, 1934, p. 55.

[3] One of these points must be "unstable" (in the Marshallian sense) representing merely a "passing equality of supply and demand", but not equilibrium. The first and the third points will be stable, however, i.e. these will be real equilibrium positions.

[4] *Elements*, 6th ed., pp. 68-70. Also Wicksell, *Über Wert Kapital und Rente*, pp. 61 ff.

backward-falling demand curve to cut the supply curve in more than one, and so at least in three, points. But since backward-falling demand curves (unlike the backward-rising supply curves) only occur in very rare cases,[1] this case of multiple equilibria should not be regarded as more than a curiosum.

(ii) We may assume, however, that the basic curves are not "normal-shaped", i.e. either (*a*) that the principle of an increasing marginal rate of substitution does not obtain for either the utility or the production functions *throughout* (as a general rule) or (*b*) that this principle, for one or the other of these functions, does not obtain *at all*.

In the second case (*b*), clearly no equilibrium is possible. If either the psychological indifference curves are concave throughout or the production indifference curve convex throughout, an "equilibrium position" (characterised by the parallelism of the tangents of these curves) could at best be regarded as a position of minimum satisfaction but not a position of maximum satisfaction.[2]

The situation, however, is different if the condition of convexity and concavity, respectively, is only partially broken. Here we shall limit ourselves to the case where the production indifference curve is thus "queer-shaped": since the consideration of the other case (where the psychological indifference curves are aberrant) is both more complex and of much more dubious significance.

A production indifference curve[3] in which sections of concavity are interspersed with sections of convexity always involves multiple equilibria, in the sense that there is always more than one point at which the tangent of this curve is parallel to the tangents of the psychological indifference curves. In the terms of the Marshallian, particular equilibrium analysis, the multiple equilibria in this case are due to "forward-falling", as distinct

[1] Cf. Hicks, *op. cit.*, p. 68, for the conditions necessary for a backward-falling demand curve (in his terminology, a rising demand curve).

[2] *Ibid.*, p. 57.

[3] The term is not really suitable (since it implies an "indifference" which in this case has no meaning) and has only been chosen to emphasise the fact that it is a counterpart to the psychological indifference curves. It has also been called the "curve of obstacles" or the "co-efficient of transformation", neither of which is more attractive than the one given in the text. What the curve really shows is the technical rate of substitution between various goods at the margin, under varying distributions of production.

from "backward-rising", supply curves.[1] But whereas backward-rising supply curves merely involve the possibility, but not the necessity, of multiple equilibria, in the case of forward-falling supply curves multiple equilibria will always be present,[2] i.e. there will always be more than one arrangement which satisfies the conditions of equilibrium. This, however, cannot be shown with the aid of the particular equilibrium analysis, since the position of the demand curves will be different in the alternative situations.

If, however, the situation is one where equilibrium is reached immediately (case (*a*) above), normally only one of these positions will be a true position of equilibrium, since one of these points will be generally preferred to all the others. Only if the production indifference curve becomes tangential at more than one point to the *same* indifference curve (and this condition has not much sense in the case of the community!) will it be a true case of multiple equilibria.[3]

If, however, the position is only gradually reached (case (*b*) above), the possibility of multiple equilibria will always be present whenever the production curve has more than one peak (irrespective of whether these peaks touch the same indifference curve or not) because once a start has been made along one road there will be no tendency to reverse the route even if the peak towards which another road is leading is higher. In these cases, therefore, multiple equilibria will always be present whenever there are states of increasing returns to single industries, i.e. whenever there are stages of diminishing technical marginal rates of substitution. In these cases, therefore, the final situation will be "indeterminate" in the sense that it will depend upon the direction which happens to be adopted initially; though equilibrium may still be

---

[1] Similarly it could be shown that "queer-shaped" psychological indifference curves yield "forward-rising" as distinct from "backward-falling" demand curves. The terms "backward-rising", "forward-falling" and "forward-rising", "backward falling," respectively, are taken from Mr. Kahn (*Review of Economic Studies*, Vol. I, No. 1, pp. 71 ff).

[2] Except in cases where the psychological indifference curves are not asymptotic to the axes but turn away from them after a certain point. In this case multiple equilibria do not necessarily follow from queer-shaped production curves.

[3] It will, of course, be equally true in cases where the multiple equilibria are due to "backward-rising" supply curves, that in so far as one of these positions is preferred to the others, only one of them will be a "true position" in cases where "equilibrium is reached immediately".

determinate on our definition of the term, since all the possible equilibrium positions may still be deduced from the data of the initial situation.

IV

If, however, the conditions enumerated above in Section II, under (*a*) and (*b*), are not satisfied, equilibrium will always be indeterminate, as the successive moves undertaken in order to reach equilibrium will influence the nature of the final position. The situation, of course, may still be one which is tending towards an equilibrium, i.e. towards a system of prices which in the absence of independent changes, will maintain itself indefinitely; but the point at which price-movements ultimately come to rest can no longer be deduced from the data of the initial situation.

The question which we now have to answer is whether this will be necessarily so; whether, if the equilibrium system of prices is not put in operation immediately, the succeeding price-changes will necessarily end up in reaching some equilibrium position.

As we have already pointed out, it follows from Marshall's analysis that if the initial price differs from the true equilibrium price, changes will become necessary (a further set of transactions will take place at a different price); but these price-changes will always be in the *direction* of the equilibrium price and there will always be some final price which "brings about equilibrium", i.e. which puts an end to the process of exchange. This, however, relates to the case of "market equilibrium", i.e. to a given period of time in which there are a given volume of goods available and given wants to be satisfied. When we were dealing with "long-period normal equilibrium", however (i.e. given rates of supply of the ultimate resources, and given structure of wants recurring in every period), we were assuming a "constant carry-over" from one period to the next, and thus postulated the same initial situation at the beginning of every period.

This assumption of a "constant carry-over" conceals another assumption (which it includes, but with which it is not identical), namely that the quantities (demanded and supplied) react instantaneously on price changes; since if the quantitative reaction to a certain price change of a certain "day" only takes place on the length of the time-lags—is the same on the demand side as on the supply side. In the following analysis we shall treat only these two cases of complete discontinuity and continuity.

I. Where the adjustments are completely discontinuous, stability (or "definiteness") of equilibrium will depend on the relative elasticities of demand and supply; according to what may be called "the cobweb theorem" of Professor Henry Schultz and Professor U. Ricci.[1]

Let us assume that a shift in demand from DD to $D'D'$ changes the price from P to P_1, which is not an equilibrium price, since

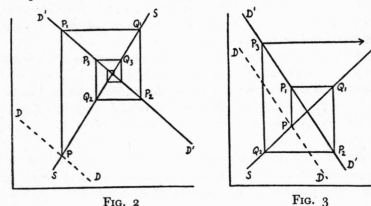

FIG. 2   FIG. 3

the true long run supply corresponding to this price is Q_1. After a time, depending on the adjustment period, supply will therefore change to Q_1, and price will then change from P_1 to P_2.[2]

---

[1] Schultz, *Der Sinn der statistischen Nachfragekurven*, p. 34, and Ricci, "Die synthetische Ökonomie von Henry Ludwell Moore", *Zeitschrift für Nationalökonomie*, 1930, p. 649. It is evident that this theorem is only applicable to cases of "completely discontinuous adjustments", or to the case (which Professor Schultz had in mind) where adjustments are completely discontinuous on the side of supply and instantaneous on the side of demand.

[2] Under our present assumptions that ruling prices are always expected to remain in operation, and thus no stocks for future sale will be carried, the price-reaction to changes in supply must always be instantaneous; since we can either assume that (1) *demand* reacts instantaneously to price-changes, in which case price will also react instantaneously to changes in supply: or (2) that demand-reactions take time, in which case the *immediate price-reaction* to changes in supply will be greater than the ultimate price-reaction. Under the assumption that adjustments are completely discontinuous, the slowness of demand-reactions to price-changes manifests itself in reducing the elasticity of the demand curve, and thus alters the situation in the direction of instability—since the relevant demand curve is the one which shows the amounts taken at various prices *immediately* after the (rate of) supply has changed. Whether the true (long period) demand curve will then have any relevance or not,

determinate on our definition of the term, since all the possible equilibrium positions may still be deduced from the data of the initial situation.

IV

If, however, the conditions enumerated above in Section II, under (*a*) and (*b*), are not satisfied, equilibrium will always be indeterminate, as the successive moves undertaken in order to reach equilibrium will influence the nature of the final position. The situation, of course, may still be one which is tending towards an equilibrium, i.e. towards a system of prices which in the absence of independent changes, will maintain itself indefinitely; but the point at which price-movements ultimately come to rest can no longer be deduced from the data of the initial situation.

The question which we now have to answer is whether this will be necessarily so; whether, if the equilibrium system of prices is not put in operation immediately, the succeeding price-changes will necessarily end up in reaching some equilibrium position.

As we have already pointed out, it follows from Marshall's analysis that if the initial price differs from the true equilibrium price, changes will become necessary (a further set of transactions will take place at a different price); but these price-changes will always be in the *direction* of the equilibrium price and there will always be some final price which "brings about equilibrium", i.e. which puts an end to the process of exchange. This, however, relates to the case of "market equilibrium", i.e. to a given period of time in which there are a given volume of goods available and given wants to be satisfied. When we were dealing with "long-period normal equilibrium", however (i.e. given rates of supply of the ultimate resources, and given structure of wants recurring in every period), we were assuming a "constant carry-over" from one period to the next, and thus postulated the same initial situation at the beginning of every period.

This assumption of a "constant carry-over" conceals another assumption (which it includes, but with which it is not identical), namely that the quantities (demanded and supplied) react instantaneously on price changes; since if the quantitative reaction to a certain price change of a certain "day" only takes place on the next day or the day after, we can no longer postulate the same initial situation at the beginning of every day. This problem of the time-lag between quantitative and price-changes does not arise, therefore, at that stage of the enquiry. It must be examined, however, as soon as the assumption of a "constant carry-over" is dropped. And once allowance is made for the fact that in the real world functional adjustments take time and different forces in the system may operate with different velocities of adjustment, it may become possible to construct cases—*under the assumption that ruling prices are always expected to remain in operation*, which is assumed throughout the present article—where the successive reactions lead away from, rather than approach, an equilibrium position.[1]

The question, therefore, whether in any given case, equilibrium will be "definite" or "indefinite" (i.e. whether it will be approximated to or not) appears to depend on the velocities of adjustment of the factors operating in the system. It is this factor, therefore, which we have to examine in some detail.

The "velocity of adjustment" may be alternatively defined as the time required for a full quantitative adjustment to take place (either on the supply side or on the demand side) corresponding to a given price-change[2]—i.e. the time elapsing between the establishment of a certain price and the full quantitative adjustment to that price—or the rate at which the quantities (demanded or supplied) change per unit of time in response to price-changes. (The first may conveniently be termed the "adjustment period", and the second the "unit-velocity" of adjustment.) Given this rate (the unit-velocity), given the magnitude of the initial price-change and given the elasticities of the curves,[3] the time required

---

[1] On the place of the factor "velocity of adjustment" in the general theory of equilibrium, cf. Rosenstein-Rodan, "Das Zeitmoment in der mathematischen Theorie des wirtschaftlichen Gleichgewichtes", *Zeitschrift für Nationalökonomie*, Vol. I, No. 1. Also, "The Rôle of Time in Economic Theory", *Economica*, February, 1934. Cf. also Fasiani, *Velocita delle variazione della demanda e dell' offerta e punti di equilibrio stabile e instabile*, *Atti della R. Acad. de scienze di Torino*, 1932.

[2] Which is not the same thing as the reaction of price to an initial change in supply or demand. (Cf. Rosenstein-Rodan, *op. cit.*, p. 89.) But since these latter velocities, although different from, yet depend on the velocities of the quantity reactions to initial price-changes (the velocity of price-reactions to supply-changes being the reciprocal of the velocity of demand-reactions to price-changes and vice versa), they are not separately treated in the present analysis. Cf. also p. 30 note 2 below.

[3] By elasticities we mean here the elasticities of "long-period-curves", i.e. curves showing the quantities supplied or demanded, per unit of time, corresponding to each price, after *all* adjustments have been made to that price.

for full adjustment (the adjustment period) will also be determined. Allowance should be made, however, for the possibility that these unit-velocities may themselves be interdependent—i.e. the rate at which quantities change per unit of time may itself depend on the magnitude of the initial price-change.

An analysis which makes full allowance for all these factors would necessarily be very complex. We can simplify it considerably, however, by making certain assumptions. We may either assume that the unit-velocity is always the same, whatever the magnitude of the initial price-change; or, alternatively, that the unit-velocity is always directly proportional to the magnitude of the initial price-change—in which case the adjustment period will be independent of this factor.

We shall also neglect the fact that the curves themselves shift during the process of adjustment (if they did not, the final position in so far as it is definite, would also be determinate, i.e. independent of the path followed). But the introduction of this factor would only complicate the analysis, without altering the nature of the results.

Finally, we have to take account of the fact that adjustments always proceed at more or less frequent intervals—that they are more or less continuous. The quantity of anything demanded or supplied may change once a day, once a week, a month, or a year —depending on such factors as the technical period of production, etc. We shall call an adjustment *completely discontinuous* if the full quantitative adjustment to a given price-change occurs all at once, at the end of a certain period. (E.g. a change in the price of rubber may not influence the rate of supply for a period of seven years, at the end of which the full quantitative reaction may take place at once. Or a change in the price of corn, by inducing farmers to change the area sown, will make its effect felt a year later when the new harvest comes to the market.)[1] Similarly, we shall call an adjustment *completely continuous* if it proceeds at a steady rate in time, or if the time-lags between the appearance of successive quantitative changes are such as can be neglected. The latter will always be the case when the degree of discontinuity—

[1] If, therefore, there are differing elasticities for the Marshallian long and short periods, this always implies that adjustments are continuous, or, at any rate, less than completely discontinuous.

the length of the time-lags—is the same on the demand side as on the supply side. In the following analysis we shall treat only these two cases of complete discontinuity and continuity.

I. Where the adjustments are completely discontinuous, stability (or "definiteness") of equilibrium will depend on the relative elasticities of demand and supply; according to what may be called "the cobweb theorem" of Professor Henry Schultz and Professor U. Ricci.[1]

Let us assume that a shift in demand from DD to $D'D'$ changes the price from P to P_1, which is not an equilibrium price, since

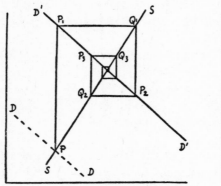
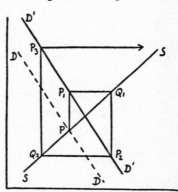

FIG. 2   FIG. 3

the true long run supply corresponding to this price is Q_1. After a time, depending on the adjustment period, supply will therefore change to Q_1, and price will then change from P_1 to P_2.[2]

[1] Schultz, *Der Sinn der statistischen Nachfragekurven*, p. 34, and Ricci, "Die synthetische Ökonomie von Henry Ludwell Moore", *Zeitschrift für Nationalökonomie*, 1930, p. 649. It is evident that this theorem is only applicable to cases of "completely discontinuous adjustments", or to the case (which Professor Schultz had in mind) where adjustments are completely discontinuous on the side of supply and instantaneous on the side of demand.

[2] Under our present assumptions that ruling prices are always expected to remain in operation, and thus no stocks for future sale will be carried, the price-reaction to changes in supply must always be instantaneous; since we can either assume that (1) *demand* reacts instantaneously to price-changes, in which case price will also react instantaneously to changes in supply: or (2) that demand-reactions take time, in which case the *immediate price-reaction* to changes in supply will be greater than the ultimate price-reaction. Under the assumption that adjustments are completely discontinuous, the slowness of demand-reactions to price-changes manifests itself in reducing the elasticity of the demand curve, and thus alters the situation in the direction of instability—since the relevant demand curve is the one which shows the amounts taken at various prices *immediately* after the (rate of) supply has changed. Whether the true (long period) demand curve will then have any relevance or not,

Again, after a time, supply will move from Q_1 to Q_2 (the supply corresponding to P_2) and price from P_2 to P_3. The successive stages of adjustment present the appearance of a cobweb (see Figs. 2 and 3), which will be contracting or expanding according as the demand curve is more elastic than the supply curve or vice versa. From this the following propositions can be derived:

(i) If demand is elastic relatively to supply, the cobweb will be contracting; equilibrium will be "definite".

(ii) If supply is elastic relatively to demand, the cobweb will be expanding; equilibrium will be "indefinite".

(iii) If the elasticity of supply and demand are the same, there will be a constant range of fluctuations.[1]

It is easy to see why this proposition is true only in cases where adjustments are completely discontinuous. For if quantities move slowly but steadily in response to price, the successive movements of quantities will change price and thus the direction of the movement, *before* the full adjustment has been made to the previous price. In this case the elasticities of the long-period curves will have little or no influence in determining the question of stability.

II. In the case of continuous adjustments the question of stability will depend not on the relative elasticities but on the relative velocities of adjustment of demand and supply. This can be seen from the following simple consideration. Let us divide the

will depend on whether the adjustment period on the demand side will be less, or greater, than the adjustment period on the supply side. In the former case the price will alter *before* the supply-reaction has taken place; and will thus diminish the range of succeeding fluctuations in supply.

[1] [The above conditions refer to the special case where the elasticity of both the demand and the supply curves is constant throughout their length. In other cases the necessary conditions cannot be expressed in terms of a simple general rule. (i) In the case of straight line demand and supply curves (such as those shown in Figs. 2 and 3), contraction or expansion is a matter of the relative *slopes* of the two curves, and not of their elasticities. The cobweb will be contracting when the demand curve is flatter than the supply curve, and *vice versa*. (ii) In the case of non-linear curves of varying elasticity, the cobweb will be contracting or expanding when the elasticity of the demand curve is *consistently* higher or lower than that of the supply curve, for all prices. (iii) In all other cases no general rule can be formulated, and it is possible that the cobweb could be an expanding one within certain ranges of price-fluctuations and a contracting one outside that range, so that the movement approaches a limit cycle, whatever the nature of the initial disturbance. It is also conceivable that the opposite should be the case; then the stability condition will be satisfied for small disturbances and not for large ones.]

"period of adjustment" (the period during which prices and quantities move in response to an initial price-change) into a series of sub-periods which are small enough to make quantitative adjustments completely discontinuous within that sub-period. Suppose that the smallest period to register any quantitative change in demand or supply is a "day"—then one day is the period within which adjustments can be regarded as "completely discontinuous", within which, therefore, prices must be steady, or rather can only change once, at the end of the day. We can then construct such "ultra-short-period" demand and supply curves which show the quantity demanded or supplied at any price, assuming that this price has been in operation only for a day. There will always be one point on these short-period curves which will correspond to the long-period demand (or supply) at this price;[1] but, otherwise, the elasticity of these curves will depend not on the elasticity of the long-period curves but on the velocities of adjustment. That factor whose unit-velocity is greater will have the more elastic curve. Applying, then, Professor Schultz's theorem to each of these sub-periods separately, we get the following results:

(i) If the velocities of adjustment are greater on the demand side than on the supply side, movements will lead towards an equilibrium, i.e. equilibrium will be "definite".

(ii) If the velocities of adjustment are greater on the supply side than on the demand side, movements will lead away from equilibrium, i.e. equilibrium will be "indefinite".

Since on general grounds we may expect supply reactions rather than demand reactions to be slow, and since cases of completely discontinuous adjustments are rare, inherent instability (in so far as the above conclusions are correct) may rather be regarded as a special case—so long as the fundamental data are such that they yield stable situations (i.e. so long as the basic curves are not completely "queer-shaped"). And it may not be out of place to emphasise once more the fact that all these conclusions have been

[1] Since any such curve can only be drawn from a given long-period price as the starting-point, i.e. one such short-period curve can be drawn from every point of the long-period demand (or supply) curve.

derived on the assumption that all economic decisions are made on the basis of ruling prices alone, without any regard to future price-changes; though in any actual situation, the presence of some foresight may always be expected. The existence of foresight, however incomplete, will always change the situation in favour of stability so long as the expectations of price-changes are in the right direction (in the direction in which prices actually move), though it will change the situation in favour of instability if expectations are in the wrong direction. Once, however, the assumption of the constancy of fundamental data is removed and allowance is made for the fact that the data change, and often change unexpectedly, there is no longer any reason to assume that the expectation of future price-changes will generally be in the right direction. Instability in the real world[1] then appears as the result of *wrong* anticipations.

[1] Whether in any actual case anticipations will be in the right direction or not, will depend partly on the nature of the change and partly on the efficiency of the institutions of the market whose function it is to anticipate future price movements. Given the forecasting ability of a speculative market, anticipations of future price-changes are as a general rule much more likely to prove correct when they are due to localised causes than when they are of a more general "monetary" character. Cf. Dr. Hicks' analysis in *Gleichgewicht und Konjunktur, loc. cit.*, esp. pp. 446 ff.

2

THE EQUILIBRIUM OF THE FIRM[1]

1. THE exploration of the conditions of equilibrium of the individual firm has in recent times occupied to an increasing degree the attention of economists. This, as should be evident, was a necessary development of the so-called "particular equilibrium" method of analysis developed by Marshall and especially of the concept of the "supply curve": the postulation of a definite functional relationship between price and rate of supply in the various industries. The latter, though an integral part of the Marshallian system, was by no means such a straightforward self-evident concept as its counterpart, the demand curve. The reasons for this asymmetry are not far to seek. The assumption that buyers respond to price stimuli in a definite and unequivocal manner (which is all that the demand curve implies) can be deduced from the general proposition that they have a definite system of wants and act in accordance with it; that is to say, it can be directly derived from the general postulates of the subjective theory of value. But the assumption that sellers do the same is a much more complex affair—at any rate in a world where production is carried on on a co-operative basis. It implies that there exists a mechanism which translates technical and psychological resistances into cost computations in such a way that a definite amount of a commodity will be offered by each producing unit in response to any price. It implies, therefore, that there is a definite relationship between the costs incurred and the amount produced for each individual source of supply and between price and the number of such producing units; and finally between price and some derivative of the cost function of the individual producing unit. Briefly, then, it assumes two things: perfect competition[2] and the existence of a definite cost function

---

[1] Originally published in *Economic Journal*, March, 1934.

[2] Under "perfect competition", here and in the following, we simply mean a state of affairs where all prices are given to the individual firm, independently of the actions of that firm.

for each firm. (The assumption of perfect competition is, of course, also necessary in the case of the demand curve. But on the demand side this can more or less be treated as a "datum"—at least in so far as the demand for consumers' goods is concerned[1]—for it follows from the facts that in buying individuals act alone[2] and that the contribution of a single individual to the social income and, thus, his individual spending power, is relatively small. But the nature of the conditions of competition on the supply side, as is now increasingly realised, is itself something to be explained.) In order to arrive at the supply curve for an industry, therefore, it must be shown that corresponding to each price there will be a definite number of firms in the industry and a definite amount produced by each *when all firms are in equilibrium*.[3]

Moreover, the importance attached to the nature of the supply function in post-Marshallian economics, the division of industries into those of increasing, constant and diminishing supply-price, and the distinction between external and internal economies, which postulated different cost functions for individual firms and for the aggregate of firms composing the industry, made it more than ever necessary to analyse the conditions of equilibrium for the individual firms *before* any postulates were made about the supply function of an industry. For only when the necessary functions are found which determine the behaviour of individual firms and some formal conclusions have been arrived at about the forms which these functions can actually take and when the inter-relations of these cost functions have been analysed, only then can

[1] The demand for producers' goods (derived demand functions), on the other hand, are more like supply functions in this and the following respects.

[2] This is not to be interpreted as saying that "co-operative buying" is not feasible. But the advantages of buyers' co-operation consist solely in marketing advantages (in "exploiting" sellers), while the advantages of sellers' (producers') co-operation follow from the principle of the division of labour and exist independently of any additional marketing advantage which can thereby be gained.

[3] Both Marshall and Professor Pigou appear to argue that an "industry" can be in equilibrium without all the firms composing it being simultaneously in equilibrium. This is true in one sense but not in another. If it is assumed that firms have a finite life like individuals, that they gradually reach their prime and then decline, it is, of course, not necessary that all the firms' outputs should be constant when the industry's output is constant. But if the growing output of young firms is to cancel out the declining output of old ones on account of something more than a lucky coincidence, it is necessary to assume that all firms are in equilibrium, i.e. that they produce the output appropriate to the ruling prices, to their costs and *to their age*. The introduction of a third type of "variable" (i.e. the firm's age) merely implies that equilibrium must also be established with respect to this; it certainly does not imply that equilibrium need not be established with respect to the other variables.

we derive those supply curves of various shapes which the simple two-dimensional diagram at once suggests to the mind.[1]

2. Marshall realised that it was necessary to describe the mechanism with the aid of which the reactions, which the supply curve exhibits, actually come about; and this, I believe, was the reason which led him to the concept of the "representative firm". His purpose was therefore not the establishment of a concept which has analytical significance as such, but rather the construction of a mental tool with the aid of which the reaction-mechanism postulated by the supply curve can be, if not analysed, at least rendered plausible. The representative firm was therefore meant to be no more than a firm which answers the requirements expected from it by the supply curve. In the words of Mr. D. H. Robertson: "In my view it is not necessary . . . to regard it (i.e. the representative firm) as anything other than a small-scale replica of the supply curve of the industry as a whole."[2] In this sentence, I believe, Mr. Robertson has admirably summarised the real weakness of the Marshallian concept; perhaps more so than he would himself care to admit. It is just because the representative firm was meant to be nothing more than a small-scale replica of the industry's supply curve that it is unsuitable for the purpose it has been called into being. Instead of analysing at first the conditions of equilibrium for individual firms and then deriving from them, as far as possible, the conditions of equilibrium for an industry, Marshall first postulated the latter and then created a *Hilfskonstruktion* which answered its requirements.

Professor Robbins has shown[3] that Marshall's concept of the representative firm (apart from the defect that it is nowhere in the *Principles* adequately defined) is open to the *prima facie* objection that it introduces elements which are not consistent with the

[1] With the growing realisation of the difficulties confronting any attempt at a workable definition of the concept "commodity", doubts arose concerning the legitimacy of the concept of a single "industry" which are probably more important and fundamental than the objections raised in the present article. But as the results of our investigation do not depend upon the validity of this concept, while its use considerably simplifies the analysis, we shall assume for the purposes of the present article that production can be divided up between a definite number of "standardised" commodities, each of which is sufficiently unlike the other to justify the use of the word "industry" applied to it.

[2] "Increasing Returns and the Representative Firm", *Economic Journal*, March, 1930, p. 89.

[3] "The Representative Firm", *Economic Journal*, September, 1928.

general assumptions upon which economic theory is based. We are here asked to concentrate our attention upon a particular firm, which, whether it is conceived as one selected from a large number of actual firms or merely some sort of average of all existing firms, is supposed to fulfil a special rôle in the determination of equilibrium in a way which other firms do not. "There is no more need for us to assume a representative firm or a representative producer than there is for us to assume a representative piece of land, a representative machine or a representative worker."[1] Professor Robbins' criticism only affects Marshall's particular solution, however, and shows that the kind of short cut Marshall attempted will not do. It enhances rather than obviates the necessity for analysing the conditions of firm-equilibrium as such.

Since Marshall's time the analysis of the equilibrium of the firm has been carried to a much higher stage of refinement. In one respect, however, later constructions suffer from the same deficiency as Marshall's. They also assume cost-conditions for the individual firms which *fit in* with the postulates made about equilibrium rather than prove how the cost functions of individual sources of supply make possible, under a given system of prices, a determinate equilibrium for the industry. Explicitly or implicitly the equilibrium of the firm is made dependent upon the equilibrium of the industry rather than the other way round.[2] And although, in this particular branch of economics, attention has more and more concentrated upon the equilibrium of the individual firm,[3]

[1] *Ibid.*, p. 393.

[2] Cf. especially the definition of the "equilibrium firm" by Professor Pigou, ". . . whenever the industry as a whole is in equilibrium in the sense that it is producing a regular output y in response to a normal supply price, p, [it] will itself also be individually in equilibrium with a regular output x_r" (*Economics of Welfare*, 3rd ed., p. 788). Professor Pigou does not, however, make clear whether (a) the concept of the "equilibrium of the industry" necessarily involves the concept of the "equilibrium firm" (he merely says that "the conditions of the industry are compatible with the existence of such a firm"), and (b) whether the existence of an equilibrium firm is a sufficient condition for the equilibrium of the industry. In our view, the conception of an "equilibrium of the industry" has no meaning except as the simultaneous equilibrium of a number of firms; and consequently the conditions of the latter must be analysed before the concept of the "equilibrium of the industry" and the categories of industries of increasing, constant and diminishing supply-price can be established.

[3] Cf. especially the writings of Professor Pigou, Mr. Shove, Mr. Harrod, Mr. and Mrs. Robinson in England, Professor Viner, Professor Yntema and Professor Chamberlin in the United States, Dr. Schneider and Dr. von Stackelberg in Germany, Professor Amoroso in Italy.

it has never been called into question, so far as the present writer is aware, whether the assumption of a determinate cost schedule (upon which the whole theory of supply rests) can be derived from the premises upon which static analysis, in general, is based. It is the purpose of the present paper to show that the conception of such a determinate cost function, obvious and elementary as it may seem, involves unforeseen difficulties as soon as an attempt is made to analyse the factors which actually determine it.

3. We propose to start in a roundabout way, by postulating at first the two assumptions on which the Marshallian supply curve is based: namely, perfect competition[1] and the existence of a definite functional relationship between the costs incurred and the amount produced by the individual firm;[2] and then to examine whether it is possible to find a form for this cost function which will make these two assumptions compatible with each other. We shall see that an analysis of the factors which determine the form of this cost curve will lead us to doubt the legitimacy of the concept itself. We shall also see later on that our results retain some interest even after the assumption of perfect competition is dropped.

As is well known, the requirement of the firm's cost curve under perfect competition is that it must slope upwards after a certain amount is produced[3]—an amount which is small enough to leave a sufficiently large number of firms in the field (for any given total output of the industry) for the conditions of perfect competition to be preserved. For the short-run analysis this presents no difficulties. In the short-run (by definition) the supply of some factors is assumed to be fixed, and as the price of the other

---

[1] If competition is imperfect, only the amount produced *under given conditions of demand* can be determined, but there is no definite relation between *price* and supply. Mrs. Joan Robinson employs the concept of the supply curve even under conditions of imperfect competition (*The Economics of Imperfect Competition*, Chapter VI), but a perusal of her book shows that she merely retains the name of the latter for an analysis of the former.

[2] We ought to start, in an analysis of this sort, by attempting to define a "firm". This, however, would render the treatment unnecessarily complicated and, as will be seen later on, a definition, sufficient for the purpose, emerges by itself in the course of the analysis (see below).

[3] This was first pointed out by Cournot (*Researches*, p. 91). Marshall's remarks in a footnote (*Principles*, 8th ed., p. 459) concerning Cournot's alleged error on this point were wholly unjustified. I am indebted to Dr. J. R. Hicks for this point.

(freely variable) factors is given, costs per unit[1] must necessarily rise after a certain point.[2] (This follows simply from the assumption, frequently styled "the law of non-proportional returns", that the degree of variability of the technical coefficients is less than infinite—which is just another way of saying that there are different kinds of factors.) But such a short-run curve will be hardly sufficient for our purpose. Unless we can assume that the "fixed factors" are fixed by Nature and not as a result of a previous act of choice (and it is hardly legitimate to make such an assumption in the case of an individual firm), we must again enquire why the fixed factors came to be of such a magnitude as they actually are. The problem of equilibrium again presents itself.

We must start, therefore, at the beginning, i.e. the problem is essentially one of long-run equilibrium. All factors which the firm employs are therefore assumed to be freely variable in supply and all prices to be given. What will be the shape of the cost curve? Will costs per unit vary with output, and if so, how?

(i) If the assumption of complete divisibility of all factors is dropped we know that cost per unit, for some length at any rate, must necessarily fall. This is due to the fact that with increasing output more and more indivisibilities (actual and potential) are overcome, i.e. *either* the efficiency of the actually employed factors increases *or* more efficient factors are employed whose employment was not remunerative at a smaller output.[3] Given

---

[1] Under "costs" here and in the following we include only such payments for the factors which are necessary in order to retain those factors in their actual employment, at a given efficiency. The remuneration of "fixed" factors (i.e. factors which are rigidly attached to the firm) form, therefore, no part of costs. (Fixity of supply implies both (a) that the factor is available to the firm irrespective of its remuneration, and (b) that its efficiency is not a function of its remuneration.)

[2] They must also necessarily fall up to a certain point if the fixed factors are also indivisible. Indivisibility and fixity of supply are, however, two entirely distinct properties which are frequently not kept apart, as both give rise to fixed costs, i.e. costs which do not vary with output. But on our definition of costs, only the remuneration of indivisible factors whose supply is not fixed enters into costs; while indivisible factors of fixed supply, although no part of costs, influence costs (through changing the physical productivity of the other factors) in a manner in which factors of fixed supply which are not indivisible do not. (Factors of the latter category can only influence costs *upwards*, not *downwards*.) The relevance of this distinction in connection with the present paper will become clear later on (see § 7, pp. 47-8 below).

[3] It appears methodologically convenient to treat all cases of large-scale economies under the heading, "indivisibility". This introduces a certain unity into analysis and makes possible at the same time a clarification of the relationship between the different kinds of economies. Even those cases of increasing returns where a more-than-proportionate increase in output occurs merely on account of an increase in the amounts

the state of knowledge, however, a point must be reached where all technical economies are realised and costs of production therefore reach a minimum. Beyond this point costs may rise over a certain range, but (if, in accordance with our assumptions, factors continue to be obtainable at constant prices) afterwards they must again fall until they once more reach their minimum at the same level as before. The optimum point can then only be reached for certain outputs, but there is no reason why the successive optimum points should not be on the same level of average costs. Indivisibilities, causing rising costs over certain ranges, thus do not explain the limitation upon the size of the firm so long as *all* factors are freely variable and all prices are constant.

(ii) It has been suggested, alternatively, that there are external diseconomies under which (as pecuniary diseconomies are ruled out by definition) must be meant the limitation upon the supply of such factors as the firm does not directly employ but only indirectly uses. (Cf. Pareto's example of the rising costs to transport agencies owing to traffic congestion.) But such external diseconomies (assuming that they exist) are again not sufficient for our purpose. By definition, they affect all firms equally,[1] and therefore do not explain why the output of the individual firm remains relatively small (the number of firms in the industry relatively large), as they only give a reason why the costs of the industry should be rising, but not why the costs of the individual firm should be rising *relatively to the costs of the industry*. The diseconomies, therefore—in order that they should account for the limitation upon the size of the firm—must be *internal*.

(iii) It follows clearly from these considerations that (as diminishing returns to *all* factors together are not conceivable) the technically optimum size of a productive combination cannot be determined if only the prices of the factors and the production function of the commodity are known. Knowledge of these only

of the factors used, without any change in the proportions of the factors, are due to indivisibilities; only in this case it is not so much the "original factors", but the specialised functions of those factors, which are indivisible.

[1] If external diseconomies affect different firms unequally, this merely explains why some firms should expand relatively to others, but not why their size should be limited. (Similarly in the case where different firms have different access to external economies.)

enables us to determine the optimum proportions in which to combine the factors but not the optimum amounts of these factors. In order to determine, therefore, the optimum size of the combination it is necessary to assume that the supply of at least one of the factors figuring in the production function should be fixed— in which case the optimum size (or at any rate the maximum amount of the product which can be produced at minimum costs) becomes determinate as a result of the operation of the law of non-proportional returns.[1]

Moreover, it is necessary that the factor whose supply is "fixed" for the firm should at the same time have a flexible supply for the industry—otherwise the industry would have to consist of one firm or at least a fixed number of firms. It is not the case, therefore, of a factor which is rent-yielding for an industry (a special kind of land, for example, which, though its supply for the industry is fixed, must have under the assumption of perfect competition a definite supply-price for the individual firm!), but rather the reverse: a factor which *is* rent-yielding (price-determined) for the firm but has a definite supply-price for the industry. In this case, therefore, the fixity of supply must arise, not from a natural limitation of the amount available, but from a special peculiarity of the firm's production function; that is to say, there must be *a* factor, of which the firm cannot have "two" units— just because *only one unit* can do the job.

It has been suggested that there is such a "fixed factor" for the individual firm even under long-run assumptions—namely the factor alternatively termed "management" or "entrepreneurship". As it follows from the nature of the entrepreneurial function that a firm cannot have two entrepreneurs, and as the ability of any one entrepreneur is limited, the costs of the individual firm must be rising owing to the diminishing returns to the other factors when applied in increasing amounts to the same unit of entrepreneurial ability. The fact that the firm is a productive combination under a single unit of control explains, therefore, by itself why it cannot expand beyond a certain limit without encountering increasing costs. The rest of this paper will be taken up by a

[1] It would be sufficient for the determination of the optimum size if one of the factors had a rising supply curve to the firm. This, however, is not compatible with the assumption of perfect competition.

discussion of the problems arising out of this suggestion: what is meant by entrepreneurship as a factor of production? Is its supply really fixed in the long run? And finally, does it justify the construction of a determinate long-run cost curve of the required form?

4. The term "entrepreneurship" as a factor of production is somewhat ambiguous—or rather more than ambiguous, possessing as it does at least three distinct meanings. What is generally called the "entrepreneurial function" can be either (1) risk—or rather uncertainty-bearing; or (2) management, which consists of two things: (a) supervision, (b) co-ordination. The latter two are not generally kept separate, although, in the writer's view, to distinguish between them is essential to an understanding of the problem. Supervision is necessary in the case of co-operative production (where several individuals work together for a common result) in order to ensure that everybody should do the job expected of him—in other words, to see that contracts already entered into should, in fact, be carried out. Co-ordination, on the other hand, is that part of the managerial function which determines what sort of contracts should be entered into: which carries out the adjustments to the given constellation of data. Which of these three functions can be considered as having a "fixed supply" in the long run?

The first of these functions—uncertainty-bearing—can be dismissed offhand, from our point of view. Because whatever measure of uncertainty-bearing it will ultimately be found most convenient to adopt—the theory of risks and expectations is as yet too undeveloped for us to talk about a "unit" of uncertainty-bearing—it is highly unlikely that it will be found to have a fixed supply for the individual firm. The mere fact that with the rise of joint-stock companies it was possible to spread the bearing of uncertainty over a great number of individuals and to raise capital for an individual firm far beyond the limits of an individual's own possession, excludes that possibility.

Nor is it likely that management possesses these unique characteristics—in so far as this term refers to the function of supervision. Supervising may require a special kind of ability, and it is probable that it is a relatively indivisible factor. It may not pay to employ a foreman for less than fifty men and it may be most economic to employ one for every seventy-five; but is there any reason why it should not be possible to double output by doubling both, foremen and men? An army of supervisors may be just as efficient (provided it consists of men of equal ability) as one supervisor alone.

This is not true, however, with regard to the co-ordinating factor: that essential part of the function of management which is concerned with the allocation of resources along the various lines of investment, with the adjustment of the productive concern to the continuous changes of economic data. You cannot increase the supply of co-ordinating ability available to an enterprise alongside an increase in the supply of other factors, as it is the essence of co-ordination that every single decision should be made on a comparison with all the other decisions already made or likely to be made; it must therefore pass through a single brain. This does not imply, of course, that the task of co-ordination must necessarily fall upon a single individual; in a modern business organisation it may be jointly undertaken by a whole Board of Directors. But then it still remains true that all the members of that Board will, in all important decisions, have to keep all the alternatives in their minds—in regard to this most essential mental process there will be no division of labour between them—and that it will not be possible, at any rate beyond a certain point, to increase the supply of co-ordinating ability available to that enterprise merely by enlarging the Board of Directors.[1, 2] The efficiency

[1] The essential difference between supervising and co-ordinating ability is that in the case of the former, the principle of the division of labour works smoothly: each supervisor can limit his activities to a particular department, or a particular sub-department, and so forth. In the case of a Board of Co-ordinators, each member of that Board will have to go through the same mental processes, and the advantages of co-operation will consist solely in the checking and counter-checking of each other's judgments. If the Board consists of men of equal ability, this will not materially improve the quality of their decisions; while if the abilities of the different members are markedly unequal, the supply of co-ordinating ability could probably be enlarged by dismissing the Board and leaving the single most efficient individual in control. In practice, of course, a certain amount of co-ordinating activity will be undertaken by Departmental Managers alone in large businesses, but this will always refer to such "infra-marginal" cases where the weighing of *all* alternatives is manifestly superfluous. Only such decisions, however, which affect the "margins" fall under the heading of co-ordination, properly defined. (Cf. Professor Knight's distinction between the "important decisions" always reserved for the entrepreneur, and the "routine work" of management. *Risk, Uncertainty and Profit*, Chapter X *passim*. For a fuller treatment of "marginal" and "infra-marginal" acts of choice, cf. Rosenstein-Rodan, art. "Grenz-nutzen", *Handwörterbuch der Staatswissenschaften*, 4th ed., Vol. IV, pp. 1198 ff.)

[2] Cf. the analysis on the problem of co-ordination in E. A. G. Robinson, *The Structure of Competitive Industry*, pp. 44 ff.

of the supply of co-ordinating ability can be increased by the introduction of new technical devices, e.g. by a better system of accounting; but given the state of technical knowledge and given the co-ordinating ability represented by that enterprise, the amount of other factors which can be most advantageously employed by that enterprise will be limited, i.e. the supply of co-ordinating ability *for the individual firm* is fixed.

It follows from these considerations that for theoretical purposes the most satisfactory definition of a firm is that of a "productive combination possessing a given unit of co-ordinating ability" which marks it off from productive combinations (such as an industry) not possessing this distinguishing peculiarity. It is the one factor which in the long run is "rigidly attached to the firm", which, so to speak, lives and dies with it; whose remuneration, therefore, is always price-determined.[1,2] On this definition, firms whose co-ordinating ability changes, while preserving their legal identity, would not remain the same firms; but then all the theoretically relevant characteristics of a firm change with changes in co-ordinating ability. It might as well be treated, therefore, as a different firm.

5. We have found, therefore, that the firm's long-run cost curve is determined by the fixity of supply of the co-ordinating ability represented by it. Further considerations, however, so far from lending support to the usual representation of this cost function and the supply function which is based upon it, lead to

[1] The case of the salaried General Manager of modern joint-stock companies presents difficulties which the present writer by no means professes to have solved. Professor Knight (*op. cit.*) seems to take the extreme view that control always rests with those who bear the ultimate risks; while the salaried managers are only concerned with routine work. This is manifestly untrue in certain cases, if "control" is to be interpreted as the "making of important decisions". Also, we have to take into account the possibility that the efficiency of a given unit of co-ordinating ability should vary with the amount of profits it receives—though just in the case of the entrepreneur this is very unlikely. In so far as it does, however, the supply of co-ordinating ability will be variable and the entrepreneur's remuneration (or rather that proportion of it which is necessary to maintain him in a given degree of efficiency) will enter into costs. All these, however, though they put difficulties in the way of the definition we have chosen, do not affect the rest of the argument.

[2] Which does not imply, of course, that co-ordinating ability is rigidly attached to an industry—as a given unit of co-ordinating ability (and thus a firm) can always leave one industry and turn to another. Similarly, there are factors which are rigidly attached to the industry, but not to the firm: specialised kinds of machinery, for example, which can only be used by the industry in question, but which a firm will not continue to employ if they yield a greater product in combination with a different unit of co-ordinating ability than they do for the firm which originally possesses them.

the conclusion that this very fact renders the cost function of the individual firm indeterminate. For the function which lends uniqueness and determinateness to the firm—the ability to adjust, to co-ordinate—is an *essentially dynamic function*; it is only required so long as adjustments are required; and the extent to which it is required (which, as its supply is fixed, governs the amount of other factors which can be most advantageously combined with it) depends on the frequency and the magnitude of the adjustments to be undertaken. It is essentially a feature, not of equilibrium but of disequilibrium; it is needed only so long as, and in so far as, the actual situation in which the firm finds itself deviates from the equilibrium situation. With every successive adjustment to a given constellation of data, the number of co-ordinating tasks still remaining becomes less and the volume of business which a given unit of co-ordinating ability can most successfully manage becomes greater; until finally, in a full long-period equilibrium (in Marshall's stationary state), the task of management is reduced to pure supervision, co-ordinating ability becomes a free good and the technically optimum size of the individual firm becomes infinite (or indeterminate). There is thus no determinate ideal or equilibrium position which a firm is continuously tending to approach, because every approximation to that situation also changes the ideal position to which it tends to approximate. It is not possible, therefore, to derive the firm's cost function from the economic data—i.e. from a given system of prices and a given production function: because the nature of that production function, or, rather, the relative position which the factor "co-ordinating ability" occupies in that production function, is not given independently of equilibrium, but it is part of the problem of equilibrium itself.[1]

It is possible, of course, that if the frequency and the magnitude of the adjustments to be undertaken remain the same (in other words, the degree to which economic data are changing per unit of time is constant), the theoretically optimum size of the individual firm might remain constant. But even if it were possible

[1] Similar ideas are expressed by Professor Chamberlin concerning his curve of selling costs (*The Theory of Monopolistic Competition*, p. 137). Professor Chamberlin, however, does not draw the consequences which, in our view, follow from these in regard to his own analysis.

GOSHEN COLLEGE LIBRARY
GOSHEN, INDIANA

to formulate a kind of theory of "static-dynamics" where, having once found a suitable measure of economic change (a kind of compound variable made up of the degree of variation of all the different data and weighted according to some arbitrary standard), the magnitude of the latter could be assumed to remain constant, the above conclusion by no means follows necessarily. For the optimum size would still be dependent upon the nature of the change and upon the degree to which adjustments to each given constellation of data can be made in a given time (in other words, the degree to which the path actually followed deviates from the equilibrium path).[1] Thus the mere introduction of dynamic change does not render the situation any more determinate than it was without it. It might mean, however, that in the actual world, the average size of individual firms will remain more or less the same because the inherent tendency of the size of the firm to expand will be continuously defeated by the spontaneous changes of data which check it.

6. What conclusions follow, from a theoretical point of view, from these considerations? It follows, first, that under static assumptions[2] (i.e. a given constellation of economic data) there will be a continuous tendency for the size of the firm to grow and therefore *long-period static equilibrium and perfect competition are incompatible assumptions*. Even if conditions of perfect competition obtain in any given situation, that situation cannot become one of equilibrium so long as the conditions of perfect competition remain preserved. It follows, secondly, that the existing organisation of the economic system, the division of the productive organisation into a great number of independent units under a single control, is essentially one adapted to the existence of dynamic change and imperfect foresight; and therefore the institutional pattern borrowed from a dynamic world cannot readily be applied

[1] Only if all future changes, and the consequences of these changes, are completely foreseen by everybody, will the situation be different; but then it will be analogous to a continuous long-run equilibrium and co-ordinating ability will be unnecessary. For the conception of a dynamic equilibrium with complete foresight see Hicks, "Gleichgewicht und Konjunktur", *Zeitschrift für Nationalökonomie*, Vol. IV, No. 4.

[2] The sole significance of static assumptions in this connection is that in this case the tendency to equilibrium is not dependent on the degree of foresight. All our conclusions also apply to a dynamic world with complete foresight. (Cf. also Knight, *op. cit.*, p. 287: "To imagine that one man could adequately manage a business enterprise of indefinite size and complexity is to imagine a situation in which effective uncertainty is entirely absent.")

to a theoretical static society where every kind of dynamic change is absent. It follows, lastly, that all concepts which are derived from the twin assumptions of a determinate static equilibrium and perfect competition (such as that of a determinate, reversible supply function) are open to the *prima facie* objection that they are derived from assumptions which are mutually inconsistent. In fact, the idea of a determinate equilibrium corresponding to each given constellation of "tastes" and "obstacles" becomes questionable in a world where the existence of indivisibilities offers advantages for co-operative production.[1]

7. We started off by enquiring into the cause which makes the cost curve of the individual firm rise relatively to the costs of the industry and thus makes a determinate equilibrium under perfect competition possible. We came to the conclusion that there is no such thing. We now have to drop the assumption of perfect competition and assume, in accordance with the conditions in the real world, that a firm can, at any rate beyond a certain point, influence by its own action the prices of the goods it is buying and selling. The limitation upon the size of the firm no longer presents any problem. It is sufficiently accounted for by the supply and demand curves with which it is confronted. But the element of indeterminateness, which the isolating assumption of perfect competition enabled us to detect, still continues in force when the basic assumption is removed. In so far as the relative place of co-ordinating ability is still not given by the production function, but depends on, and changes with, the relation of the

---

[1] It is at least questionable whether the same conclusions would hold in a world of perfect divisibility, where *all* economies of scale are absent; and it is to be remembered that it was under this assumption that the conception of equilibrium of the Lausanne School was elaborated. We have seen that the extent to which co-ordination is needed, in any given situation, depends on the volume of business (i.e. the scale of operations of the individual producing unit); and in a world where the scale of operations offers no *technical* advantages, economies could be gained by reducing that scale further and further until the need for co-ordination (i.e. the need for a specialised function of control, of decision-making) was completely eliminated. (This is not to be interpreted as saying that each "infinitesimal" unit would not have to co-ordinate its own activities —in the sense of "equalising its alternatives on the margin"—but these would be completely similar to the co-ordinating activities undertaken by each individual on the side of consumption. There would be no need for co-ordinators, i.e. factors of production specialised in the function of co-ordination. It was with this idea in mind that we found it legitimate to assume earlier in this article [cf. p. 35, especially footnote 2] that in buying, individuals act alone and thus treat perfect competition on the demand side as a datum.) In such a world, therefore, there would be no organisation of production into firms, or anything comparable to it; and perfect competition would establish itself merely as a result of the "free play of economic forces".

actual situation to the equilibrium situation, it still remains true that the cost curve of the individual firm, and consequently its position of equilibrium in relation to a given system of supply and demand curves, is indeterminate.

On closer scrutiny, however, there appears a line of escape for those who believe that the position of equilibrium under imperfect competition is otherwise determinate. Co-ordinating ability may be regarded as a fixed factor, but it is not, or at least it need not be, regarded as an indivisible factor.[1] Although it is not possible to increase the amount of factors applied to a unit of co-ordinating ability beyond a certain limit without loss of efficiency, there is no ground for assuming that there will be increasing returns to the other factors if they are applied in less than a certain amount to a unit of co-ordinating ability.[2] A certain business manager may not be able to manage more than a certain volume of business, in a certain situation, with undiminished efficiency, but why should he not be able to manage *less* equally well?[3] Thus the indeterminateness in the amount of co-ordinating ability required per unit of product does not affect the downward-sloping portion of the cost curve, it merely affects the upward-sloping portion. Now, under conditions of imperfect competition, only the downward-sloping section of the firm's cost curve is relevant from the point of view of the determination of equilibrium, as in equilibrium the firm's average cost curve must be falling.[4]

On further consideration, however, this point turns out not to be very serious. The costs which, in equilibrium, must be falling are average total costs, including the remuneration of uncertainty and co-ordinating ability (including, therefore, all profits which cannot be eliminated by the forces of competition); it is not a condition of equilibrium that marginal costs or even average costs,

---

[1] Cf. footnote 2 on p. 39 for the distinction between "fixed" and "indivisible" factors.

[2] There might be increasing returns for other reasons (if the factors themselves are indivisible), but this does not concern us here.

[3] "Co-ordinating ability" can also be assumed to be an indivisible factor if the type of decisions which entrepreneurs have to make varies in accordance with the volume of business and if an individual entrepreneur is better fitted for the making of some kinds of decisions than other kinds. If this assumption is preferred, the rest of the argument in the present paragraph becomes irrelevant.

[4] Cf. Chamberlin, *The Theory of Monopolistic Competition*, Chapter V, and Joan Robinson, *The Economics of Imperfect Competition*, Chapter VII.

in our definition of the term,[1] should be falling[2] while those sections of the cost curve, where these are rising, will be indeterminate. Moreover, it is possible to argue that changes in the amount of co-ordinating ability required per unit of product will affect "normal profits" in Mrs. Robinson's definition[3] (i.e. the amount of profits necessary to induce new firms to come into the industry), and thus change the position of the demand curves with which existing firms are confronted. In case this is true, not only the equilibrium amount produced by a given firm will be indeterminate, but also the number of firms in the industry, given the conditions of the demand for goods and the supply of factors.

8. There remains, finally, a more practical question to be answered: What is the effect of the elements of indeterminateness above analysed on the actual world? How can their influence be evaluated in terms of what some writers call "the instability of capitalism"? And here we can conclude our investigation with a more reassuring note.

In relatively "quiet" times, i.e. in times when tastes and the rate of saving are steady, technical innovations rare and changes in the population small, we may expect the actual size of "representative" firms to expand. If the system is one in growth (i.e. if capital and population are increasing), this will probably take place without a diminution in the number of existing firms. It is in any case questionable how far this tendency for the individual firms to expand can actually lead to a diminution in the number of firms. Although if "relatively static conditions" prevail long enough the number of firms existing must fall, and fall rapidly, it is very questionable whether in any actual case the process could be carried far. In the first place, the fall in the scarcity of co-ordinating ability represents, from the point of view of society as a whole, a reduction in real costs. It implies an increase in the "bundle of utilities" which can be produced out of a given amount of resources. It is quite possible, therefore, that the increase in the amount produced by the representative firm should run *pari passu* with an increase in the social product and should not

[1] Cf. footnote 1, p. 39. The importance of choosing this definition lies in the fact that it draws attention to the purely tautological nature of the conclusions arrived at by including price-determined remunerations under the cost-items.

[2] On this point cf. Mr. Harrod's note on "Decreasing Costs", *Economic Journal*, June, 1933.   [3] *The Economics of Imperfect Competition*, p. 92.

D

necessitate any diminution of production elsewhere. In the second place (and this seems more important), the growth in the size of some firms, due to the fact that they periodically revise their ideas of their own cost curves (which is what the change in co-ordinating ability comes to), throws new co-ordinating tasks upon other firms (to whom this must appear as a change of data), and even if it does not oblige them to reduce their output, at least it will check their growth. For this reason alone it is not to be expected that the process of expansion will be smooth and continuous, even under purely static conditions.

The reverse is true in times of "disquietude", when changes of data become more frequent and more far-reaching. But while the tendency to expand in quiet times mainly acts in the long run through changing the supply of the long-period variable factors (because so long as plant, machinery, etc., are given, the tendency to expand is effectively blocked by the limitation upon the amount of other factors which can be combined with them),[1] the tendency to contraction may affect short-period output, by raising the prime costs (marginal costs) curve.

All this must in no way be construed as an attempt by the present writer to put forward yet another theory of the trade cycle. Although if all major causes of fluctuations were absent there would exist a certain range of fluctuations due to the causes above analysed, in the author's view these are completely covered up in the real world by the more violent fluctuations which emanate from other causes—just as the ripples on the sea which emanate from the movement of ships (and which would make their effect felt over wide ranges if the sea were absolutely quiet) are fully absorbed by the more powerful waves which are due to the winds and the movements of the moon. When compared with the instabilities due to the monetary system, the rigidities of certain prices and the uncertainty of international trading conditions, the instability caused by the vagaries of the factor "co-ordinating ability" must appear insignificant.

---

[1] Save in the case where the long-period factors are divisible, i.e. consist of small units, and where, therefore, their supply can be expanded, though not contracted, within a short period. For example, in a factory which uses a great number of highly durable machines it is always possible to increase their number in a short period, but it may not be possible to diminish it until some of them wear out.

Part II

THE THEORY OF IMPERFECT COMPETITION

3

MRS. ROBINSON'S "ECONOMICS OF IMPERFECT COMPETITION"[1]

I

RECOGNITION that the unrealistic assumptions in regard to the nature of competition form one of the main deficiencies of the traditional theory of value, and are directly responsible for some of the apparent inconsistencies between the conclusions of theory and experience, constitutes one of the most significant advances of post-war economic thought. Traditional theory—tacitly rather than explicitly—was built upon the assumption that the elasticity of demand for the product of an individual producer with respect to the price charged by any other producer is either zero or infinite. In reality it is neither. Different producers are not selling either "identical" or "different" products, but "more or less different" products—the demand confronting them being neither completely sensitive nor completely insensitive to the prices charged by other producers.

This necessitates a new analysis of the determination of value; and Mrs. Robinson sets out in this book[2] to provide us with such an analysis. But the performance at once exceeds and falls short of the promise; the contents of the book cover a field different from that which we were led to expect from the title page. She neglects the intricate problem of the interaction of the price and output policy of rival producers and the dependence of each producer's equilibrium position on his own anticipation of this interaction (usually called the "problems of duopoly") alto-gether, though these ought to occupy a central position in the treatment of any competitive situation which can rightly call itself "imperfect"; she also excludes "marketing costs" from con-sideration—by the simple device of deducting such expenditures from the producer's demand curve—although, whatever views

---

[1] Originally published in *Economica*, August, 1934.
[2] *The Economics of Imperfect Competition*, by Joan Robinson, Macmillan, 1933.

one may hold about these, there can be little doubt that their emergence is one of the most characteristic features of an "imperfect market". In the circumstances it is not surprising that her book—after a most intriguing introductory chapter giving all the reasons for the necessity of a new approach to the theory of value—inevitably becomes a treatise on monopoly; a treatise most admirable in its lucidity, sharpness and the wealth of its material, but nevertheless a treatise very much on well-established lines. There is an elegance in the manner of presentation and the proof of her propositions about which any pure mathematician might justly feel proud; and for these reasons alone more than one part of her book—such as the analysis of Price Discrimination in Book V—is destined to remain for a long time the standard text on their subject. There is, in fact, hardly a single proposition on the theory of monopoly, treated by Mrs. Robinson, where she does not succeed in simplifying and improving upon the existing method of presentation; and there are quite a number of propositions—such as those dealing with the effect of monopolies on distribution—where she succeeds in carrying our knowledge a great deal further. No student of the theory of monopoly could fail to obtain a firmer and more inclusive grasp on the subject by reading her book, or to be grateful to her for saving the necessity of resorting to inferior or more cumbrous sources. But of "imperfect competition proper", of the problems peculiar to the type of situation presented by her at the beginning, there is little to be found; and such as there is is too tautological to improve our insight very much. In fact, one almost has the feeling that Mrs. Robinson could have written much the same book if Mr. Sraffa's path-breaking article (to which she acknowledges so much debt) had never been written; and if the problem of "highly substitute but not identical" commodities had never presented itself in the course of the discussion on increasing returns.

All this, however, is not meant as a criticism of the book itself; it could at best be regarded merely as a criticism of its title. For in the field which the book really covers it represents a brilliant intellectual achievement; and after reading some 350 delightfully instructive pages, it is hardly fair to complain that we have learnt something different from what we expected to learn or even from what she expected to teach us. For we have learnt quite a lot; and what we did learn was very well worth learning.

If one can make any general criticism, it does not so much concern her own propositions as the way she disposes of her predecessors. Some of the references to Marshall, for example, may be regarded as a trifle ungenerous, especially since she herself emerges—though I feel sure Mrs. Robinson would not admit this —as a true champion of Marshallian orthodoxy; and this sometimes in a field where Marshall himself might well have preferred to be unorthodox. Mrs. Robinson professes ultimate faith in the power of revelation of Plane Co-ordinate Geometry, in the handling of which she is a superb master; but her geometry— despite all the new curves and all the new properties discovered about them—is really ultra-Marshallian. In a sense, it represents the ultimate logical outcome of the Marshallian method. Whether this method is also the most convenient one for the analysis of the problems she wants to apply it to, still remains to be seen; in our view the apparatus of the "curves" becomes progressively less useful as one makes the basic assumptions more realistic; since it then becomes increasingly difficult to exhibit the conditions of equilibrium by functions of one variable. But it is the road she herself has chosen; and as her chapters on "objections" show, she has few illusions about the difficulties that confront it. Her all too noticeable endeavour to dissociate herself from Marshall thus compares ill with the latter's constant attempts to associate himself with Ricardo.

II

Of all Mrs. Robinson's results, unquestionably the most valuable are to be found in Books VII-IX, which deal with the extension of the marginal-productivity theory of distribution to monopoloid situations. With the aid of the now famous elasticity-formula Mrs. Robinson can derive the monopolist's demand curve for a factor of production and thereby solve the general problem of distribution under a régime of monopolies. She thus shows that (assuming at first perfect competition in the markets for the factors themselves) hired factors of production will tend to receive their "marginal value products", i.e. the net increase in the value of output created by the addition of a single unit of a factor; which is always less (except under perfect competition) than the value of their own net product (since by their own contribution they reduce the value of the product of all earlier units). The tendency, therefore, shown by Wicksell,[1] towards an equality in the level of remuneration of the same resources, both in contractual and non-contractual employments, will not be necessarily realised if competition is not perfect—even if there is no "institutional monopoly" in the sense that any of the required resources are under a single control. For while the hired factors will receive less than the value of their marginal physical products, the profits of the entrepreneur—the remuneration for the use of his own resources —will always be higher than the value of the marginal productivity of those resources multiplied by their amount. (This will also be true in cases where the entrepreneur earns no more on his own labour and capital than what he could earn by hiring them out; only then the marginal productivity of his own resources in their given employment will be *less* than it is elsewhere.)[2] In denoting the difference between the values of the marginal net products and their actual remuneration as the measure of the "exploitation" of factors, we should not forget, however, that this difference is not something which factors could always receive if only the entrepreneur acted in a way a state of perfect competition would force him to act. For in cases where the average variable costs are falling, payment on the scale of the values of marginal productivities would actually involve the entrepreneur in losses. The sum of the values of the marginal products of hired factors is then greater than the total product.

[1] *Lectures*, p. 125.

[2] A strict proof of this proposition requires the assumption of a "homogeneous and linear" production function. This can be assumed, however, even where "economies of scale" are present, so long as we assume that the fall in costs is due to the indivisibility of factors actually used and not the introduction of *new* factors as the scale of output is increasing; or, if it is due to the latter, that the "factors" are classified according to the specific form in which they are used and not according to the "original" resources from which they arise (e.g. a specific machine is regarded as a separate factor, and not the units of "capital" and "labour" which the machine represents). Then the sum of the marginal productivities of the factors, multiplied by their respective amounts, will be equal to the total product, and the marginal productivity of the "indivisible factor" will be negative so long as the average cost of all other factors is falling as output is increasing.

So long as we assume perfect competition in the markets for the factors themselves, factor prices, though not equal, will, at any rate, be exactly proportional to the value of their respective marginal productivities;[1] and consequently hired factors will be combined with each other in the same ratio as under perfect competition. This is no longer true, however, when the factor markets themselves are imperfect; and in consequence hired factors are subjected to "monopsonistic" as distinct from "monopolistic" exploitation. The marginal value product of factors will then tend to equal not their price, but their marginal cost, which is higher than price; and factors will no longer be combined in proportions at which their relative marginal productivities correspond to their price ratio (except in the special case when their elasticities of supply are all equal). Moreover, it can be shown that this change in the proportion in which factors are combined caused by imperfections in the factor markets implies a reduction in productive efficiency. For assuming a given total supply of all resources, variability of technical coefficients, and any given ratio in which different commodities are produced, it can be proved that the aggregate output will then be at a maximum when the factors in each employment are combined in such proportions that the ratio of the marginal physical productivities of the factors is everywhere the same. This condition remains fulfilled even if factors are everywhere subjected to "monopolistic exploitation" (however much the elasticities of demand for different commodities differ); it is unfulfilled as soon as "monopsonistic exploitation" enters the field. The latter brings about therefore a purely technical wastage of resources which is absent in the case of the former.[2]

Moreover, there is a difference from the point of view of policy, since the effects of monopolistic exploitation on labour are unavoidable while monopsonistic exploitation on the other hand can be countered by collective bargaining or any similar device

---

[1] Since for all factors the difference between the value of the marginal product and price is in the ratio of $\frac{\epsilon}{\epsilon-1}$ where ϵ is the elasticity of demand for the commodity.

[2] There may still be, in this case, a "technical wastage" of a different kind: if, on account of the generation of excess capacity, too little of the hired factors is combined with the residual factors (i.e. the entrepreneur's own resources). We shall examine this question on a later occasion.

which makes the supply curve of labour to the individual employer horizontal. It would be a mistake, however, to draw too much upon this particular argument for the purposes of trade union policy. For it is difficult to think of cases where "monopsonistic" as distinct from "monopolistic" exploitation should still be considerable.[1]

Unfortunately, Mrs. Robinson's manner of exposition just in these parts of the book is not quite so admirable as the standard in which the rest of the book is written. Here, at any rate—perhaps just because these parts are full of new ideas—the exposition could be considerably simplified. There was surely no necessity for her purposes to introduce the concepts of average *net* and marginal *gross* productivity, which must cause considerable headaches to those who are not used to her own ways of thinking; nor for the measurement of factors in terms of "efficiency units", which, on closer inspection, proves to be a very tricky concept indeed. For *different* factors of production can only be grouped together under "corrected natural units" if the elasticity of substitution between them is infinite; otherwise the multiplier by which their "natural units" must be "corrected" is indeterminate (depending partly on the ratio of the number of their natural units and partly on the amount of other factors with which they are combined). Mrs. Robinson seems to be aware of this difficulty, as her footnotes on pp. 332 and 344 show. But where are we to find resources between which the elasticity of substitution is infinite and which are yet normally classed as different factors? Surely it is more usual to err in the opposite direction.

III

Lack of space makes it unfortunately impossible to examine Mrs. Robinson's analysis of "competitive equilibrium" in Book III—which is the most relevant part of the book from the point of view of imperfect competition theory. We shall hope to return to it on a subsequent occasion. Here I should like to confine myself

---

[1] Theoretically by the introduction of collective bargaining wages could be raised by a percentage equal to $\frac{100}{E}$, without causing unemployment (where E is the elasticity of supply of labour to the individual employer).

to two points which concern not so much her actual conclusions as the technique adopted.

(i) The first of these concerns her concept of an "industry" (under conditions of imperfect competition). It implies the assumption that the products of different firms consist of a "chain of substitutes" surrounded on each side by a "marked gap" within which the demand for each firm's product is *similarly sensitive* with respect to the price of *any* of the others. The "boundary" is thus defined as the limit beyond which this sensitiveness ceases or at any rate becomes a different order of magnitude. No doubt for each *particular* producer there exists such a boundary. But there is no reason to assume (except in some very special cases, involving a peculiar grouping of consumers) that this boundary is the *same* for any group of producers; or that the sensitiveness of demand for the products of any particular producer is of the same order of magnitude with respect to the prices of *any* group of his rivals. Some producers will be "nearer" to him, others "farther off". If the demand for cigarettes in a particular village shop is more affected by the price of beer in the opposite public-house than by the price of cigarettes in the shop at the nearest town, which of the two would Mrs. Robinson lump together into "one industry": the seller of cigarettes plus the seller of beer in the village, or the seller of cigarettes in the village plus the seller of cigarettes in the town?[1]

(ii) The second concerns her concept of a demand curve confronting an individual producer. The traditional "market demand curve" for a certain product is *not the same sort of thing* as the demand curve which is relevant in determining the actions of the individual producer. The first denotes a functional relationship between the price and the amounts bought from a particular producer. The second concerns the *image* of this functional relationship as it exists in the mind of the entrepreneur. The two may differ widely. The second may be much more, or much less,

[1] Mrs. Robinson is no doubt aware of the arbitrary nature of the assumptions underlying her concept of an "industry". But I doubt if she allows for the extent to which these assumptions are indispensable for her subsequent constructions. For it is only under the assumption that there is a large group of firms between which the preferences of consumers are evenly divided (i.e. the "cross elasticities of demand" are of the same order of magnitude) that we can draw up a demand curve for the product of each; since it is only then that we can assume that a change in price by a single producer will not significantly affect the demand for any other single producer. Cf. p. 60 below.

elastic than the first; it may be discontinuous while the "real demand curve" is continuous.[1] It is easy to say that the general assumption of "perfect knowledge" eliminates this difference. But it is important to remember that such an assumption is something quite different and logically much less satisfactory in the case of imperfect competition than in the case of perfect competition. (1) In the case of the latter, it only implies that people know the relevant prices (in the present or in the future) quoted in the markets. In the case of the former it implies a knowledge of hypothetical situations to which the price-mechanism may give no indication at all. (2) The "real demand curve" confronting the individual producer might be (and if the above argument is correct, generally will be) indeterminate; since it depends on the way *other* producers react to his actions (this reaction can take the form *either* of a change of price *or* of a change in the quality of the product, both affecting in different ways the first producer's demand), and these reactions under a régime of monopolistic competition, cannot be derived unequivocally from the data.[2] The "imagined demand curve", on the other hand, becomes determinate as soon as it exists in the producer's imagination— and since something always must exist there[3] the question of indeterminateness simply does not arise in this case. If on the other hand, by assuming perfect knowledge we make the two coincide, not only do we make the analysis unnecessarily unrealistic, but we introduce complications (by rendering the

[1] Since entrepreneurs generally have no more than a very vague idea of their own demand curve it is more reasonable to assume that this "imagined demand curve" is a discontinuous one. In which case marginal revenue may be equal to marginal cost at several outputs. The two may even cut each other at a point where marginal revenue is equal to price.

[2] Mrs. Robinson, following a suggestion of Professor Pigou, draws up a demand curve under the assumption that not the prices, but the "conditions of supply" of all other commodities are given and which then shows "the full effect upon the sales of a particular firm resulting from any change in the price it charges" (p. 21). But *this* method of drawing up demand curves is only legitimate under conditions of perfect competition. For it is only under perfect competition that the marginal cost curve becomes the supply curve of the individual firm. (On p. 22, on the other hand, she says that "we ignore the fact that the price charged at any one moment may alter the position of the demand curve in the future" from which one would infer that she regards the *prices* of all other products as given.)

[3] If the entrepreneur has *no* idea of his own particular demand curve at all, this is equivalent to an "imagined demand curve" which is completely horizontal up to the amount actually sold, and then becomes completely vertical. It therefore consists of a single "step". The better "idea" the entrepreneur has of his own demand curve the more of such steps will his imagined demand curve consist.

"imagined demand curve" indeterminate) which can be avoided.[1] (3) Moreover, imperfect knowledge regarding the "real demand curve" is consistent with a state of equilibrium in a sense in which imperfect knowledge in regard to prices is not. So long as a producer sells as much at a given price as he expects to sell, his erroneous ideas concerning the elasticity of demand at that price are quite immaterial. The "imagined" and the "real" demand curve are thus merely required to meet at one point—I admit, at the critical point—otherwise they may show the wildest divergence without upsetting equilibrium. This not only implies that in the absence of perfect competition ignorance may persist with impunity; it also implies that under monopolistic conditions people's subjective estimates of their situation (apart from their actual situation) constitute one of the independent determinants of equilibrium.

Recent work in the theory of duopoly has also made it clear that that baffling question can only be satisfactorily treated by explicitly allowing for the entrepreneur's estimates of his rivals' reactions, as distinct from the actual reaction itself. This, of course, is not easy to do by "curves". But does it not seem probable, in the light of preceding remarks, that a more thoroughgoing recognition of this factor would both unify and simplify the whole theory of imperfect competition?

[1] Professor Chamberlin, who uses the same concept in his *Theory of Monopolistic Competition*, specifically assumes "perfect knowledge," and makes the demand curve determinate by assuming that the effect of a single producer's actions on any other single producer are always negligible, and thus will not induce him to change his own policy in turn. We have seen the reasons for doubting the legitimacy of such an assumption. Mrs. Robinson says at one place (p. 23) that "we shall assume that it is legitimate to make use of a two-dimensional demand curve, without enquiring how it is drawn up" from which one could infer that she is thinking of such an "imagined demand curve". But, unfortunately, neither her definitions on pp. 20-2 nor her subsequent analysis bear out this interpretation.

MARKET IMPERFECTION AND EXCESS CAPACITY[1]

I

OF all the doctrines emerging from recent work on the economics of imperfect competition, none appears more intellectually striking or more significant from a practical point of view than the doctrine of "excess capacity". It is intellectually striking, because it admits possibilities which the traditional "laws of economics" seem to have excluded: e.g. that an increase in "supply" may be followed by a rise in price.[2] And it is practically significant, because if the main contentions of the theory are found to be correct, it affords some reasons for interfering with the "free play of competitive forces" on grounds upon which traditional economic theory would have dismissed the case for interference. The theory envisages a situation where, on the one hand the market facing a group of competing firms is, for one reason or another, not absolutely "perfect", while on the other hand the entry of resources into the "industry" is free, and it shows that under such conditions "competition" (i.e. the free flow of resources into uses where they expect to obtain the largest net remuneration) will drive each producer to a situation in which he is not using its resources to the best advantage; and it will thus lead to a reduction of the physical productivity of resources all round. In a sense, it thus reverses the old argument about increasing returns and monopoly; it not only says that falling costs will lead to monopoly but that a monopolistic or rather a pseudo-monopolistic situation[3] will automatically lead each firm to a position where it is faced

[1] Originally published in *Economica*, February, 1935.

[2] Since Marshall, we are aware of the fact that, given certain cost conditions, an increase in demand may be followed by a fall in price. But neither the Marshallian nor, so far as the present writer is aware, any other theoretical system left room for the possibility that, under certain market conditions, an increase in the number of sources of supply (an inflow of resources into the industry) could lead to a rise in prices.

[3] We shall see later what precisely the term "monopolistic" implies in this connection.

with falling average costs.[1] It is a highly ingenious and one might almost say revolutionary doctrine: it shows up "free competition" (i.e. the freedom of entry into any trade or industry) not in the traditional and respectable rôle as the eliminator of the unfit but in the much more dubious rôle as the creator of excess capacity. It affords an éxcellent theoretical background for the age-old cry of business-men about the "wastes of competition"—so far completely neglected by the economists. It is worth while therefore to examine this theory in some detail.

The theory is put forward both in Professor Chamberlin's recent work and also in Mrs. Robinson's book.[2] Closer inspection reveals, however, that Mrs. Robinson's version possesses a merely formal similarity with Professor Chamberlin's theory. For Mrs. Robinson includes in her "cost curves" such profits which are not competed away by the entry of new producers; and in the circumstances, her statement that "demand curves will be tangential to cost curves" and that firms will be of "less than their optimum size" is merely a statement of a tautology.[3] It does not imply "excess capacity" or anything of that sort. In the subsequent analysis we shall follow therefore mainly Professor Chamberlin's statement of the theory.

II

The main argument can be stated briefly. Although not stated so explicitly, it is really based on four assumptions. First, it is

[1] "Falling average costs", if they are to be regarded as the criterion of excess capacity, should be interpreted that in the relevant output, costs are falling *in a state of long-period equilibrium* (after *all* adjustments have been made to that output), which also implies that *variable costs* are falling (since in the long run the supply of all factors—even the resources supplied by the entrepreneur himself—can be assumed variable and consequently there are no fixed costs). Since in a state of full equilibrium short-run cost curves must be tangential to the long-run cost curve, falling long-period costs also imply that short-run total costs are falling. But the converse is not necessarily true; falling short-run total costs (the fixed costs being calculated on a "historic" basis) need not involve falling long-run costs, for the same output, and consequently these are no safe criteria for establishing the prevalence of excess capacity.

[2] Chamberlin, *The Theory of Monopolistic Competition*, Chapter V. Mrs. Robinson, *The Economics of Imperfect Competition*, Chapter 7. The theory, of course, is by no means completely new. Wicksell had already stated it (*Lectures*, p. 86) and it is also to be found, in essentials, in Cairnes' *Political Economy*, p. 115. It was outlined in P. Sraffa's well-known article ("The Laws of Returns under Competitive Conditions", *Economic Journal*, 1926). The first systematic exposition is, however, Chamberlin's.

[3] Cf. on this point G. F. Shove, "The Imperfection of the Market" (*Economic Journal*, March, 1933) an article which, in the present writer's view, contains one of the most penetrating analyses so far published on this whole subject.

assumed that there are a large number of independent producers, each selling one product only, which is "slightly different" from the products of the rest of the producers. The words "slightly different" imply, that while the demand for the product of any of the producers is highly sensitive to the prices charged by the others, yet this sensitiveness is never so great as to compel all producers to sell at the same price. It implies that a producer, by lowering his price relatively to his competitors' prices, will attract away some, but not *all* of their customers; or alternatively, that he will lose some, but not all of his own customers, if he raises his price relatively to the rest.[1] It is assumed, secondly, that *"consumers' preferences are fairly evenly distributed among the different varieties,"*[2] and since there are a large number of them "any adjustment of price or of 'product' by a single producer spreads its influence over so many of his competitors that the impact felt by any one is negligible and does not lead him to any readjustment of his own situation."[3] Thus, given the prices of all the others, a "demand curve" can be drawn up with respect to the product of each.[4] Thirdly, it is assumed that no producer possesses an "institutional monopoly" over any of the varieties produced and thus the entry of new producers "into the field in general and every portion of it in particular is free and unimpeded". Fourthly, the long-run cost curves of all producers are assumed to be falling up to a certain rate of output; in other words, it is assumed that up to a certain output, there are economies of scale. (Professor Chamberlin's cost curves are U-shaped, i.e. they begin to rise

[1] In technical terms this implies that the consumer's elasticity of substitution between the different producers' products is large, but not infinite; which is the same thing as saying that the cross-elasticities of demand (the elasticity of demand for one producer's product with respect to another producer's price) are considerable but not infinite. Looking at it in this way, monopoly and perfect competition appear as the two limiting cases, where the cross-elasticities are zero or infinite, respectively; and there can be little doubt that the large majority of industrial producers in the real world are faced with imperfect markets in this sense.

[2] Which implies, in the above terminology, that the cross-elasticity of the demand for the product of any producer is of the same order of magnitude with respect to the price of *any* of his competitors. Cf. my article, "Mrs. Robinson's Economics of Imperfect Competition", *Economica*, August, 1934, p. 339 [p. 59 above].

[3] Chamberlin, p. 83. Mrs. Robinson does not state this so definitely, but her analysis is implicitly based on the same assumptions. Professor Chamberlin states (pp. 82-3) that he only makes these assumptions temporarily in order to facilitate the exposition, and removes them later on (pp. 100-11). But, as I shall try to show, the theory in its rigid form at any rate, really stands or falls with these assumptions.

[4] In the absence of these assumptions one can speak of a demand curve only in the sense of an "imagined demand curve", cf. below.

after a certain point. But while the legitimacy of the latter assumption in the case of long-run curves appears doubtful,[1] it does not affect his argument, which merely requires that costs should be falling over a certain range.) The elasticity of the demand curve, and the cost curve of each producer, are also assumed to be the same, but this, as I shall try to show, is not essential to the main argument so long as institutional monopolies are assumed to be absent. Now, given these two curves, each producer will try to produce that output which will maximise his own profits, i.e. equate marginal revenue with marginal cost. But since marginal revenue is less than price, price will be higher than average cost (including under the latter the displacement cost of the resources supplied by the entrepreneur himself) unless average cost is also, and to a corresponding degree, higher than marginal cost (which it can only be if average costs are falling). Let us assume that this is not the case initially. Entrepreneurs in the industry will then make "monopoly profits", i.e. remuneration for their own resources will be higher than that which similar resources could earn elsewhere. This will attract such resources into the industry; new firms will come in, producing new substitutes, which will reduce the demand for all existing producers; and this process will continue, until profits are reduced to normal, i.e. the difference between the actual earnings and the displacement costs of the entrepreneur's own resources is eliminated. In the position of final equilibrium not only will marginal cost be equal to marginal revenue, but average cost will also be equal to price. The demand curve will thus be tangential to the cost curve. The effect of the entry of new competitors will not necessarily reduce the price of existing products; it may even raise them. The profits which the entrepreneur no longer earns will thus not be passed on to the consumer in the form of lower prices but are mainly absorbed in lower productive efficiency. The producers, *as a body*, could of course prevent this from occurring by reducing their prices *in anticipation* of the entry of new competitors. But since the appearance of any *single* new producer will only affect the demand of a *single* existing producer very slightly,

---

[1] Cf. my article, "The Equilibrium of the Firm", *Economic Journal*, March, 1934, p. 70 [pp. 44-5 above].

E

while similarly the reduction of price of a *single* existing producer will only slightly affect the profits which a potential producer can expect, no producer could take these indirect effects on his own price policy into consideration.

There can be little doubt that given these assumptions the theory is unassailable. Any criticism therefore must be directed against the usefulness and the consistency of the assumptions selected.

III

1. The first of these concerns the assumptions made about the interrelations of the demand for the products of various producers (which are substantially the same as those underlying Mrs. Robinson's concept of an "imperfectly competitive industry").[1] No doubt, in most cases, the products of various producers selling the same sort of goods are not perfect substitutes for each other in the sense that the slightest price difference would eliminate all demand for the products of higher-price producers. The reasons for such market imperfection may be classed under one of three headings. There may either be slight differences in the products themselves (as in the case of motor cars, wireless sets, etc., the absence of "standardisation"); or differences in the geographical location of producers in cases where the consumers themselves are distributed over an area; or finally, there may exist a certain inertia on behalf of the buyers themselves who will require either some time, or a certain magnitude in the price-difference, before they make up their minds to buy from another seller—even if they are quite indifferent as between the products of different sellers.[2]

---

[1] Cf. *The Economics of Imperfect Competition*, Chapter 1. Cf. on this point my review, *op. cit.*, p. 339 [p. 59 above].

[2] It might be objected that anything which causes a lack of indifference between buyers will make the products imperfect substitutes in relation to each other (since the consumers' attitude is the final criterion for classifying "products") and consequently no distinction can be made out between "buyers' inertia" and "product-differentiation" as causes of market imperfection. There is, however, a very good reason for keeping them separate. Whereas in the ordinary case of imperfectly substitutable commodities the consumers' elasticity of substitution between two products is symmetrical (i.e. a given change in the price ratio will cause a given change in the relative quantities demanded, whichever of the two prices has moved relatively to the other) this is by no means the case when the lack of indifference is merely due to the inertia of buyers. In the latter case, one cannot even speak of a given "marginal rate of substitution", since this rate will be different according to the direction of the change.

Whatever the cause, the effect, from the analytical point of view, will be the same: the cross-elasticities of demand will have a positive finite value. But is there any justification for the further assumption that they will also be of the same order of magnitude with respect to the prices of *any* group of rival products? Can we say that any adjustment of price or of "product" by a single producer will spread its influence evenly over all his competitors? No doubt, cases are conceivable when it would. When the imperfection of the market is due to sheer buyers' inertia *and nothing else*, we could invoke the law of large numbers and say that the buyers who no longer buy from A, will pair themselves more or less evenly with B, C, D. . . . But buyers' inertia, though an important factor in practice, is rarely found in isolation as a cause of market-imperfection. It is generally coupled with either or both of the other causes.[1] And in these cases, it is clear that the different producers' products will never possess the same degree of substitutability in relation to any particular product. Any particular producer will always be faced with rivals who are nearer to him, and others who are farther off. In fact, he should be able to class his rivals, *from his own point of view*, in a certain order, according to the influence of their prices upon his own demand (which will not be necessarily the same order as that applying to any particular rival of his). This is clear in the case where market-imperfection is merely due to differences in the geographical location of producers. It is equally true in cases of "product-differentiation". Savile Row tailors will be most influenced by Savile Row prices; they will be less concerned with fluctuations in the price of East-End clothes.[2]

"Pseudo-monopolists"—distinguished from the old-fashioned "real monopolists" merely by the fact that the cross-elasticities of demand for their product is large—thus cannot be grouped

---

[1] Moreover, the case where market-imperfection is *merely* due to buyers' inertia is not a very good one from the point of view of this theory: since it always implies the presence of institutional monopoly as well. Cf. p. 74.

[2] It is conceivable that the "scale of preferences" of different consumers should differ in just that degree as to eliminate the differences in the degree of substitutability of different products for the body of consumers as a whole. (If individual X regards product B as a nearer substitute to A than either C or D, but Y regards C as a nearer substitute than either B or D, while Z regards D as the nearest substitute to A, then the prices, B, C, D may have the same influence on the demand for A.) But this is a rather improbable supposition.

together in a lump but can at best be placed into a series. Each "product" can be conceived of as occupying a certain position on a scale; the scale being so constructed that those products are neighbouring each other between which the consumers' elasticity of substitution is the greatest (a "product" itself can be defined as a collection of objects between which the elasticity of substitution of all relevant consumers is infinite). Each producer then is faced on each side with his nearest rivals; the demand for his own product will be most sensitive with respect to the prices of these; less and less sensitive as one moves further away from him. "Product variation" by an individual producer can then itself be represented as a movement *along* the scale; and, given the position of all other producers, each producer will tend to settle at that point on the scale where his anticipated profits are the greatest. New entrants must also occupy a position on that scale, and will thus necessarily make the chain of substitutes "tighter".

The idea of such a scale can best be envisaged in the case of the simplest type of market-imperfection, the distribution of consumers over an area. Let us assume that all consumers are situated along a road (a kind of "ribbon development"), they are evenly, densely spread, and all of them have an equal desire to buy. They are completely indifferent as between the products of different sellers; or rather the only difference consists in respect to transport costs (which can be equally regarded to be borne either by the buyers or the sellers). Under such conditions, sellers will tend to settle at equidistant points from each other along the road,[1] and thus they are all "pseudo-monopolists", since no two producers sell from the same spot.[2] Looked at from the point of view of any seller, a change of price by any other particular seller (the prices of the rest being assumed as given) is less and less important for him, the further away that particular seller is situated.

[1] If only there are more than two of them, cf. Chamberlin, p. 196, where Professor Hotelling's relevant theorem is corrected.

[2] The assumption that institutional monopolies are absent implies, in this case, that any seller *could*, if he wanted to, move to the same spot as that occupied by any other seller (or so near to it as to eliminate differences in transport costs) and thus make his own product "indistinguishable" from that of the other. Neglect to distinguish between these two cases of "monopolies" has been the source of much confusion in the past.

It follows from this, first, that even when the number of producers is large (the chain of substitutes tight) it cannot be assumed
that the effect of a single producer's action will spread itself *evenly*
over a large number of his rivals and will be negligible for each of
them individually. The other producers' prices and "products"
thus cannot be assumed as given in drawing up the demand
schedule for the first; and the real demand curve for a single
producer's product is thus indeterminate (depending on any of
the large numbers of possible reactions in which his rivals might
indulge).[1] The problems of "duopoly" are thus not merely con-
comitants of a situation where there is a "small number of
producers", but arise in all cases where producers are selling
substitute products, since the fact of imperfect substitutability
necessarily involves the presence of the scale, and thus of the
"small number". "Duopoly" is thus seen not as a special class by
itself but rather as "the leading species of a large genus".

Secondly, it can just as little be assumed that "new products"
(the products of new or prospective entrants) will stand in the
same or similar relation with *all* existing products. A new product
must necessarily be placed in between two existing products; and
will thus make considerable inroads into the markets of its nearest
neighbours. Thus a producer, if far-sighted, will take the effect of
his own actions not merely on his existing competitors into consideration but also on his *potential competitors*.[2] He will act on the
basis of an "imagined demand curve" which shows the amount he
can sell at different prices *in the long run*, under the assumption
that his competitors' products, prices and the number of his

[1] This does not imply that each producer will not base his policy upon certain
ideas concerning the relation between the demand for his product and its price. But
this "imagined demand curve" is based on certain expectations concerning his rivals'
behaviour as a result of changes in his own policy; irrespective of whether these
expectations are correct or not. Such an imagined demand curve is always determinate (since something must always exist in the producer's own mind). But it is a
different sort of thing from the demand curves of traditional analysis which always
implied an *objective* relationship between price and the quantity demanded. For a
fuller treatment of the distinction between a real and an imagined demand curve, cf.
my previous article quoted above, *Economica*, August, 1934, p. 340 [pp. 59-60 above].

[2] If a producer takes into account the consequences of his own policy on his *existing*
competitors, this will probably induce him to charge a higher price than otherwise
(will make his imagined demand curve less elastic). But if he takes *potential competition*
into account, this will probably induce him to charge a price lower than otherwise
(make his imagined demand curve more elastic). "Potential competition" implies
both (*a*) the appearance of a new rival, (*b*) the possibility of product-adjustment
rather than price-adjustment by an existing rival.

competitors are all adjusted to his price. If a producer knows that if he charges a high price to-day a competitor will appear to-morrow whose mere existence will put him in a *permanently worse position*, he will charge a price which will afford him only a low profit, if only he hopes to secure this profit permanently; i.e. he will act in a manner *as if* his own demand curve were very much more elastic than it is. And this "foresight" will, or at any rate may, prevent him from being driven to a state of excess capacity.[1]

2. Moreover, it can be shown that even if none of the producers takes the indirect effects of his own policy into consideration,[2] "potential competition" will never succeed in making the in-dividual demand and cost curves tangential, if economies of scale exist; while the possibility of product-differentiation will by itself never prevent the establishment of perfect competition if eco-nomies of scale are completely absent. Demand curves and cost curves therefore will only become necessarily tangential to each other when "demand curves" have also become horizontal.

In order to prove this, let us again take the simplest case of market imperfection which is at the same time the one most favourable to the "excess capacity" theory—when it exists solely on account of the spreading of consumers over a large area. Let us again assume that consumers are evenly distributed over the whole area; that they have no preferences whatever as between the different sellers; and that the cost functions of all producers are identical. The demand curves of individual sellers will be downward-sloping solely on account of the increase in transport costs as more is sold. Let us assume that producers are situated at equal distances from each other and that they all make profits (sell at prices which more than cover average displacement costs).

---

[1] Whether it will do so or not, will depend on the relative willingness and ability to bear losses—on behalf of the existing producer and the new entrant. For let us assume that a producer reduces his price in anticipation of the entrance of new com-petitors. If the new producer comes in nevertheless, *at the ruling price*, both will be involved in losses. But there will be some higher price at which both will make some profits; and if the new entrant can induce the old producer to raise his price to that level he can thereby secure his place on the "scale" permanently. If, on the other hand, the old producer persists in charging the low price, one of them will have to drop out. (In so far as buyers' inertia is present at all, there is always a presumption that such a price-war will cost less to the old producer than the new one.)

[2] I.e. they all act on the basis of an imagined demand curve which corresponds to a real demand curve drawn on the assumption that the prices and products of all other producers remain the same, irrespective of what the first producer is doing (which is the assumption underlying Professor Chamberlin's demand curves).

Let us assume that new producers enter the field. Each producer's market will be smaller; the elasticity of demand, at any price, higher than before. But if we assume that economies of scale are completely absent (i.e. long-run cost curves are horizontal) profits will never be eliminated altogether so long as the elasticity of demand is less than infinite. For each producer can always recover some of his lost profits by reducing output up to the point where marginal revenue equals marginal cost (which in this case, also equals average cost). The inflow of new producers will continue, leading to a continuous reduction in the output of existing producers and a continuous increase in the elasticities of their demand until the latter become infinite and prices will equal average costs. There the movement will stop. But each firm will have reduced his output to such an extent that he has completely lost his hold over the market.

We see therefore that the mathematical economists in taking perfect competition as their starting point, weren't such fools after all. For they assumed perfect divisibility of everything; and where everything is perfectly divisible, and consequently economies of scale completely absent, perfect competition must necessarily establish itself solely as a result of the free play of economic forces. No degree of product-differentiation and no possibility of further and further product-variation will be sufficient to prevent this result, so long as all kinds of institutional monopolies and all kinds of indivisibilities are completely absent.

Let us now introduce indivisibilities and economies of scale. The movement of new firms into the field will then not continue until the elasticities of demand for the individual producers become infinite; it will be stopped long before that by the increase in costs as the output of producers is reduced. *But there is no reason to assume that it will stop precisely at the point where the demand and cost curves are tangential.* For, on account of the very reason of economies of scale, the potential producer cannot hope to enter the field profitably with less than a certain magnitude of output; and that additional output may reduce demand, both to his nearest neighbours and to him, to such an extent that the demand curves will lie *below* the cost curves and all will be involved in losses. The interpolation of a third producer in between any two producers may thus transform profits into losses. *The same reason therefore which prevents competition from becoming perfect—i.e. indivisibility—will also prevent the complete elimination of "profits".* It will secure a "monopolistic advantage" to anybody who is first in the field and merely by virtue of priority. The ultimate reason for this is that it is not the original resources themselves, but the various uses to which they are put that are indivisible—you can divide "free capital" but you cannot invest *less* than a certain amount of it in a machine—and consequently the investment of resources cannot be so finely distributed as to equalise the level of marginal productivities.[1]

The above argument does not hold if we assume, as Professor Chamberlin assumed at the start, that consumers' preferences are *evenly distributed* over the whole field; and consequently the entry of a new firm affects *all* existing firms to an equal degree. Then the demand for each is only reduced by an insignificant amount by a single new entrant; and consequently the number of firms could increase with impunity until profits are completely wiped out and the demand curves become tangential.

That Professor Chamberlin is aware of our first objection is clear from his analysis of chain-relationships on pp. 102-4 of his book. That he is also aware of the second is clear from certain remarks in connection with spatial competition on p. 199. It would be most unfair therefore to criticise him on a point of logic—since the logic of Professor Chamberlin's analysis is indeed excellent. What he does not seem to be aware of is the degree of unreality involved in his initial assumptions, and the extent to which his main conclusions are dependent on those assumptions.

3. So far we have not mentioned the most frequent and conspicuous objection against the "excess capacity" theory: that it assumes "identical cost and demand curves" for the different producers. In our view, this is no valid criticism on Professor Chamberlin's assumptions. The identity of the demand curves

[1] This brings out clearly also the objection against Mrs. Robinson's "normal profits". We see how the level of profits in each firm—the difference between its actual remuneration and the displacement cost of its earnings—is determined by the degree of indivisibility which acts as a "protective shield" against intruders. There is no more reason to assume these profits to tend to a normal level than there is to assume that the extent of indivisibilities is the same in all cases.

merely ensures that the *prices* of different producers will be identical. But since producers are free to vary the quality of their product as well as their price, differences in elasticity will not save producers from being driven to a position of "tangency"— although they may reach this position by selling at different prices. The identity of the cost curves—*in the required sense*—follows on the other hand from the assumption of the absence of any institutional monopoly. It is assumed, that is to say, that every producer *could*, if he wanted to, produce commodities completely identical to those of any other producer—if he does not, this is merely because he would not find it profitable to do so.[1, 2] Such institutional monopolies may consist of patents, copyrights, trade-marks or even a trade-name. They may be conferred by law, by ownership, or merely by the will of the public. If the public *prefers* to buy from Messrs. Smith and Robinson and thus the name of the seller becomes part of the "quality of the product", then Messrs. Smith and Robinson have an institutional monopoly of their products. They possess something which others cannot possess. Similarly, if the entrepreneur *owns* resources which are *relatively* better fitted for the production of some varieties than the resources over which other entrepreneurs have command, he has exclusive control over resources which to that extent are unique: and this also implies the presence of some institutional monopoly.[3] Consequently, in the absence of these, since the relative costs of producing different varieties must be the same for the different producers, their cost curves, *for each single variety*, must also be identical.

It might be objected that "institutional monopoly", thus defined, covers a much larger number of cases than what is generally understood by this term. Indeed, one could make out a nice distinction between the possession of an "absolute"

[1] Professor Chamberlin does not state this explicitly; but this is the only logically consistent interpretation one can give to his assumption that "the entry of new producers into the field in general and every portion of it in particular is free and unimpeded".

[2] This implies in our terminology that every producer is free to move along and settle at any point of the "scale"; he can get therefore "as near to" the products of any other producer as he wants without incurring higher *relative* costs.

[3] In order to avoid misunderstanding it must be pointed out that the absence of institutional monopoly does not imply that the abilities of each entrepreneur, and consequently the *absolute levels* of their costs, are identical.

monopoly (when no other producer is able to produce a completely identical product at *any* cost) or a comparative or "partial" monopoly (when no other producer is able to produce the same product at the same relative cost). But as all products are more or less close substitutes for one another, this distinction becomes analytically unimportant since it comes to the same thing whether producer B can produce merely a "more or less close substitute" to A—or whether he can produce the *same* product but only at a higher cost than A.[1] Anything therefore which imposes higher costs on one producer than another (whether it is due to the possession of unique resources by one entrepreneur or whether it is merely due to buyers' inertia[2] imposing a special cost of entry on new producers) implies, to that extent, the presence of institutional monopoly.

Such institutional monopolies of course are never completely absent. Their presence—though, as we have seen in the last section, by no means essential—may even be directly responsible for a large part of market imperfection, as Professor Chamberlin himself so convincingly shows in his appendix in favour of "unfair trading". They cannot therefore usefully be assumed absent when a situation is analysed which is often largely bound up with them. And what does the situation look like when they are not absent?

If the "scale of differentiation" of the consumers can be regarded as given (as e.g. in the previous example, when the degree of substitutability of different products was rigidly determined by the level of transport costs) institutional monopoly, to the extent to which it is present, will prevent the generation of excess capacity—since, to that extent, profits earned by one producer cannot be competed away by another producer. Many types of institutional monopolies, however, by themselves increase the degree of market imperfection, and to that extent are favourable

---

[1] In both cases producer B will obtain smaller total receipts for the same total outlay.

[2] What we designated above as "sheer buyers' inertia" (i.e. that consumers require either a certain lapse of time, or a certain minimum of price-difference before they change over from one seller to another, even if they are otherwise completely indifferent between the different sellers' products) is merely a special case of institutional monopoly; since it always imposes a differential advantage on the existing producer relatively to the new entrant. The mere existence of specialised durable plant, however, does not imply such a differential advantage in the long run, although it may prevent adjustments being undertaken in the short run.

to the generation of excess capacity.[1] The sudden appearance of buyers' inertia, for example, has the double effect of reducing the elasticity of demand for the individual products and of imposing a cost of entry on potential competitors; these two opposing tendencies may cancel out, or the net effect may go in either direction.

To sum up the results of the above argument. The extent to which excess capacity may be generated as a result of "free competition" (under the assumption that the existence of economies of scale will prevent this competition from becoming perfect) will depend: (i) on the degree of "short-sightedness" or "far-sightedness" of producers (how far they take potential competition into account in deciding upon their price- and product-policy). This is a question of business psychology rather than economics. (ii) The extent to which institutional monopolies are present. This, as we have seen, will tend to prevent the generation of excess capacity if it leaves the scale of differentiation unaffected; while it will have an uncertain effect if it increases the scale of differentiation as well. (iii) The extent to which the market-situation resembles a "chain relationship" (in Professor Chamberlin's terminology), i.e. the extent to which the various cross-elasticities of demand differ in order of magnitude. Only in the special case when they are all of the same order of magnitude will Professor Chamberlin's conclusion (that demand curves will be tangential to cost curves) necessarily follow. At the same time, there is a presumption that some degree of excess capacity will be generated even if profits will not be completely competed away since "indivisibilities", by themselves, will not offer a strong enough shield to prevent *some* rise in costs as a consequence of the intrusion of new competitors. Many of the objections therefore which can be brought against the theory if put forward in its

---

[1] The difference between these two types of institutional monopolies (the one which affects merely the relative costs of different producers, and the other which affects the elasticities of the demand curves for products as well) can best be elucidated by examples. A legal patent for a certain cheap process of producing ordinary window glass will not lead the consumers to differentiate between glass produced by one process or another. It will merely have the effect of imposing higher costs upon anybody who does not possess the patent. A trade-mark protecting a certain soap or medicine, however, may lead the consumers to differentiate between different soaps or medicines; and thus reduce the elasticity of demand for the products of each producer.

rigid form (that demand curves will tend to become tangential with the cost curves), do not affect the fundamental proposition that the effect of the competition of "new entrants" and consequent reduction of the level of profits earned may take the form of a rise in costs rather than a reduction of prices.[1]

4. So far we have not touched upon another abstract assumption which Professor Chamberlin has made, i.e. that each producer produces only a single product. In reality the majority of producers produce a series of different products, if products are to be defined by the same rigid market-criteria as were applied in the earlier parts of this paper. And at first sight at any rate, it does appear as if the spreading of production over a series of different products is the way in which producers can overcome the effect of those indivisibilities which form the *conditio sine qua non* of imperfect competition. If there is not a sufficiently great demand to produce one product on an "optimal scale", the producer may still utilise his plant fully by producing two or more products, rather than building a smaller, sub-optimal plant or leaving his existing plant under-employed. In this way, indivisibilities will be overcome; and consequently excess capacity will not make its appearance either. The effect of "competition from outside" will be to induce producers to produce a larger series of products, rather than to reduce the scale of output as a whole.

In our view this line of reasoning is not strictly accurate; for even if it is admitted that varying the number of different kinds of products produced provides one line of adjustment for the entrepreneur, this does not imply that the essential consequences of this type of situation (that increased competition will lead to an increase in costs) can thereby be avoided. Whether they will or

[1] Professor Chamberlin's analysis is most valuable also in throwing light upon the probable consequences of all monopolistic agreements which refer to selling prices rather than quantities produced. It explains why, if a uniform taxi-fare is imposed, one will find too many empty taxis about. Or if the code of "professional etiquette" prevents doctors and lawyers from undercutting each other, sooner or later they will all complain that they are "under-employed". Or if manufacturers' cartels or trade associations impose a uniform price or a uniform "profit-margin" on retailers, one will find too many tobacco shops round the streets. It should also make us very sceptical about any remedying of the evils of imperfect competition by compulsory rationalisation, cartellisation, or any type of interference with price-competition. For measures which intend to prevent the alleged evils of "price-cutting" not infrequently tend to aggravate the real evils which they are supposed to remedy.

not, will depend on the nature of the cost function of the jointly produced products.

Commodities, of course, will only be produced jointly if it is cheaper to produce them jointly than separately. For certain commodities (such as wheat and straw) this is always the case: whatever is the amount produced of each (or rather whatever is the amount of resources engaged in producing them); irrespectively therefore of whether the economies due to scale are attained or not. These are the cases of "by-products" where more than one commodity emerges as a result of a single productive process. Certain other commodities, however, may be jointly produced simply because the demand for any of them is not large enough to be produced on a scale which should enable the realisation of the economies of scale; while some of these economies can be retained by utilising a larger plant for the production of several commodities. For such commodities joint production will only be profitable at certain outputs, and will become unprofitable as soon as the demand for each or any of them is sufficiently large to enable the economies of scale to be secured in the case of separate production. This is the case simply because the indivisible factors (buildings, machinery, etc.) which are responsible for these economies, are never completely specialised; and can be used, more or less effectively, for the production of several things simultaneously.

Since, however, in most cases, indivisible factors are not completely unspecialised either, such a "spreading of production" is always attended with some cost; i.e. the physical productivity of a *given* quantity of resources calculated in terms of *any* of the products will always be less, the greater the number of separate commodities they are required simultaneously to produce. That this is the case for a large proportion of jointly produced commodities is shown by the fact that the development of an industry is always attended by "specialisation" or "disintegration", i.e. the reduction of the number of commodities produced by single firms.[1]

Assuming that the cost functions of jointly produced commodities are of this nature, how does the equilibrating process

---

[1] Cf. Allyn Young, "Increasing Returns and Economic Progress", *Economic Journal*, 1929.

work itself out under our previous assumptions? For simplicity, we can postulate that there is a given number of firms, and initially each of them produces only one product and all are making profits (not necessarily to the same degree). Let us suppose that one of them finds it profitable to produce another commodity, highly competitive with the products of some other producers. These latter producers will now find the demand for their products reduced; and *this* may make it profitable for them to engage in the production of a second, or even a third, commodity —even if this was not profitable before. This in turn will induce other producers (possibly our "first" producer) to do the same, which in turn will lead to a further "spreading of production" by competing producers. Assuming always that producers merely take the *direct* effects of their actions into consideration (i.e. act upon an imagined demand curve which regards the prices and the products of all other producers as given)[1] this process will continue, so long as producers continue to make some profits; and so long as the loss caused by a reduction in the amount of resources engaged (if the reduction in the output of one commodity were not compensated by an increase in the output of another) is greater than the loss caused by a further "spreading of output". A precise formulation of this process would require either some very cumbrous language or some rather involved mathematics; but without resorting to either, it is easy to see what conditions the final equilibrium will involve. The demand curve for each single product will have become very much more elastic[2] (since each producer now produces a very much smaller share of each product, or "type of product"); profits will have been wiped out and the general level of costs of each product, or type of product, will have become higher. There will not be much "excess capacity" in the sense that, given the *number* of different products produced simultaneously by each firm, an increase in the output of all of them would reduce costs per unit. Yet there

[1] This implies in this case that producers ignore not only any adjustment of price or of product by other producers as a result of their own policy, but also any effect upon the demand for some of the other commodities produced by themselves.

[2] It can become infinitely elastic only when the "spreading of output" involves *no* additional cost at all. In this case the "economies of scale" refer to the amount of resources used by single firms rather than those engaged in the production of certain products; and for each single product, conditions of perfect competition might be brought about even if the total number of firms is small.

will be a "technical wastage", since the physical productivity of resources will be less than what it would be if each producer produced a smaller number of products and a larger proportion of the total output of each; a policy they undoubtedly would prefer if all of them could foresee the ultimate, as distinct from the immediate, consequences of their actions.[1]

IV

We have seen therefore that in all cases where economies of scale are present over certain ranges of output and where market imperfection exists (in the sense that highly and yet imperfectly substitutable commodities are on sale), "increased competition" (i.e. an increase in the number of firms in a particular industrial field) might lead to a reduction of technical efficiency rather than to a reduction in price or an increase in aggregate output; while in cases where firms can vary the number of different products produced, this might come about even without an inflow of "new firms". In both cases this result was seen to depend on a certain "short-sightedness" of producers who act on the basis of the immediate industrial situation confronting them rather than following out the further consequences of their own policy. The prevalence of such short-sightedness can be sufficiently accounted for, however, partly by the producers' ignorance of those further consequences and partly by the uncertainty as to the extent of far-sightedness with which their actual and potential competitors are endowed.

It is extremely difficult to deduce any general conclusions from the above analysis as to the effect of the generation of excess capacity upon economic welfare in general—in whatever arbitrary way this concept may be defined. If the money-value of the National Dividend is to be made its criterion (calculated on the basis of some *given* price-level), then no doubt, it could be increased, in some fields quite considerably, by compulsory "standardisation", cartel-agreements, the restriction of entry or any similar measure enabling producers to realise more fully the

---

[1] There may be another reason, apart from this type of "short-sightedness", why producers would prefer a policy of many-product production: and this is the reduction of risk, especially important in cases of fashionable articles, where they cannot calculate with any precision how the public will take any particular variety.

"economies of scale". The recognition of this fact, however, as yet far from warrants the advocacy of such measures. Apart from the ill-effects on distribution (and in a world of wage-rigidities, upon employment) which such processes of monopolisation inevitably involve, the public would be offered finally larger amounts of a smaller number of commodities; and it is impossible to tell how far people prefer quantity to diversity or vice versa.

Neither is it permissible to argue, on the other hand, that the generation of excess capacity is itself the result of consumers' choice; since it only comes about by creating a greater diversity of commodities: and consequently that its emergence is evidence that the public, to that extent, prefers "variety" to "cheapness". This line of reasoning would only be permissible if consumers were actually confronted with the choice of having *either* a smaller range of commodities at lower prices *or* a larger range at higher prices. In fact, they never are in a position to choose between these alternatives: they are offered either the one or the other, but never both. To expect the consumers to be so "far-sighted" as to concentrate on the purchase of a few varieties merely in the hope of thereby reducing prices in the future, is an assumption which even the highest level of abstraction should avoid.

5

PROFESSOR CHAMBERLIN ON MONOPOLISTIC AND IMPERFECT COMPETITION[1]

IN a recent issue of the *Quarterly Journal* Professor Chamberlin published an article[2] aiming at bringing to the fore "a number of misconceptions either vaguely current or held by specific writers" as to the nature of monopolistic and imperfect competition, and also to show "the dissimilarities" between different theories in the same field.[3] The purpose of the article was thus mainly one of clarification; in fact it revealed the existence of much more far-reaching differences than the present writer would have thought possible in that particular branch of economics which Professor Chamberlin himself so largely helped to create.

In Professor Chamberlin's view, the theory of "imperfect competition" as put forward by Mrs. Robinson and other English authors is something different from the theory of "monopolistic competition" as discussed by himself and his followers. Such differences can be of three kinds. There is, first of all, the difference in terminology—and here Professor Chamberlin lays great stress on the suitability of his own expression. There are, or can be, differences in doctrine—in treatment and exposition, and in the conclusions reached; and such differences, of course, are unavoidable with a new subject, especially in two books which were independently written and published almost simultaneously. Finally, there can be a difference in the subject-matter of the theories, i.e. in the *real phenomena* with which they purport to deal, and if Professor Chamberlin had a difference in this sense in view (and what else can the term "dissimilarities" imply, as against "misconceptions"?) he certainly has not succeeded in establishing that it exists. If differences of this last type were present, the two

[1] Originally published in the *Quarterly Journal of Economics*, May, 1938. A reply by Professor Chamberlin (not reprinted here) was published in the same issue.
[2] "Monopolistic or Imperfect Competition?", *Quarterly Journal of Economics*, August, 1937.
[3] *Ibid.*, p. 558.

F

theories could peacefully "co-exist", side by side, just as a theory of interest can co-exist with a theory of wages. But barring this kind of difference, all "dissimilarities" must be in the nature of "misconceptions"; they must all be capable of elimination, once the scientific method employed is agreed upon.

Ignoring for the present the differences of the first type, and denying the existence of those of the third, we are left with differences of the second type; and here Professor Chamberlin presents a truly formidable array. Specifically, he distinguishes between six misconceptions and three dissimilarities, but a careful summary of his paper could subdivide it even more. I hope the reader will excuse me if, instead of following Professor Chamberlin's paper point by point, I deal with the matters raised in a somewhat arbitrary order of my own.

I

In the first part of his paper, as I see it, Professor Chamberlin makes four important points, all closely related to one another. The first relates to the conditions of equilibrium under imperfect competition, the second concerns the relation of market imperfection to the number of firms, the third the relation of increasing returns to imperfect competition, and the fourth the compatibility of freedom of entry with the existence of monopolistic (or imperfect) competition. I shall attempt to deal with them in this order.

(1) The first of these is a relatively minor matter and is only mentioned because of its importance in connection with the subsequent points. Professor Chamberlin attacks the view that " 'imperfect' and monopolistic competition are in some special way related to the marginal revenue curve",[1] and he criticises Mrs. Robinson's view that full equilibrium "requires a *double* (his italics) condition, that marginal revenue is equal to marginal cost and that average revenue (or price) is equal to average cost".[2] "In reality," he argues, "there is no double condition at all; the equation of price with average cost is quite sufficient, because it necessarily includes the equation of the marginal items, whereas the reverse is not true. Instead of containing 'the heart

[1] *Loc. cit.*, p. 558.   [2] *The Economics of Imperfect Competition*, p. 94.

of the whole matter' the marginal curves would appear to be quite subordinate."[1] This assertion seems all the stranger since two pages later, he takes great trouble to deny it.[2] It is there made clear that "the solution of tangency [i.e., the equality of average cost with average revenue] flows from certain heroic assumptions which are later dropped, and is to be regarded as of only limited direct applicability, being mainly an expositional device". It is here asserted, therefore, that what is essential for equilibrium under monopolistic competition is equality of marginal cost and marginal revenue, whereas the equality of the average curves is merely an "expositional device".[3]

"The heart of the whole matter", which places the marginal revenue curve in such an important position, is the relation of price to marginal cost. It is the nature of this relation which distinguishes a state of competition that is pure from one that is impure: in the one case price will be equal to marginal cost, in the other it will be higher than marginal cost. But in order to know the relation of price to marginal cost, we have to know the elasticity of the demand curve at the relevant point, i.e. we have to know the position of marginal revenue. Moreover, the only simple criterion that enables us to distinguish between *degrees* of impurity in competition is the relative magnitude of price and marginal revenue, i.e. the actual elasticity of demand at the equilibrium level of output. If Professor Chamberlin had borne this in mind—it is not easy to do if one thinks only in terms of average curves—some of his later strictures, as we shall see, might never have arisen.

(2) In the second place, he denies the proposition (an idea which he finds has "an astounding—and disconcerting—vitality")[4] that the degree of market imperfection depends on the numbers of firms in any given section of the competitive field, "in the sense

[1] Chamberlin, *loc. cit.*, p. 559.
[2] *Ibid.*, p. 561.
[3] But quite apart from this denial, Professor Chamberlin's statement that "in reality there is no double condition at all" cannot possibly stand. Equality of price with average cost by no means necessarily implies the equality of marginal revenue and marginal cost, as Professor Chamberlin himself was well aware at the time he wrote the *Theory of Monopolistic Competition*. The one equality only carries with it the other equality in a special case—when the elasticity of the average curves is equal at the same point where their values are equal. The "solution of tangency" is merely an expression of Mrs. Robinson's "double condition" in geometrical terms.
[4] *Ibid.*, p. 562.

that with larger numbers the demand curves for the individual firms would become more and more elastic until conditions of pure competition were reached".[1] Since this proposition, in my view, is fundamental to an understanding of the theory, his reasoning requires detailed examination. He uses three arguments. The first is based on a confusion between changes in the size of a competitive field, originating on the side of demand, with changes in its "competitive density", originating on the side of supply. The second is based on a misunderstanding of the concept of "density" and of changes in this density. The third—and fundamental— argument is based on a confusion between the *slope* of a curve and its *elasticity*.

Professor Chamberlin argues, first of all, that in certain cases an increase in the number of firms need not affect the demand schedules of already existing firms. "If we think of stores distributed over an area, their number may increase by an expansion of area rather than because of a denser population within it."[2] This is perfectly true but equally irrelevant. In this case, the demand curves of already existing firms remain the same as they were, simply because the increase in the number of firms occurred as a *consequence* of an increased demand. The proposition which he criticises assumes *given* conditions of demand, and examines an increase in the number of firms due to the profits made by existing firms. Even if the increase in demand took the form of an increase in the density of population and, in consequence, the increase in the number of firms were associated with a general increase in the elasticities of the demand curves, this would be no more an argument in favour of the proposition than Professor Chamberlin's example is an argument against it.

His second argument deals with "non-geographical problems", and asserts that since new varieties of products always appeal to *some* new buyers, their effect is analogous to that of the increase in demand in the previous example.[3] So long as the new varieties appear on account of a spontaneous increase in the sources of

[1] *Loc. cit.*, p. 562. Professor Chamberlin uses the expression "differentiation of the product" where I used the term "degree of market imperfection". He must, however, have had the degree of competition in mind; otherwise the sentence is meaningless. Nobody asserted, of course, that product differentiation would gradually disappear with a continued increase in the number of firms.

[2] *Ibid.*, p. 563.   [3] *Ibid.*, p. 563.

supply, and not an initial rise in demand, it is quite irrelevant *where* the new buyers come from. Their effect will always be to raise the cross-elasticities of demand for *some* of the existing products; and this is all that the concept of a "commodity scale" and of new firms coming "in between" the old ones implies. It is not, of course, necessary that new products should take their place between *two* existing products; and the example of gas refrigerators and menthol cigarettes completely misses the point. The "competitive field" of the real world is *n*-dimensional and not one-dimensional. There are a large number of ways in which products can be more or less alike or more or less different. To regard it as "one-dimensional", as Professor Chamberlin's narrow interpretation supposes, is merely an "expositional device", and in no way part of the argument. Had he thought of the problem in terms of the cross-elasticities of demand of competing products that surround any particular product—the only way in which *density* in any given section of the competitive field can be defined—it would have been obvious to him that an increase in the number of varieties produced, which is *not* in response to an initial change in demand conditions, must have the effect of increasing this density.

But perhaps the real source of Professor Chamberlin's confusion is found in the last section of the paragraph: "that large or small numbers indicate nothing *necessarily* as to the degree of substitutability between the products concerned . . . is perhaps most clearly evident from the fundamental proposition that the number of producers in any field depends first of all upon how broadly the field is defined."[1] The number of stars in any section of the universe also depends on what we regard as the section. But not so with the density of stars. And in the argument under discussion, large or small *numbers* were always meant to refer to a *given section*, i.e. they meant to imply differences in density.

We now come to Professor Chamberlin's last argument in this connection, which is the really crucial one. Even if we assume that the products come "closer together", with a larger number of producers, he argues, "the result is not necessarily a closer approach to pure competition".[2] "If high profits lead to an increase in the number of sellers, so that the curve moves to the left, it will

[1] *Ibid.*, p. 563.   [2] *Ibid.*, p. 564.

remain of the same *slope* so long as the rate at which buyers value convenience does not change."[1] In the footnote that is attached to this sentence, he admits that the elasticity of demand at any particular price will "evidently increase as the curve moved to the left",[2] but proceeds immediately to dismiss the significance of this fact by pointing out that "this does not involve a flattening out of the curve". Thus the argument which started off by denying the proposition that "curves become more and more elastic with an increase in numbers" ends up by admitting it and introducing by the back door an entirely different one—that curves do not necessarily "flatten out" with an increase in numbers!

The relevant fact, of course, is that such a shift of the curve to the left will increase the elasticity of demand at the equilibrium level of output and will therefore bring price *nearer* to marginal cost. Hence it will necessarily reduce the degree of market imperfection, in the sense in which this was defined above and in which, I thought, everybody was agreed by now that it should be defined.[3]

[1] Chamberlin, *loc. cit.*, p. 564. This refers to an assumed case where producers and their customers are located along a line and the demand curve for the product of any one firm will be a straight line the slope of which is determined "by costs of transport or by the valuation per unit distance put upon convenience".

[2] *Ibid.*, p. 564, note 9. The footnote as printed says "it would evidently diminish". I understand, however, as is indeed obvious from the context, that the word "diminish" is due to a misprint.

[3] I can think of only two explanations for Professor Chamberlin's position. The one is that he is applying results obtained under the special case of zero costs to the general case. If costs are zero (Cournot's mineral springs!) it will indeed be true that the shift of the curve to the left will not increase the elasticity of demand at the new output, simply because in this case elasticity must always be unity: the zero-cost producers will always reduce the price by so much as to restore the elasticity to the previous level. If costs are positive, however, a continuous shift of the curve to the left will be associated with a continuous increase in the ratio of marginal cost to price.

The second possible explanation is that he regards the slope of the demand curve, and not its elasticity, as a measure of the impurity of competition. Since under pure competition curves must be horizontal, it is obvious that unless curves get "flatter" we cannot get "nearer" to the purely competitive ideal! If this is the explanation, it is a great pity that Professor Chamberlin should have allowed his geometry to run away with him. The *slope* of a demand curve, though not its elasticity, is a matter of the scale of drawing. The reason why the demand curves for individual firms in a perfectly competitive industry are horizontal, while the "industry demand curve" is not, is simply that in the diagram for the individual firm units of output are represented on a very much bigger scale than in the industry-diagram. (Even so, the "horizontal" position of the demand curve should never be taken literally. It does not imply that an increase in output by an individual producer can have *no* effect on price; it is merely a geometrical projection of the assumption that individual producers' influences on market prices are so small that they *regard* prices as given.)

If Professor Chamberlin had redrawn his output-scale as the individual firm's output moved to the left, his desire to see the demand curve gradually flattened out would have also been satisfied. (This is not to deny, of course, that the slopes of the

It can only be hoped that despite Professor Chamberlin's protest, the idea that elasticities increase as the number of firms gets larger will continue to have an astounding vitality. As we shall see presently, it is a most fruitful idea.

(3) After this it is scarcely surprising that Professor Chamberlin denies an inherent connection between monopolistic competition and increasing returns (economies of scale). He denies my proposition[1] that, if full divisibility of all factors is assumed and consequently economies of scale are completely absent, the free play of economic forces would necessarily establish perfect competition. His argument is again based on the failure of the demand curves to "swing round" to a horizontal position as they are being pushed to the left. He admits that if costs per unit *do not* rise, as the output of the firm is reduced, the multiplication in the number of firms, and the consequent reduction in the scale of output of each, will not be sufficient to eliminate profits, *so long as competition remains imperfect.* "But if the demand curves do *not* become horizontal, as I argued in general above, infinite divisibility leads to an absurd result: the influx of firms would simply continue indefinitely (because there would always be profits under constant costs); and the final outcome would appear to be an infinite number of infinitesimal firms. . . . The conclusion must be that the general assumption of infinite divisibility *contributes nothing towards the flattening of the demand curve, and hence* [my italics] does not convert monopolistic into pure competition."[2]

It should be obvious from our previous reasoning that perfect competition no more requires the existence of an "infinite number of firms" in this case than it does in any other case. As the number of firms increases and demand curves move to the left, price necessarily moves nearer to marginal cost (which in this case is also equal to average cost). There comes a point where producers no longer take into account their own influence upon price and proceed to *equate* price with marginal cost. At this point further movement will cease and pure competition is established. We can

demand curves can change owing to a change in the demand function, even if the scale of output is given. But the sense in which demand curves *must* flatten out in order to approach the conditions of pure competition is only the sense in which the scale of output *must* be redrawn as actual output gets smaller and smaller.)

[1] *Economica*, February, 1935, p. 42 [p. 71 above]. Chamberlin, *loc. cit.*, p. 563.
[2] *Ibid.*, p. 565.

represent this situation by a horizontal demand curve if we like, but this would be no more than a geometric expression of the assumption that producers take prices as given. The important point is that unless economies of large scale, or rather the diseconomies of small scale production, set a limit to the inflow of competitors, or "institutional monopolies" afford peculiar advantages to particular individuals, there can be no equilibrium until producers equate price with marginal costs; and equality of price with marginal cost *is* pure competition.[1]

It is not suggested, of course, that economies of scale in the real world are ever *completely* absent, that there is such a thing as "perfect divisibility". Professor Chamberlin's statement[2] that if the assumption of divisibility is inconsistent with the existence of economies of scale, "it is the former, and not the latter, which must give way", really misses the point. The value of this proposition is as a *didactic principle* which enables us to make generalisations about the factors which determine the *nature* of the competitive situation; it is not dependent upon the actual existence of infinite divisibility. If we know that without economies of scale there can be no imperfect competition, we also know that the degree of market imperfection depends, *inter alia*, on the extent to which there are economies of scale. If these economies are rapidly exhausted (at a relatively low level of output) the likelihood of there being a low degree of imperfection in competition is high, and vice versa. It also depends upon the consumers' sensitiveness to product differentiation. If this sensitiveness is great, and in consequence the possibilities of product-variation are large, the economies of scale that are compatible with pure competition must be much more insignificant (must be exhausted more rapidly) than in the case where such possibilities are limited. The proposition is valuable also in enabling us to separate out the *purely economic* causes of "monopolies" from the *institutional* causes;

---

[1] At what point this will be reached—how many firms there will be—depends, of course, upon the attitude of producers, and especially their foresight. If they foresee what is happening, they will bring down prices to the level of costs before their market largely disappears. In that case pure competition will be consistent with a relatively small number of firms.

[2] *Loc. cit.*, p. 565, note 3.

but for an elucidation of this we must turn to Professor Chamberlin's next point.[1]

(4) In his *Theory of Monopolistic Competition*, Professor Chamberlin showed how the equilibrium for a group of firms is determined under the assumption that "entrance to the field in general and to every portion of it in particular was free and unimpeded".[2] In a subsequent paper I pointed out[3] that this implies that every producer *could*, if he wanted to, produce commodities completely identical to those of any other producer, and that the relative costs of producing different commodities for different producers must be the same. Professor Chamberlin, I am glad to see, agrees that "logically, this is what 'free entry' in its fullest sense must mean". He proceeds immediately, however, "to change his views in the matter", and to take the view that free entry "*is quite incompatible with a differentiated product*".[4] "With respect to the *particular product* produced by any individual firm under monopolistic competition, there can be no 'freedom of entry' whatever. No one else can produce a product identical with it, although he may be able to produce others which are fairly good substitutes for it. Under monopolistic competition, then, there can be freedom of entry only in the sense of a freedom to produce substitutes; and in this sense freedom of entry is universal, since substitutes are entirely a matter of degree."[5]

There are no reasons given for this *volte-face*, beyond the assertion itself, and this makes it rather difficult to guess the underlying chain of reasoning. But let us suppose that two producers *could* produce a completely identical product; that they have no trade names, or that the consumers pay no heed to them; that the

---

[1] The argument in note 3, p. 561, designed to show that "increasing returns" are neither a *necessary* nor a *sufficient* condition for monopolistic competition, contains a logical *non sequitur*. "They are not necessary", says Professor Chamberlin, "because it is possible . . . that marginal revenue and marginal cost intersect above and to the right of the point of minimum average cost. They are *not* sufficient because a *horizontal demand curve* makes equilibrium within the 'increasing returns' phase of the cost curve *impossible*." (My italics.) In plain English this last sentence proves exactly the opposite of what he intended to prove. Since pure competition is impossible with increasing returns, increasing returns must be a *sufficient* condition for imperfect competition! If the above analysis is correct, then in the absence of institutional monopolies, they must also be a *necessary* condition for imperfect competition.

[2] *Monopolistic Competition*, p. 111.

[3] *Economica*, February, 1935, pp. 43-4 [pp. 72-3 above].

[4] Chamberlin, *loc cit.*, pp. 556-67.

[5] *Ibid.*, p. 567.

cost curves of the two producers are exactly the same, but that the demand for the product happens to be not large enough for *both* producers to produce it on a scale that would leave them a profit on it. The *joint* cost curve of the two producers lies *above* the demand curve, but the individual cost curve of either lies *below* it. Would Professor Chamberlin argue that the product would not be produced at all, or that both producers would produce it, forming a "duopoly" until they are relieved from this sad state by the bankruptcy court? And suppose that our two producers by slightly varying their product (say one producing bath soap with lavender scent and the other with verbena) find that there is a sufficient market for both of them to carry on, and proceed to do so, would Professor Chamberlin really argue that they are inconsistent with the assumptions? Or would he simply say that they do not deserve the name of monopolistic competitors? Unless he supplies more convincing reasons for the incompatibility of full freedom of entry with an imperfect market his new views on this matter can scarcely command universal assent.

I particularly regret that Professor Chamberlin should have changed his views on this point. To have shown that the monopoloid situations of the real world are quite compatible with full "freedom of entry", that is to say with the complete absence of particular advantages vested in particular people, I have always regarded as one of the great achievements of the *Theory of Monopolistic Competition*. Up to the publication of this book, the idea of "monopoly" was inevitably linked up, in the economist's mind as well as in the public mind, with the idea of "privilege"; the *behaviour* of monopolists might well have been described in terms of marginal curves, but the causes for the *existence* of monopolists were generally sought in the possession of some unique advantage. Professor Chamberlin's theory of product-differentiation has shown us that monopoly is purely a matter of degree; and that monopolies of various degrees can exist without any "unique advantage" at all, merely because the demand for a *single variety* of product is small relatively to the economies of scale in its production. To have shown that the limitations on competition can be due to purely economic causes, to the conditions of production and of consumption, and not only to the operations of that sinister group of individuals, the "institutional monopolists", the owners of patent rights and of mineral springs, was a great step forward in economics; and it should be placed to Professor Chamberlin's credit, despite his present disclaimer.[1]

Nor would I share Professor Chamberlin's view that the concept of "freedom of entry" is "not very useful and may even be misleading in connection with monopolistic competition".[2] To be sure, in a strict sense everything is a substitute for everything else, and hence *some* freedom of entry is universal. It is very important to know, however, how large is the range of substitutes over which, in any particular case, entry is closed, that is, to distinguish between different degrees of such freedom. If "further research is to proceed with sound understanding of the issues", surely one of its objects should be to explore the extent to which institutional causes (restriction of entry) and economic causes (increasing returns) are operative in the formation of particular monopolistic situations. By doing away with the concept of "freedom of entry", we shall no longer be able to distinguish between such "monopolies" as the company store in a company town, which owes its position to privilege, and Henry Ford, who owes his position (largely if not entirely) to the economies of large scale production.

II

In the second part of his paper, Professor Chamberlin discusses the question "what monopolistic competition *is*, and in particular, how it is different from imperfect competition".[3] "Imperfect and monopolistic competition have been commonly linked together as dealing with the *same subject*. [My italics.] Their similarities seem to be adequately appreciated; their dissimilarities hardly recognized."[4] A careful perusal of the ten pages devoted to this question, however, fails to bring out any evidence in support of the contention that the two theories relate not to the same subject,

---

[1] Professor Chamberlin's view, that under full freedom of entry, profits must for all firms be reduced to a minimum (p. 567), ignores the fact that economies of scale offer a protective shield to profits, even if entry is free in the fullest sense. Cf. on this my "Market Imperfection and Excess Capacity", *Economica*, February, 1935, p. 42 [pp. 71-2 above].
[2] *Ibid.*, p. 567.   [3] *Ibid.*, p. 570.   [4] *Ibid.*, p. 573.

but to different subjects. What Professor Chamberlin really contends, is that there is a difference in "approach", in economic *Weltanschauung*, between Mrs. Robinson and himself; but the reader could hardly fail to carry away the impression that here, at any rate, Professor Chamberlin has fallen a victim to the general tendency among producers in an imperfectly competitive market —a tendency he so convincingly describes—and is trying to differentiate his product too far. "Monopolistic" competition, à la Chamberlin, is a "blending between competition and monopoly",[1] while "imperfect" competition, à la Mrs. Robinson, regards "monopoly (in its ordinary sense) and competition . . . as mutually exclusive".[2] "If I seem to exaggerate at all the importance of this difference in conception between us, it is because I have become convinced that it is the key to an understanding of many other differences in treatment of the problems involved."[3]

Now I do not think that this difference in fundamental conception really exists. Professor Chamberlin himself produces only two pieces of evidence in support of it. The first is that Mrs. Robinson, after considering the alluring possibility of arranging "actual cases in a series of which pure monopoly would be the limit at one end and pure competition at the other", rejects this as "involving insuperable difficulties".[4] "The comparison should be made here with *Monopolistic Competition*, pages 63 and 64, where this view is specifically embraced as the corner-stone of the theory."[5] The second is that the expression "imperfect competition" avoids the necessity of regarding competition and monopoly as overlapping, and holds "interference with one's [traditional] categories of thought at a minimum".[6]

Unfortunately Professor Chamberlin nowhere defines what he means by a state of monopoly in the sense in which this is different from a state of monopolistic competition. If he did, the difficulties of arranging actual cases as a series between monopoly and competition would have at once been apparent. The only way in which "pure monopoly" could be defined would be a state of

[1] Chamberlin, *loc. cit.*, pp. 558, 570.   [2] *Ibid.*, p. 573.   [3] *Ibid.*, p. 573.
[4] *The Economics of Imperfect Competition*, pp. 4-5, Chamberlin, *loc cit.*, p. 574.
[5] *Ibid.*, p. 574.   [6] *Ibid.*, p. 572.

affairs in which the demand curve for the "monopolist" was completely independent from the price of any other commodity or group of commodities; and monopoly in the sense not only does not exist, it is not even conceivable, since it would conflict with our basic assumptions about the nature of human wants.[1]

We have seen above that the *degree* of imperfection of competition can be measured by the elasticity of individual firms' demand curves. But this measurement certainly cannot be used to denote the relative strength of the "monopoly" and "competitive" elements in a given situation, in the sense which Professor Chamberlin has in mind. Quite apart from the fact that it would lead to the absurd conclusion of regarding the limiting case of "pure monopoly" as one where the elasticity of demand is zero (and prices are infinite, I suppose!), it is certainly not true that lower elasticities of demand are a necessary indication of the greater relative strength of "monopoly" elements and a greater weakness of the forces of competition. This merely implies that producers do not think it *worth while* to compete on the basis of price; it does not imply that they do not, or cannot, compete on a different basis (such as product-differentiation and advertisement). Low elasticities of demand are quite consistent with intense competition, in the ordinary sense.[2]

[1] Mrs. Robinson made this point very clear in the place quoted by Professor Chamberlin. If reference was made to her "rejection" of regarding actual cases as intermediary between monopoly and competition, the reasons given for this should have also been dealt with.

[2] I should like to take this opportunity of replying to a criticism made by Professor Cassels in an earlier number of the *Q.J.E.* (May, 1937, p. 439). Professor Cassels, not without justification, pointed out that in my paper on *Excess Capacity*, I did not make explicit recognition of the fact that Professor Chamberlin did not intend to apply the term "excess capacity" to *all* cases of falling cost, but merely to those cases where the market-situation is such that each producer regards his competitors' prices as identical with his. This is perfectly true; but my failure to delimit the phenomenon of "excess capacity" to those cases was not due to an oversight of Professor Chamberlin's distinction, but to a doubt of its validity. It is true, of course, that the extent to which excess capacity may be generated will depend, *inter alia*, on the elasticity producers believe they have; and it will be all the greater, the smaller is this elasticity. But the point I wanted to bring out was that the demand curve which is relevant here is the "imagined demand curve", and that it is impossible to generalise about the nature of this curve on the basis of the criteria Professor Chamberlin has employed. It is quite possible, for example (a possibility Professor Chamberlin has not taken into account), that precisely in those cases—the presence of the "small group"—which he has reserved for this phenomenon of "excess capacity" the producers should take *potential competitors* into account, and not (or not only) the price-reactions of existing competitors, in which case the estimated elasticity of demand will be high and the degree of excess capacity will be kept low. Nor would I agree to the view that the distribution of resources which would come about if all producers regarded their competitors'

It is not "monopolistic competition" which is an "intermediate case between monopoly and competition"; it is the old theory of monopoly which is revealed, in the light of more recent theory, as a doctrine relating merely to a *single aspect* of "monopolistic competition". What Professor Chamberlin's book has shown us is, not that competition and monopoly are no longer to be regarded as "mutually exclusive alternatives", but simply that the distinction between competition and monopoly is no longer valid. And in this sense, I am sure, Professor Chamberlin's "approach" commands general agreement. Mrs. Robinson herself made this amply clear in her book: "No sooner had Mr. Sraffa released the analysis of monopoly from its uncomfortable pen in a chapter in the middle of the book than it immediately swallowed up the competitive analysis without the smallest effort."[1] I really cannot see where the fundamental difference in *Weltanschauung* comes in.

If a distinction is to be drawn, it should be drawn on a rather different basis. The man in the street regards the monopolist as the possessor of some institutionally conferred privilege. I have argued before that *all* monopolies of ownership (whether they relate to a specific mineral, a patent right or a trade mark cherished by consumers, or to the possession of a unique brain) fall logically under this category; and that the degree of freedom of entry depends on the strength of these "institutionally conferred" privileges.[2] There is no reason why the economist, for once, should not make a concession to everyday usage and reserve the term "monopoly" to denote the possession of such privileges.

There remains, finally, the question of terminology. The reader will have observed that in this paper, not without intention, the expressions "monopolistic competition" and "imperfect competition" have been used quite promiscuously. On previous occasions, not realising that such "unmistakable preference" for

prices as constant has any claim to being regarded as an "ideal" distribution. There are no objective criteria which would enable us to determine what is an ideal distribution, i.e. the extent to which consumers really prefer "variety" as against "cheapness" in a régime where prices are not everywhere equal to marginal costs. (Cf. Chamberlin, *Monopolistic Competition*, pp. 93-4; Cassels, *loc. cit.*, pp. 436-8.)

[1] *The Economics of Imperfect Competition*, p. 4.

[2] Cf. my "Market Imperfection and Excess Capacity", *Economica*, February, 1935, p. 44 [pp. 73-4 above]. As there pointed out, some degree of "institutional monopoly" would arise from mere buyers' inertia alone.

a term that is "purely negative" commits one to a particular point of view,[1] I generally used the expression "imperfect competition". The underlying motive was a simple one. For reasons that ought to be obvious, "imperfect competition" is a more familiar expression in England, while the term "monopolistic competition" is more familiar in the United States. That such differences in terminology should persist on the two sides of the Atlantic is, perhaps, regrettable; but so long as they are not confined to Professor Chamberlin's and Mrs. Robinson's theories, but extend to a much wider range of objects, such as lorries, braces and constables (trucks, suspenders and cops) they do not seem to call for special comment. If I may, however, end up with a small constructive suggestion, would it not be possible to find room for the use of *both* expressions side by side? If my suggestion concerning the use of the term "monopoly" found general acceptance, and "restriction of entry" were regarded as an *independent* cause of limitations on competition, the term "imperfect competition" could be reserved for situations which are free from "monopoly" elements altogether (i.e. where there is full freedom of entry and the limitation is due to economies of scale in production); while "monopolistic competition" would refer to those situations where the limitation is due to "monopoly" elements (i.e. to restrictions of entry). This would enable us to look upon the "limited competition" of the real world as a blend, in different degrees, between the limiting cases of purely imperfect and purely monopolistic competitions; and it would also be in accordance with the relative importance the authors of the two expressions now seem to attach to these two forces in causing the phenomena they describe.

[1] In the Preface to the *Theory of Monopolistic Competition,* Professor Chamberlin states: "The title of this book is apt to be misleading, since I have given to the phrase 'monopolistic competition' a meaning slightly different from that given it by other writers. Professor Young once suggested 'The Theory of Imperfect Competition', and this, although it had to be discarded as inaccurate, comes close to describing the scope of the subject."

6

THE ECONOMIC ASPECTS OF ADVERTISING[1]

1. AN enquiry into the economics of advertising can be conceived in two ways: either as an analysis of the factors which determine the scale of advertising expenditure in different trades, or as an enquiry into the *effects* of advertising on the distribution of resources between different uses, on costs and prices. Looked at in the first way, the problems to be investigated form a branch of the general theory of competition; they concern such questions as, Why is it that competitive advertising develops in some industries and not in others? What determines the amounts spent on such advertising either absolutely or relatively to price? What determines the price of advertising per unit of publicity (e.g. the column inch rate of newspapers)? etc.

The second approach takes advertising expenditure as given, and examines the effects of advertising on the welfare of the community. Here a sharp distinction must be drawn between the direct functions of advertising and its incidental effects, i.e. its indirect contribution to welfare through the changes which it helps to bring about in the economic organisation of society. It is, roughly speaking, true of any kind of economic activity that in addition to the satisfactions (or utilities) it creates directly—through the provision of goods or services—it also induces other effects ("external" economies or diseconomies) by affecting, favourably or unfavourably, the efficiency of resources engaged in producing other goods and services. The peculiarity of advertising lies only in the fact that here these "external effects" are

[1] Originally published in the *Review of Economic Studies*, 1949-50, Vol. XVIII, No. 45.

This paper was written in 1943, as a preliminary statement of the economic issues connected with advertising, for an investigation on the effects of advertising on welfare which was to be undertaken by the National Institute of Economic and Social Research. In view of the magnitude of the task that was shown to be involved, this project was later abandoned, though the statistical results of the enquiry were published by the Institute (cf. Kaldor and Silverman, *A Statistical Analysis of Advertising Expenditure and of the Revenue of the Press*, Cambridge University Press, 1948). The paper is published here with certain abbreviations, but with only slight verbal changes in the text.

regarded as much more important (by its champions and perhaps also by its antagonists) than the direct effects.

2. The main purpose of the present enquiry lies undoubtedly in this second approach: the effects of advertising on welfare, rather than the "causes" of advertising. It is impossible, however, to keep these two aspects rigidly separate; and in the course of analysing the effects of advertising on economic organisation, the question of why advertising features so much more prominently in some trades than in others and how advertising is itself a part of a wider category of "selling costs" may have to be gone into in some detail.

THE DIRECT FUNCTIONS OF ADVERTISING

3. The social function of advertising is undoubtedly the provision of information concerning the prices and qualities of goods and services available in the markets. As a provider of market information it is therefore most closely related to other forms of provision of market information, such as stock-exchange and other market price lists, railway guide books, etc.,[1] and rather less closely to all the other services concerned with the dissemination of knowledge—newspaper, periodical and book publishing, education in schools and universities, etc. Advertising differs, however, from other services concerned with the dissemination of information (as well as most other goods and services) in three important respects:

(i) The "seller" of any particular piece of advertising—the one who provides the service—is always the same economic unit as the seller of the goods and services to which the advertising relates. Hence the advertising service and the goods and services that are advertised should be regarded as in joint, or rather in "common supply".[2]

(ii) The price of "advertising-service" to the "buyer" is always nil, i.e. the information itself is freely provided, the cost of providing the information being incorporated in the price of the commodities advertised. Advertising is therefore a particular case

[1] In a wider sense, all these are forms of "advertising". What distinguishes them from advertising in the narrower sense here used is that the cost of providing the information is not borne by the sellers of the commodities advertised, but by the public.

[2] The term "common supply" is preferable, since "joint supply" refers to a situation where several commodities emerge as a result of a single process of production.

of subsidised commodities (commodities sold below cost) and the economic motive for the subsidy is always the expected consequential increase in the demand for complementary goods and services.[1]

A Digression on Subsidised Commodities. Subsidised commodities may be defined as all commodities sold below the marginal cost of production, commodities provided freely being a particular class of subsidised commodities. Most services provided by the Government are subsidised commodities in this sense, their cost being either incorporated in the price of other commodities, or met by compulsory levies on income; and there are a wide group of subsidised commodities provided by private enterprise as well. There are at least four different reasons for the existence of subsidised commodities, three of which relate mainly to those provided by public authorities:

(1) The nature of the service being such that its provision benefits everyone indiscriminately, irrespective of whether he "bought" the service or not. (Security, defence, street-lighting, etc., may all be regarded as falling in this category.) In this case, the services can only be provided by taxation, and not by individual purchase and sale.

(2) Commodities may be subsidised because the community recognises that their supply involves "external economies" to a far greater extent than the average of commodities, and hence their social cost is proportionately lower than their private cost. A particular instance of this is expenditure on education and research. (On the principles of the economics of welfare, the optimum degree of subsidy on any particular commodity is the one which brings its price, relatively to the prices of other commodities, into equivalence with its relative marginal social cost.)

(3) Subsidising commodities may be a convenient method of bringing about a change in the distribution of goods and services between persons. The provision of free milk and school meals, and the subsidies on various foods, all fall in this category.

(4) Finally, goods and services may be subsidised by the "many-product firm", because the aggregate profits of the firm

---

[1] In so far as an increase in the supply of a particular service leads to an increase in the demand for other goods and services, the goods and services in question can be looked upon as in joint or complementary demand.

will be greater if some of its commodities are sold below cost, and others above cost, than if each commodity or service were sold at a price which merely reflects its own cost and own demand and takes no account of the consequential changes in the costs and demands of other goods and services provided by the firm.[1] Apart from the case of by-products—where one cannot really speak of a subsidised price, since the costs of the several products cannot be dissociated from each other—subsidised commodities occur in all those cases where the demands for different things are in complementary relation to each other, and where a reduction in the price of a "minor" commodity or service leads to such an expansion of the demand for a "major" commodity or service, sold by the same firm, that the total amount spent on both will be greater than if the price concession had been spread over both proportionately. Examples for this are innumerable. They take the form either of the subsidiary goods and services being sold separately, but at a loss (e.g. the Standard Oil Co. in the nineteenth century sold oil-lamps at a nominal price, in order to increase the consumption of oil; gas and electricity companies often sell, or hire, equipment to consumers at a nominal price; department stores have "loss-leaders" or deliberately incur losses on subsidiary services, such as restaurants, etc.) or of selling a bunch of commodities and services together, instead of pricing them separately (the miscellaneous services which distributors provide free of charge to customers, etc.). Clearly most "selling costs" fall under this heading.[2] Advertising is a particular case

[1] An individual commodity or service is here thought of as something which *could* be provided and sold separately, whether or not it is so provided.

[2] Cf. also § 35, pp. 129-30. It is a debatable point whether the economics of all this commodity subsidisation is consistent with the "rational conduct" of the *homo oeconomicus* or not. Thus, with a perfectly rational man one would have to assume that the decision on the use of a particular method of illumination, such as oil (or gas, or electricity) would be based on the total cost of using the article, and not on a particular part of this cost; and therefore the stimulus imparted to oil consumption by the reduction in the price of lamps could be no greater than if the price of oil had, instead, been reduced by a corresponding amount, in which case it would only "pay" to incur losses on a subsidiary commodity, if it would have equally paid to reduce the price of the "main" commodity. But whether it is consistent with rational conduct or not, there is no doubt that business-men believe that demand functions do behave in this peculiar manner, and there is no need for us here to go behind the demand curves. Also, the above argument could hardly be applied to advertising, since the subsidiary service provided in this case is knowledge concerning the main product; and it cannot be argued that the consumer's demand function for a particular commodity is unaffected by the degree of his knowledge in relation to it.

belonging to the former category where the subsidiary service is retailed entirely free of charge, but separately, with a view to enhancing the demand for the main product. (It belongs to the former category, rather than the latter, since the advertising is freely provided to everybody, irrespective of whether they buy the main commodity or not.) The newspaper industry provides another example of subsidised commodities, belonging to this class; here the service provided to the public is subsidised (the papers are sold to the public below cost), in order to enhance the demand for advertising space, by the advertisers. Advertising, therefore, is a subsidised commodity which itself subsidises other commodities, in so far as the advertising is done through media (such as the Press, or radio) which provide other services as well.

There are two important points to be made in connection with subsidised commodities belonging to category (4):

(*a*) Commodity subsidies provided by private firms always presuppose a state of imperfect competition or monopoly; they cannot occur under perfect competition. The reason for this is that under conditions of perfect competition the prices of all commodities and services are given to the individual firm, and all demands are infinitely elastic, so that a change in the rate at which any particular commodity is supplied by the firm cannot have any repercussion at all on the terms on which the firm can sell other commodities. Under perfect competition, the demand for any commodity, or any separate part of a composite commodity, is "given" to the firm; hence it could never pay a firm to sell a particular commodity below its own marginal cost. It follows also that under perfect competition, all separate (or rather separable) parts of a composite commodity would be priced separately; or if they happen to be sold together, the price of the whole could never be different from the sum of the prices of its parts, any one of which could equally be obtained by the buyer separately, if he so desired. Subsidies and joint-pricing are the main distortions of the price structure of a system of monopolistic competition, as compared with the hypothetical price structure of a purely competitive system.[1]

(*b*) On the principles of the economics of welfare, commodity

[1] Cf. also § 36, p. 130.

subsidies (along with commodity taxes) involve a maldistribution of resources between different uses, unless they are offset by corresponding differences between marginal private cost and marginal social cost. This is so because the optimum distribution of resources which maximises welfare relative to a given pattern of consumers' preferences (and also a given pattern of income distribution between persons) is necessarily the one which secures the equality of price and marginal social cost, for all commodities.[1]

(iii) The expenditure on "advertising service" can be varied, not only by varying the *amount* of information supplied, or the number of consumers of this information (i.e. the number of people to whom it is supplied), but also by varying the elaborateness of advertising techniques involving increased advertising expenditure per consumer, through putting the same information across "more forcibly". Whereas with the other services supplying information more expenditure generally means the supply of more information, or the supply of the same amount of information to more people,[2] with advertising, increased expenditure may only mean the more frequent repetition of the same information, or its spreading over a larger area (larger letters, with more space between them, larger-sized illustrations) or drawing upon the support of wider and richer emotional associations. Hence the common distinction between "informative" and "persuasive" advertising. This distinction, like everything else in economics, is one of degree. All advertising is persuasive in intention[3] (i.e. it is supplied with a view to finding prospective buyers), and all is informative in character (in the sense that it supplies *some* information, even if it is only the name of some firm or product).

[1] A brief note may be necessary on the terms "private" and "social cost", as here used. The marginal private cost of a commodity is the increase in outlay, as recorded by the individual producing unit, following upon the expansion of production by a small increment. The marginal social cost of any particular commodity a, measured in terms of some other commodity b, is the amount of b which under the given conditions of production has to be given up (or sacrificed) in order to expand the production of a by a marginal increment. If the expansion of the production of a involves no inevitable reduction in the output of other commodities, its marginal social cost is clearly zero. In a state of full employment, where the expansion of production in some directions necessarily involves reductions in others, the marginal social cost of a commodity will equal its marginal private cost if (a) the marginal costs of individual factors are equal to their prices; (b) the change in output leaves the productivity of resources engaged elsewhere unaffected (i.e. there are no external economies or diseconomies).

[2] With the possible exception of increased outlay on newspaper headlines.

[3] With the exception perhaps of certain legal and personal announcements.

But with some advertising, the motive of persuasion is very large, while with others (such as classified advertising, price-lists or directories) it is relatively small. Modern display advertising contains relatively little information, but it is designed to force the information which it does contain to the attention of the public by its sheer prominence.

4. It follows from the above considerations that the expenditure on advertising cannot be justified—on the purely formal plane of economic theory—in the same way as the expenditure on other commodities and services, merely by reference to the principle of "consumers' sovereignty"—i.e. by accepting consumers' preferences as the ultimate criterion of all economic activity.[1] For advertising, being a subsidised commodity, is not supplied *in response* to consumers' demand; the scale of expenditure on advertising—unlike the scale of expenditure on goods and services which are not subsidised—is not determined by the preferences of the customers, as registered through the price-mechanism, but by purely extraneous considerations. Profitability is a test of consumers' preferences only in a purely competitive system where the price-mechanism accurately registers the pull of competing attractions.[2]

This does not necessarily mean that the expenditure, from a social point of view, is wasted (in the sense that it brings no utility—or a utility considerably less than the cost); it means, however, that it needs to be justified by considerations other than profitability. In an analogous manner to the goods and services provided through the public purse, the question whether it is wasteful or not must be determined by reference to the presumed social utility of the service which the expenditure provides.

5. An examination of the social utility of a particular service

[1] Whether consumers' preferences should, in fact, be accepted as the ultimate criterion is another question that cannot be gone into here. In accepting "consumers' sovereignty", welfare economics makes two postulates, neither of which is universally true: that consumers act rationally, and that their individual preferences are independent of each other. These questions, however, are not really relevant to the point made in the text, viz. that advertising outlays cannot be justified by the criterion of consumers' preferences, even if the latter is accepted as the ultimate criterion.

[2] The same mental confusion which regards any economic activity as being in response to consumers' preferences, merely because that activity happens to be profitable, is encountered in many other contexts—e.g. when it is argued that the increase in distributive costs in the inter-war period was merely a reflection of the consumers' desire for "greater service".

which is *not* provided in response to market demand must attempt to answer three questions: (1) Is there a genuine need for it? (2) Does it fulfil this need in a satisfactory manner as to quality? (3) Is the scale of expenditure on it justifiable or excessive?

6. There can be no question as to the genuine need for information concerning the price, and especially the quality, of commodities available for purchase. This need becomes all the greater the more important are the complex and durable products of industry in the consumers' budget, goods which the individual consumer buys only infrequently—perhaps only once in a lifetime—so that he cannot acquire the necessary information merely by experience; and which are, by their nature, so complex that their quality can only be judged by an expert. There is no doubt, also, that if advertising were *not* provided freely, the consumers would be quite willing to pay for the supply of market information (as they already do in some cases, for example, railway guides), though there is reason to believe that the consumers, on the whole, tend to underestimate the benefits of increased knowledge and a strong case might be made out for enlarging the service by means of a subsidy.

7. There is no doubt, therefore, that advertising has a social function to fulfil. What requires consideration is whether it fulfils this function in a satisfactory manner, and without an unnecessary waste of resources which might have been devoted to other uses. As a means of supplying information, it may be argued that advertising is largely biased and deficient. Quite apart from the making of deliberately faked claims about products which legislation and professional etiquette have never yet succeeded in suppressing, the information supplied in advertisements is generally biased, in that it concentrates on particular features to the exclusion of others; makes no mention of alternative sources of supply; and it attempts to influence the behaviour of the consumer, not so much by enabling him to plan more intelligently through giving more information, but by forcing a small amount of information, through its sheer prominence, to the foreground of consciousness.

All these defects arise not because advertisements are supplied freely, but because they are supplied by interested quarters—

the economic units intending to sell the products advertised. In the world of commodities the "authors" write their own reviews; and because all this review-writing in turn provides subsidies to others, the professional review-writers (i.e. the Press) refrain from reviewing their productions at all. The value of the information offered about commodities depends, in precisely the same manner as the value of the information offered about books or plays, or anything else, on its objectivity and impartiality. But impartial and unbiased information could only be provided if the writers of advertisements were financially independent of the products advertised. The natural source for supplying the public with current information about commodities is the Press, which already supplies current information on all other things, and it is at least arguable that if Press-advertising had not developed, the newspapers would gradually have devoted an increasing proportion of their space to giving information on consumers' goods, in the same way as they supply information on plays, horse-races, or the Stock Exchange. The charge that can be made against advertising as a method of supplying market information is therefore not only that it fails to provide enough information or unbiased information, but that its development has indirectly led to the suppression of other channels of information about commodities; and that in consequence the public may actually be provided with *less* information than it would have obtained without it, at a much higher cost to the community.[1]

8. This brings us to the question of the scale of expenditure on advertising. We find that the cost of providing this highly inadequate and defective information-service is exorbitantly high.

---

[1] We must sharply distinguish here, of course, between the purely informative element in advertising and the persuasive element (which belongs to another branch of the argument). If, to take an example, XX, Ltd., spend large sums annually on advertisements, saying "XX is Good For You", this may be an effective method of increasing the sales of XX beer, but the informative content of the advertisement is merely this: "XX, Ltd., believe that the consumption of XX is beneficial to health." Whether this is a valuable piece of information or not, its information-value is exhausted as soon as the public are first told of it. Any further repetition of the message, and its display in prominent form, does not serve the purpose of information but of persuasion; it serves the purpose of inducing the public to believe it as well, and to keep it in the foreground of consciousness. While as a means of persuasion it may be very effective, its information value is zero. (Moreover, assuming the message to be true, it might reach the public in many other ways—through the recommendation of doctors, for instance—it does not necessarily follow that without the advertisement the public would have remained ignorant of it.)

The total national expenditure on all forms of advertising before the war may be put at £90 million.[1] Of this sum, probably not more than £20 million can be put down as the *net* subsidy, paid through advertising, to the news-gathering and informative services of the Press.[2] This leaves the sum of, say, £70 million as the total expenditure on advertising alone. As a proportion of the national income this is certainly not very large. But the proper test to apply here is not the relation of this expenditure to the national income, but (*a*) its relation to the expenditure on all other services concerned with the increase and dissemination of knowledge; (*b*) its relation to the probable cost of providing an adequate information service about commodities, if this service were provided in some other manner.

The total national expenditure, in 1938, on all services concerned with the increase and the dissemination of knowledge might be put at some £310 million, made up as follows (some of the figures are rough estimates):

	£ million
Total Income of all Schools..	125
Total Income of Universities and Colleges	8
Scientific and other Research, outside Universities and Colleges ..	6
Libraries and Museums	4
Total Expenditure on all forms of Newspapers and Periodicals[3] ..	87
Total Expenditure on New Books ..	10
Advertising (net)	70
	310

Not the whole of this sum can be put down as the cost of providing "information", some part of the expenditure on books and periodicals in particular is more properly allocable as "entertainment" (i.e. novels, stories, etc.). But it is difficult to draw the line with precision, or to separate out this item statistically. Even so, the share taken up by the cost of providing market information in the form of advertising is shown to be disproportionately large—it is nearly as great as the whole cost of providing current information in all fields through all forms of the Press,

[1] Cf. Kaldor and Silverman, *A Statistical Analysis of Advertising Expenditure and of the Revenue of the Press*, National Institute of Economic and Social Research, Cambridge University Press, 1948, Chapter II.

[2] Net after deducting all costs, direct and indirect, of providing the advertisements and of the contribution of advertising to the profits of the publishing industry.

[3] This includes the retail value of all newspapers and periodicals sold, plus the net subsidy (taken at £20 million) from advertising.

and over half the total cost of education in all schools and universities together.

Of this £70 million, probably not more than £15–£20 million can be put down to "informative" advertising in the narrower sense, such as price-lists, directories and the classified advertisements of newspapers, leaving about £50–£55 million to all forms of "display advertising". It is this latter sum which would have to be compared with the possible cost of providing an adequate service of information to the public about commodities, if this service were provided independently, and not financed through a subsidy from the producers of the individual goods advertised. The cost of providing an adequate team of investigators, with laboratories—where necessary—for commodity-testing, could hardly exceed £5 million (the pre-war expenditure on *all* forms of research), while the cost of putting the information before the public (through, e.g., the newspapers devoting a certain proportion of their space to it) could hardly be more than a tenth of the present total cost of the services provided by newspapers and periodicals, that is, some £8–£9 million. Thus the cost of an independent information service about commodities—quite disregarding the great improvements in the quality and the quantity of information which it would bring about—could only amount to a fraction of the present cost of advertising to the community.

9. In view of this, it would hardly be justified to spend a great deal of time on this particular aspect of the problem of advertising. A great deal of evidence could no doubt be collected about the informative value of display advertising; the degree of truth and falsehood in advertisements; the extent to which the consumer turns to advertisements as a source of information; the extent to which advertisements appeal to "emotions" rather than to the "intellect", etc. It would probably be found that this informative value varies greatly as between different trades, even within the general category of display advertisements—at one end of the scale being advertisements relating to sales by department stores, which disseminate market information in a strict sense, and tend to reduce market imperfection; at the other end of the scale, advertisements which have a negative informative value, because they induce false beliefs in the consumer about the

capabilities of particular products, such as many advertisements of patent medicines and foods. But investigations of this sort could hardly alter the broad picture which emerges from a general consideration of the problem; and in any case, few would care to justify the methods, and the scale of expenditure, of modern advertising by reference to the services of information which it provides. If advertising is to be justified it must be by reference to its indirect consequences rather than to its direct benefits; it must be justified by demonstrating that improvements in productive and distributive efficiency resulting from advertising more than offset both the direct cost of advertising and the balance of further social losses caused by distortion of demand, etc.

THE INDIRECT EFFECTS OF ADVERTISING

10. As mentioned in paragraph 1, p. 96, the main arguments which are advanced in favour of advertising (and, perhaps, also the main arguments advanced against advertising) are not concerned with the function of advertising as a service to the community, but with its indirect effects upon the working of the economic system as a whole. The arguments advanced in favour of advertising are (briefly) that advertising increases the efficiency of production and distribution both by lowering costs of production and distribution per unit of output (by more than the cost of advertising) and by raising quality; that it increases the general level of output by stimulating activity and reducing unemployment; that it reduces the amplitude of fluctuations by stabilising demand; that it makes for better labour relations in industry; that it increases consumer satisfaction because of the pleasure derived from advertisements and because (by promoting the sale of branded goods) it makes for greater convenience of shopping; and, finally, that by the subsidy it pays to the newspaper industry it promotes a free and independent Press. The arguments advanced against advertising (other than the fundamental one dealt with above) are, to a large extent, the direct opposites of these claims: that advertising increases the power of monopoly, with all its evils; that it tends to reduce the general level of activity by raising prices relatively to costs; that apart from the expenditure on advertising itself, it stimulates

wasteful expenditures in other directions; that it increases the instability of the economic system by increasing the amplitude of fluctuations; that it creates a false sense of values and leads to a constant tendency for actual satisfaction to fall short of expectation; generally, that it leads to inefficient distribution by consumers of their expenditure and that it jeopardises the freedom and independence of the Press.

11. The most important of these supposed effects, beneficial or otherwise, must operate through the influence of advertising on the demand for the commodities advertised. It is only by making the demand for a commodity, or for a particular product of a firm, different from what it would have been without advertising, that advertising activity can have any consequential influence upon efficiency, quality, or the level of employment. Hence, before the latter can be dealt with, the question of the effect of advertising on demand must first be considered.

Here a sharp distinction must be drawn between the effect on the general demand for an advertised commodity, and the effect upon "selective demand", i.e. upon the share of the general demand falling on the product of a particular firm. The former might be insignificant, while the latter is considerable (though it is unlikely to be the other way round; if the former is significant, the latter is likely to be significant as well); and the analysis of the economic effects of these reactions must proceed on different lines.

The Effects of Advertising on the General Demand for Commodities

12. As regards the effects of advertising on general demand (i.e. the extent to which advertising changes the consumers' structure of preferences between different goods and services) it is clearly impossible to lay down any generalisations. In the case of the introduction of some new commodity, such as the vacuum cleaner, the wireless, or the refrigerator, advertising might clearly help in securing the more rapid adoption of the commodity for general use by spreading knowledge about it more quickly than would have been done otherwise.[1] This, however, is an initial effect, whereas the important question is whether *continued* advertising exerts a steady influence on the demand for a commodity already

[1] On this point, cf. also p. 126, note 2.

in general use. On *a priori* grounds one would expect that the sale of certain classes of commodities would be greatly reduced in the absence of advertising—commodities such as patent medicines, hair treatments, etc., or certain types of patent foods, like breakfast cereals or health beverages. It is much more doubtful whether advertising has a significant effect on the consumption of more fundamental classes of commodities, such as tobacco, beer, soap, chocolate, etc.[1] When more information is available about the annual movements of consumption of individual commodities over longer periods, it will be possible to examine this question by separating out the residual variations from the effects of changes in income and changes of relative prices and correlating the former with advertising expenditures.

13. If it were found that in an appreciable number of cases advertising has had a significant effect on general demand, that alone would not, of course, afford any evidence on the effects of advertising on welfare. If the expansion of demand of advertised commodities is at the expense of the demand for non-advertised or little-advertised goods, the shift must be presumed to be due to the unequal incidence of advertising between different trades and it is impossible to say whether consumers, as a body, are better off, or worse off, as a result of the shift; except, perhaps, that it is reasonable to suppose that in neither case could the effect on welfare be very significant.[2]

14. If the expansion of demand is largely at the cost of intended

---

[1] The Borden enquiry, after an extensive investigation of a dozen commodities, here reaches a largely negative conclusion: "From the many cases analysed and from the industry studied one clear and important generalisation can be made, namely, that basic trends of demand for products, which are determined by underlying social and environmental conditions, are more significant in determining the expansion or contraction of primary demand [i.e. general demand] than is the use or lack of use of advertising. . . . Advertising has been effective in expanding demand when underlying factors favoured expansion. In other instances expansion has gone ahead irrespective of whether advertising has been used. Conversely, strong advertising has not overcome contraction of demand when underlying conditions have operated to bring contraction".
"When advertising has been used, its chief effect on primary demand has been either to speed up the expansion of demand that naturally would have come without advertising, or to check or retard an adverse trend. Consumers' wants for products have been determined by the character of consumers and by their existing environment. Advertising has not changed people's basic characteristics, nor has it appreciably changed environment." (Borden, *The Economic Effects of Advertising*, Chicago, 1942, pp. 433-4.)
[2] Except, perhaps when, as an indirect consequence of advertising, people become conscious of certain things of which they previously were unaware (e.g. the B.O. campaigns, etc.).

saving (i.e. if it raises the general propensity to consume) the situation is different; since in that case it could be argued that, in an unemployment economy, advertising increases the level of output and of employment. Some writers[1] have attempted to construct a "case for advertising" by making that assumption. But it is impossible to test this hypothesis statistically, as no method could be devised that would show what savings would have been if advertising had been less. All that it might be possible to show is—if an estimate could be made, on the lines mentioned in paragraph 12 above, of the expansion of demand for individual commodities that is attributable to advertising activity—what was the possible maximum effect on the national income, on the assumption that the *whole* of the expansion was at the cost of saving, and not at the cost of alternative consumption.

Advertising and the Level of Employment

15. On this view, advertising is looked upon as a method of raising the level of employment. In a *laisser-faire* economy where deliberate policies aiming to regulate the volume of employment are excluded, this particular feature of advertising would have to be carefully examined and weighed up against other considerations in arriving at a final judgment on the effects of advertising on welfare. But it is doubtful whether this procedure would be appropriate in the circumstances of present-day Britain. Mass unemployment is now officially recognised to be the consequence of the failure of the economic mechanism to generate sufficient effective demand to take up all the goods that the available resources of the community are capable of producing, and it has been accepted as the responsibility of the State in future to ensure (by means of fiscal and economic policies) that adequate total outlay is generated for the community as a whole, and mass unemployment is avoided. Even if it could be shown, therefore, that advertising, by stimulating spending, tends, *other things being equal*, to make unemployment less, it could no longer be taken for granted that unemployment would, in fact, be greater if the stimulus of advertising were, for some reason, withdrawn—since it could not be assumed that changes in any particular factor

[1] Cf. Rothschild, *Economic Journal*, 1942, pp. 112-21.

affecting the general level of employment would leave all the other determinants of the level of employment unchanged. This means that in investigating the effects of advertising on employment the question to be examined is not whether advertising stimulates employment as such, but whether as a method of increasing employment it is better or worse than other methods.

There is another, logically compelling, reason for this procedure. In an economy where the general level of production is determined by effective demand, and not by the amount of available resources, the ordinary rules of welfare economics are, in a sense, reversed: here "waste" is economical and economy is wasteful. In such an economy, a higher output of any particular commodity or service will not mean a lower, but usually a higher output of other things; the marginal social cost of one commodity or service, therefore, is not positive, but zero or even negative. Hence it is quite impossible on such assumptions to discuss sensibly whether any particular kind of expenditure is "wasteful" or not—on these assumptions no expenditure *can* be wasteful. If the advertising is to be justified as beneficial to the community, this must be demonstrated on more solid grounds than by saying that "since the resources devoted to it would otherwise be wasted in unemployment, it doesn't cost anything". In order, therefore, to arrive at a balanced judgment on the social benefits derived from advertising (or of anything else) the employment effects must be kept rigidly separate from the others; as regards the former, the question to be investigated is whether advertising is an appropriate and socially beneficial method for curing unemployment; while as regards the latter, the same criteria must be employed as are appropriate in an economy where the general level of production is determined by the scarcity of available resources.

16. As regards the effects of advertising on employment two considerations must be kept apart: (i) the effect of advertising on the propensity to consume; (ii) the primary and secondary effect of advertising outlay in raising incomes. As regards the latter, the primary question is whether advertising expenditures represent a form of investment, to be regarded as an "offset" to savings or not. This depends on whether advertising outlays are treated by business-men as capital expenditures, or current expenses (on

income account); in so far as it is the latter, advertising outlays must imply either an equivalent rise in selling prices, or else an equivalent reduction of current profits.[1] In neither of these cases could the expenditure on advertising be regarded as a net addition to total expenditure, and hence to total income. In case it is assumed that the cost of advertising is offset by a reduction of profits (in other words that, in the absence of advertising, selling prices would not have been lower, but net profits, as a proportion of selling price, would have been higher), there is some consequential income-redistribution from profits to salaries and wages (since a proportion of this expenditure goes into salaries and wages), and hence *some* beneficial effect on employment because a higher proportion of salaries and wages can be assumed to be spent than of profits. But, even in this case, the primary and secondary employment-creating effect of the expenditure could only be a fraction of that of an equivalent amount of loan expenditure.

17. Since the great bulk of advertising outlays is probably on income account, and not on capital account, the employment-creating effect of advertising can, therefore, mainly be sought in the psychological effects of advertising on the savings propensities of the general public. Since the savings of the lower classes are in any case inelastic (they are mostly in the form of insurance policies, etc.), the effect of advertising must be sought in the reduction of middle and upper class savings—i.e. by inducing people in these income ranges to spend on advertised goods sums that would otherwise have been saved. We have already seen that it would be very difficult to examine whether this contention is valid or not; and if valid, whether the effect is quantitatively important. But assuming that it is true, there are two things to be pointed out. First, that on general considerations, it is doubtful whether the raising of the propensity to consume of the middle and upper classes in this haphazard manner is a socially desirable way of curing unemployment. Second, that (quite apart from this consideration) it is highly doubtful whether advertising is an appropriate method for *regulating* employment, i.e. for offsetting fluctuations of activity emanating from other causes. For even if

[1] If advertising outlays are treated as part of the prime costs of production, changes in the rate of advertising outlays must be reflected in corresponding changes in the selling price; if they are treated as overheads, this need not be so in the short period.

it could be shown that advertising, in general, makes the pro-portion of income consumed higher than it would have been otherwise, it by no means follows that there is any definite relation between the scale of advertising expenditure and the propensity to consume, i.e. the employment-creating effect of the *marginal* advertising expenditure might well be zero. It would be fallacious, therefore, to assume the existence of a definite "multiplier" with respect to advertising expenditure, in a manner analogous to the multiplier in the case of loan expenditure.

18. As a matter of fact, the scale of expenditure on advertising varies positively with the general level of economic activity,[1] so that, in so far as the effect of marginal expenditure is positive, advertising itself tends to accentuate the amplitude of economic fluctuations. Hence any beneficial effect on the *average* level of employment would have to be set against the increased instability of employment. Further, in so far as, in the absence of advertising, selling prices would have been lower (and not profits higher) the positive effect on the propensity to consume of the individual consumer would have to be set against the negative effect on the propensity to consume for society as a whole, due to the changed income distribution.

19. In view of the above considerations, it does not seem promising to undertake prolonged investigations on the effect of advertising on the general level of employment. As a possible method of ensuring an adequate and steady demand for labour, advertising comes out pretty badly—as is shown by the fact that the pre-war scale of expenditure on advertising did not prevent mass unemployment, and there is no adequate reason to suppose that advertising on a greatly enlarged scale could have done so; and also by the fact that unregulated advertising activity in itself acts, if at all, in a destabilising direction, and it is difficult to see by what methods this tendency could be reversed.

20. Before leaving the question of the effects of advertising on unemployment, we might deal with the related problem of the effects of unemployment on advertising. It is sometimes argued that advertising (or, at any rate, large-scale advertising) is a

---

[1] This can be established on the basis of the American figures and the evidence in Britain points in the same way.

consequence of the insufficiency of effective demand; and that in a full-employment economy it would disappear. Now it is perfectly true that the immediate reason which makes business-men advertise is the fact that they could increase their profits by increasing their sales; under conditions where sales are limited by factors other than demand (by the amount of raw materials available, by the scarcity of labour, or of plant and machinery) there would be no point in stimulating sales by advertising. But it is most unlikely that the kind of full employment that is likely to be realised in peacetime will be such as to make it impossible, or unprofitable, for the individual firm to expand. Under conditions of extreme scarcity, as in wartime, the output of the typical firm is limited by raw-material allocations, or the difficulty of hiring more labour. It faces a "seller's market" and has no difficulty whatever in selling all that it can produce.[1] But the mere disappearance of mass unemployment in peacetime will not (and could not) imply a state of affairs where the scarcity of labour is so acute that expanding firms should be unable to expand; nor will it imply the extreme wartime scarcity of materials or equipment. The fundamental reason (as will be argued below) why the individual firm's sales, at any time, are limited by demand (and not by rising costs of production) are to be sought, not in a general insufficiency of demand and the existence of unemployment, but simply in the imperfection of the market. The forces making for advertising will continue to operate whether there is large-scale unemployment or not; indeed, they operate more strongly in times of prosperity than in times of depression. In the past, in times of boom (when there was the nearest approach to full employment) advertising activity did not tend to disappear; on the contrary it was at its height.

The Effect of Advertising on Selective Demand

21. We now come to the question of the influence of advertising on "selective demand"—i.e. on the demand for the products of a

---

[1] In conditions of *wartime* full employment, therefore (though not peacetime full employment), advertising should tend to disappear. The reasons why it did not, in fact, do so, were (*i*) business-men regarded the situation as temporary, and continued to advertise in order to maintain goodwill for the post-war period; (*ii*) the system of taxation, especially E.P.T., made advertising, from the point of view of the advertising firm, extremely inexpensive.

particular firm. This, of course, is a question of prime importance
to the business-man; and a large amount of work has been undertaken in order to determine the "pulling power" of advertising in
different trades, with different kinds of media and with advertisements relying on different kinds of appeal. With some kinds of
advertising the sales-response can be more or less exactly measured
(as e.g. with mail advertising, or Press-advertising asking for a
response through the mail) while, with other kinds, the response
can only be estimated through an analysis of time-series, where
the reliability of the estimate depends on the degree to which
irrelevant factors affecting sales can be eliminated. No doubt, in
many cases, the advertiser remains in the dark as to the effect of
his advertising outlay on his sales; no doubt, also, much advertising expenditure is "wasteful" in the sense that the sales-response
is less than adequate to compensate for the outlay. But as to the
broad fact that, by and large, advertising raises the demand curve
for the product of the firm, there can be little doubt;[1] and,
provided this "broad fact" can be taken for granted, the questions
of how (and why) this "pulling power" varies as between different
trades, and different forms of appeal—why some advertising is so
much more successful than others—fall outside the scope of this
enquiry. These questions are only of importance to the economics
of business management; from the point of view of the economics
of welfare they are irrelevant—or rather, the only question that
is relevant is whether this "pulling power" exists or not. If it did
not exist—if, in other words, the advertising outlay were a sheer
waste, from the business point of view—the question whether
advertising is profitable or not from a social point of view simply
would not arise. The latter problem arises when the former—the
profitability of advertising to the advertiser—is already taken for
granted.

22. Economists, in dealing with the problem of advertising,
generally took it for granted that advertising outlay raised the
demand curve for a particular firm, other things being equal,
including the scale of advertising outlays of rival firms. They
argued, however, that while advertising might be profitable from

---

[1] Otherwise it would be difficult to explain why firms should continue to spend large
sums, year by year, on advertising, even when their sales, over time, tend to be constant.

the point of view of any particular firm, if that firm alone adopted it, it would be a sheer waste if advertising by one firm led to the adoption of similar advertising by its rivals, since the advertising efforts of the various firms would largely cancel each other out, leaving the sales, etc., of particular firms pretty much as they were. Thus Professor Pigou:[1] "It may happen that the expenditures on advertisement made by competing monopolists simply neutralise one another, and leave the industrial position exactly as it would have been if neither had expended anything. For clearly, if each of two rivals makes equal efforts to attract the favour of the public away from the other, the total result is the same as it would have been if neither had made any effort at all."

23. It is, however, most unlikely that the general adoption of advertising in a particular trade should leave the relative position of the various firms, or even the "pattern" of the industry, unaffected; and in the reasons why this is so lies perhaps the real secret of advertising. To make this clear, let us assume that a particular trade was initially in equilibrium with *n* firms, not necessarily of the same size, but with a constant pattern of size distribution, i.e. with the size and character of the "representative firm" constant. If *all* firms adopted advertising, this would have a similar effect on the equilibrium of the industry to that of some new invention which introduced internal economies of scale: it would render the existing distribution of sales among firms unstable. The reason for this is that the shift of the demand curve resulting from advertising cannot be assumed to be strictly proportionate to the amount spent on advertising—the "pulling power" of the larger expenditure must overshadow that of smaller ones[2] with the consequence (*a*) that the larger firms are bound to gain at the expense of the smaller ones; (*b*) if, at the start, firms are more or less of equal size, those that forge ahead are bound to increase their lead, as the additional sales enable them to increase their outlay still further. Hence, after advertising has been generally adopted, and the trade settles down again to some sort of equilibrium, the pattern of the industry will have changed; sales will have been concentrated among a smaller number of firms,

---

[1] *The Economics of Welfare*, 3rd ed., London, 1929, p. 200.
[2] Cf. Marshall, *Industry and Trade*, p. 307 and note.

and the size of the "representative firm" will have increased. Or, to use a physical analogy, the introduction of advertising causes a competitive field to become "gravitationally unstable". It follows, moreover, that if the previous state of equilibrium was a "stable", and not merely a "neutral" one—i.e. if it was the result of forces tending to establish that particular pattern of output-distribution among firms, and not merely an accidental outcome of the historical development of the industry—this "concentration-effect" of advertising will be a reversible one; the continuance of the new equilibrium will depend on the continuance of advertising, and would be followed by a process of de-concentration if advertising were to cease.

Advertising and Economic Concentration

24. Indeed, the problem is not so much to explain why this concentration should occur as a result of advertising, but why it should come to a halt. If the firms were subject to internal diseconomies of scale, the process would be brought to a halt by the gradual increase in the costs of manufacture; there would necessarily come a point where further shifts in the demand curve, brought about by increased advertising, would fail to compensate for the fall in profits due to higher costs of production. The developments in managerial organisation, etc., over the last half-century or so have shown, however, that not much reliance can be placed on internal diseconomies of scale fixing an "optimum size" to the firm;[1] and in the case of constant returns to scale (and, *a fortiori*, in the case of increasing returns to scale) this process of concentration might go on indefinitely (or until complete monopoly is established) so long as the basic assumptions, that a larger expenditure on advertising exercises a greater "pulling power" than a smaller expenditure, and that the sums which particular firms can devote to advertising are more or less proportionate to their sales, remain valid. But there are reasons to suppose that beyond a certain range these assumptions cease to be valid; there comes a point where the market becomes "saturated" with

[1] It is only in the case of the one-man or one-family business that diseconomies of scale might be regarded as an important limiting factor; and here again the limitation in the amount of capital at the firm's command is probably more important than the inefficiencies due to large-scale management.

advertising and further increases of outlay will yield rapidly diminishing returns. Moreover, as the concentration process proceeds, and the surviving firms get larger in size, it becomes more and more difficult for any firm to increase its advertising outlay relatively to its competitors; since these competitors can, and would, re-act by increasing their own expenditure in turn, if necessary out of all proportion to the magnitude of their sales. Whereas the early stages of the concentration process are more or less automatic—the disappearance of the small firms proceeds automatically as a result of the increasing unprofitability[1] of their business, due to the changing character of the market—the later stages are apt to take on the character of "war", with each firm jealously guarding its own territory and being prepared, if necessary, to incur heavy losses in order to repel any attempt at intrusion by others. Hence the ultimate effect of this concentration process is much more likely to be some form of "oligopoly" (the dominance of the market by a few large firms) than monopoly.

25. If the above argument is, in general, valid—if, in other words, there is a general presumption that advertising promotes industrial concentration to a greater or lesser degree, the extent varying with the character of the individual trade in question, the "advertisability" of the particular commodity, the technical conditions of its production, etc.—the problem of the economic effects of advertising becomes (in part) one of analysing the economic effects of industrial concentration. The judgment of economists brought up on the traditional doctrines is generally adverse. Advertising is a method of differentiating, in the eyes of the consumer, the products of one firm from those of its competitors; it is a method, therefore, of reducing the scope and effectiveness of price-competition by attaching a strong element of "goodwill" to each firm. Hence, according to this argument, if the concentration is economically justified owing to economies of large-scale production, it does not necessarily follow that it would not have come about without advertising; for, in the absence of advertising, firms would have been driven to compete on the basis of price, and price-competition would have brought about the

---

[1] Both on account of the rise in costs (due to advertising) and the fall in sales, due to more powerful advertising by others.

same result, in a more beneficial way to the consumer.[1] If, on the other hand, the concentration is not justified by the existence of economies of large-scale production—if there are constant returns to scale, and, *a fortiori*, if there are diminishing returns—concentration brought about by advertising is definitely harmful; for quite apart from the rise in costs caused by advertising, there is a rise in the margin of profit, and hence in the prices paid by the consumer, due to the reduction in the degree of freedom of entry of newcomers, and the consequent increase in the degree of monopoly power enjoyed by those inside the trade. For the larger the size of, and the greater the amount of, "goodwill" attached to the "representative firm" in any particular trade, the larger is the initial outlay which must be risked by a potential newcomer who wishes to invade the market; the higher, therefore, the level of "normal profit" which insiders can enjoy without attracting new competitors.

26. This is the essence of the argument, frequently advanced, that advertising is mainly a device for strengthening monopoly power and weakening competition, and is, therefore, anti-social in its effects in much the same way, and for much the same reasons, as other institutional devices limiting competition, such as exclusive patent rights. There can be no doubt that advertising, by promoting industrial concentration, automatically enlarges the range within which firms are free to vary prices. But the view that this increased monopoly power is necessarily anti-social in its effects—which is the basic tenet of economic liberalism— assumes that a freely competitive market has the same freedom and opportunities as regards the methods and organisation of production, and the same facilities for taking advantage of innovations, as a monopolistic one. This view, however, is challenged by those who maintain that some degree of monopoly is essential in order to secure higher forms of technical organisation which require large outlays of fixed capital, and which could never be achieved in a market where entry is free.[2] This is, in my view, the real issue involved in examining the economic effects of advertising, in comparison with which other aspects of the problem are

[1] This argument is dealt with at some length below.
[2] Cf. Schumpeter, *Capitalism, Socialism and Democracy*, Chapter VIII, for a brilliant statement of the case for monopoly.

relatively insignificant. That advertising promotes the concentration of economic power cannot reasonably be doubted—indeed, if it did not, the whole discussion about the effects of advertising on the efficiency of the economic system would be irrelevant, since only by promoting concentration can advertising affect the working of the economic organisation—but the question whether this is beneficial to society or not cannot be decided by the formal arguments of economic theory. During the last forty years or so the competitive markets typical of nineteenth-century capitalism—with individual industries consisting of hundreds of small or medium-sized businesses, whose individuality was, over a wide field of industry, hidden from the consumers' view—were replaced by a new type of economic organisation, the modern oligopoly, where a few (usually less than half a dozen) firms control the vast bulk of the market. A wide range of manufactured consumers' goods (with the exception of textiles and clothing and smaller household goods) are now supplied through markets of this character. It would be idle to ascribe the *whole* of this change to the influence of advertising—the development of modern techniques of business management, the joint stock company law, the patent law, the invention of new techniques of production giving greater advantages to larger scale production, all contributed to it—but advertising was an important contributing factor; in certain cases perhaps the dominant one. Has it, on balance, enhanced economic progress? To clarify the issues in relation to the particular phenomenon of advertising, it is necessary to make a digression and examine briefly the functioning of the "competitive market" which the modern oligopoly has superseded.

Types of Market Organisation

27. In the case of certain foodstuffs and raw materials, the forces of competition gradually evolved a highly technical organisation for "clearing" supply against demand, in the shape of centralised markets ("exchanges") where the personal element in dealing (the reliance of the buyer on the personal reputation of the seller, and vice versa, commonly called "goodwill") is completely eliminated, where, therefore, all buyers and sellers are in

perfect inter-communication with each other; and where anyone, at any time, can buy or sell an amount of any particular commodity at a price which reflects the balance of pressure of total demand against total supply existing at that moment. Thus for commodities like wheat, the price in pre-war days at which a farmer in some outlying district in Canada could sell his produce, and the price at which the miller in some English town bought it, were alike determined by the world price (with appropriate deductions or additions for costs of transport, etc.), as registered by the produce exchanges of Chicago, Liverpool or Amsterdam. The prerequisite for the development of such a perfect market is the complete standardisation of the product achieved by a suitable system of grading which makes it possible to evolve a standard contract, giving full protection both to the buyer and to the seller against the non-fulfilment of any of the conditions of sale. This complete standardisation is necessary, not only in order to secure a sufficient volume of transactions in an article for which a single price can be quoted, but chiefly because only through the development of the standard contract of the "standard product" can the element of "goodwill" be eliminated and the complete unity of the market be secured.[1]

28. In the case of manufactured articles, this type of market organisation could not develop because the necessary degree of standardisation could not be achieved. Not only are the products of manufacturing industry infinitely more complex in character, and hence capable of much greater individual variation, than the staple commodities, but the range of commodities actually produced at any one time forms only a small fraction of the range of commodities potentially available; the problem of selecting what should be produced requires the function of "initiation" which the automatism of a perfect market does not provide. In the case of manufactured commodities, these marketing functions devolved—in the market organisation typical of the nineteenth century—on a special class of traders, the wholesale dealers. It was through the agency of wholesale merchants that the competition between ultimate sellers and ultimate buyers could make

---

[1] The argument in the next two paragraphs owes much to the exposition of R. G. Hawtrey, in *The Economic Problem*, especially pp. 19-23 and pp. 34-43.

itself effective throughout the length and breadth of the market. If the number of wholesalers is not too numerous, and each dealer is in touch with a number of sources of demand and a number of sources of supply, any individual buyer or seller is accorded the same kind of facility of buying and selling on the most favourable terms, as if transactions took place through a centralised market. The wholesalers' function, however, was something more than that of bringing buyers and sellers together. The specification of the things that the manufacturers were to produce was made out (in general), not by the manufacturers themselves, nor by the consumers, from whom the demand proceeded, but by the wholesale merchants. The manufacturer made things to the orders received from the wholesalers; the retailer selected his own orders from the choice of things offered by the wholesalers, and repeated the orders according to the strength of consumers' demand for the individual products. It devolved, therefore, on the wholesalers to determine what should be produced and made available to the market and to strike a balance between following consumers' requirements more closely by offering wider assortments and obtaining things more cheaply by ordering larger volumes on the same pattern. The ultimate consumer relied on his local retailer to offer him a satisfactory range of products, of dependable quality; and the retailer in turn relied on the wholesaler to supply him with what the consumers wanted. The retailer's success depended on the extent to which he could build up a local reputation for supplying "good value" for the consumers' money; while the wholesaler's success depended on the extent to which he could build up a similar "goodwill" among retailers.[1] To the extent to which individual products were "branded" (i.e. sold under a trade-name), it was the wholesalers',

[1] "The share of each dealer in the business of the market depends partly on the amount of his capital, but still more on the people accustomed to deal with him. That does not mean that those who buy from the market or sell to it will confine themselves each to the services of one dealer. But each will usually transact business only with a limited circle of dealers, each of whom will receive a fairly steady share of his custom. Everyone concerned will tend, in the absence of any reason to the contrary, to follow his established routine, and to deal in the ways he knows with the people he knows. This continuity in dealings creates what is called business connection or goodwill. It is the very stuff and substance of the dealer's business. The principal deterrent upon intruders into the market is that they have to create their goodwill from the beginning. The distinguishing characteristic of the successful merchant is the extent and solidity of his goodwill." Hawtrey, *The Economic Problem*, p. 39.

rather than the retailers' or manufacturers', names under which they were known.

"*Wholesalers' Domination*"

29. These "wholesaler-dominated" markets were competitive, in the sense that manufacturers' selling prices tended to conform fairly closely to costs of production and the more efficient manufacturers, by being able to supply the wholesaler more cheaply, could forge ahead and oust the less-efficient ones. But the efficiency of the organisation was subject to severe limitations, in several respects:

(i) In order to secure unity in the market, the number of wholesale houses had to be small, for otherwise it would have been impossible for buyers and sellers to be "in touch with" the whole field. Neither manufacturers nor retailers could deal with more than a certain number of wholesalers at the same time. A big wholesale merchant, by virtue of the larger turnover, had the double advantage of being in touch with a greater number of producers and of retailers, and thus being better situated to choose his opportunities for both buying and selling.

(ii) Since the number of wholesalers was limited, and each had his own "trade connection", competition between them was imperfect and was largely restricted to the "facilities and conveniences" offered to customers.[1] Potential competition by newcomers set certain limits to the (more or less) "conventional" profit margin maintained in a particular trade, but even these limits were periodically raised as the dealers inside the trade became larger and more firmly established. But competition between *insiders* was not in the matter of price and profit margins, but in things like efficient grading, packing, prompt fulfilment of

[1] "In the more general case, where a market is not so formally constituted and prices are not so sensitive, there tends to be a tacit understanding among dealers to respect one another's profits. A 'balance of power' is preserved, and anyone who disturbs it by a campaign of price-cutting is a common enemy. If he succeeds, the other dealers will all suffer; if he fails, all the disturbance, with the trouble and anxiety and loss caused to the dealers, will have been to no purpose. In such a market dealers will try to keep prices unchanged for considerable periods of time, even though there may be quite perceptible changes in supply and demand. They may go on selling at a uniform price, even though they are buying in a sensitive market, where prices are rarely the same for five days together, or though their sales are noticeably rising or falling. When the circumstances make a change of price desirable, they will all make the same change at the same time, either by agreement or by following the lead of a few." Hawtrey, *op. cit.*, p. 35.

orders, long credit, and—last but not least—a wide variety of choice. The great constitutional weakness of a market organisation of this type was that it did not offer premiums for standardisation, but on the contrary gave every inducement to divide production among an ever-increasing number of varieties and make the size of the *individual* order of a given specification made to the manufacturer smaller.

(iii) Although (as mentioned above) the specialised knowledge of buying by wholesalers made for the survival of the relatively efficient manufacturer, the system imposed, nevertheless, certain limitations on the growth of efficiency. The manufacturer was not in a position to initiate *large changes*, either in the matter of the scale of his organisation, or in the nature or the range of products produced. He had to rely on what orders he could get and, if his efficiency justified expansion, he had to keep in step with the wholesalers' gradual recognition of this fact; the volume of his business increased gradually as his "success" gradually enlarged his trade connection. Large changes in technique, which both required large outlays of fixed capital and could only become profitable with a greatly enlarged volume of sales, were specially risky to introduce when the sales-volume depended on the goodwill of a few buyers.

30. It was a natural development from this situation that the manufacturers should attempt to create a "goodwill" by appealing—so to speak—over the heads of the wholesalers to the ultimate buyers, the consuming public. This was only possible by providing the goods—in the form in which they reached the ultimate consumer—with brands carrying the manufacturer's name or his legally protected trade-mark. The wholesalers—not unnaturally—resisted this development, so that manufacturers' trade-marks in consumers' goods were at first confined to patent medicines and certain other products which embodied some process secured by patents. But the mere provision of a trade-mark—even when combined with distinctive package, labelling and colouring—is not a very effective method of securing "consumer goodwill"—or, rather, the goodwill which is grounded in the buying habits of the ultimate consumer is generally a less secure and more fickle thing than the goodwill of professional buyers. Since consumers

spend their income on a large number of things, and (in the great majority of cases) only an insignificant part of their income on any one article (which they prefer to buy with a minimum of fuss and bother), it is a difficult business to induce them to adopt buying habits sufficiently firm to make them demand a particular brand when purchasing a commodity from the retailers. It is here that large-scale advertising has a vital rôle to play. Advertising makes the public "brand-conscious"; it is not so much a question of making the consumer buy things which he would not have bought otherwise; but of crystallising his routine habits, of making him conscious that keeping to a certain routine in consumption means not only buying the same commodities in a vague sort of way, but sticking to the same brands.[1] It is probably no exaggeration to say that without the support of large-scale advertising this attempt of manufacturers to release themselves from dependence on wholesalers' goodwill, by building up consumers' goodwill could not have succeeded.

"*Manufacturers' Domination*"

31. Thus the growth of modern advertising is closely linked up with the manufacturers' attempt to obtain control of the marketing and distributive mechanism; and conversely the growth of "manufacturers' domination" was closely linked up with the discovery of the power of advertising.[2] With the aid of the goodwill created by advertising began that process of growth and consolidation of individual concerns—both

---

[1] The desire for change and novelty as a motive of human conduct is stressed in sociological and economic writings so much that there is a danger of overlooking the opposite motive which is even more powerful in shaping conduct in everyday life: the desire for a settled routine, of not having to decide afresh every time a new purchase is made. Departure from routine requires some conscious weighing of alternatives; it involves an effort which individuals normally like to avoid, except when the monotony following from too much routine itself becomes oppressive, in which case departure from routine becomes welcome for its own sake. Any device which enables individuals to follow a settled routine more easily and "automatically" will therefore have a powerful influence on everyday conduct, though in a subconscious kind of way; and it is by catering for this desire for routine—quite as much as, or even more perhaps, than by the awakening of "new wants"—that advertising influences conduct.

[2] According to Presbrey, *History and Development of Advertising*, pp. 337 ff. and 360 ff., manufacturers' advertising on a large scale began in the 1890s in the United States. On the evidence of the American Census figures the highest percentage rate of growth in total Press advertising was not reached until the decade 1909-19. There are no comparable estimates available as to the growth of manufacturers' advertising in Britain.

horizontally and vertically—the outcome of which was the type of economic organisation characterised above by the name of the "modern oligopoly". In the course of this development independent wholesalers were either eliminated or reduced to the function of mere distributing agents, and suppliers of credit to the retailers, with no goodwill of their own and no power of initiative. One of the main distinguishing features of this type of market organisation is that the manufacturers determine not only the factory price of their products, but also the wholesale and the retail margins of distribution; a fixed retail price becomes part of the manufacturer's brand and the practice of resale price maintenance is adopted.

It would be a mistake to suppose, however, that this process of transformation from "wholesalers' domination" to "manufacturers' domination" extended over the whole field of industry, or that the concentration process has proceeded in the different industries affected to the same extent. Of certain industries—notably textiles—it is probably true to say that the old type of organisation has remained dominant up to the present.[1] More important, perhaps, than the actual transformation in the character of older industries, was the fact that in the *new* industries—bicycles, motor-car, electrical industries, wireless, etc.—manufacturers' brand control was secured from the beginning. In all these cases large-scale advertising was present more or less from the start.[2]

32. What are the characteristic features of this new type of market organisation which distinguish it from the type discussed in paragraphs 28-29, pp. 121-4? The dominant feature is the existence of manufacturing concerns of a large size, with all its attendant advantages from the point of view of efficiency. These

---

[1] In the U.S. 36·8% of the total "intermediary trades" were handled by independent wholesalers in 1929, and 32·2% in 1935, *Does Distribution Cost Too Much*, p. 345.

[2] It was pointed out earlier, in a different connection (cf. ¶12, p. 108), that advertising in the case of such new commodities has undoubtedly helped in their more rapid adoption for general use. It could also be argued that the mere knowledge that a market can be created for a new product more rapidly by means of advertising, might induce entrepreneurs and investors to sink capital into a new project at an earlier stage (or with a lesser prospect of profit), than they would have done otherwise. It would be very difficult to submit this particular effect of advertising to any empirical test; but some notion of the importance of this kind of advertising might be obtained by an examination of how much the total outlay on advertising at any one time does, in fact, represent the advertisements of "new products".

may be grouped under four heads. First, there are the technical economies of large-scale plant, which require a certain minimum scale of operations for efficient working. The actual scale of operations of a given concern can, of course, be much larger than that which is required to secure these technical economies; the necessary minimum size probably varies greatly between industry and industry. But a firm whose scale of operations is much larger than the minimum would still be able to secure these technical economies by duplicating the "optima plant"; whereas the diseconomies that may be associated with size are not connected with technique, but only with managerial efficiency. Secondly, there are the advantages of what may be termed "internal standardisation"; of concentrating production among a smaller number of varieties, and thus getting the advantages of "long runs" in any particular line. The manufacturer who distributes his product under his own brand and who advertises on a large scale has much greater freedom in this respect than a manufacturer who produces on the orders of the wholesaler;[1] though the nature of competition might prevent him from making full use of the possibilities inherent in standardisation.[2] Thirdly, the large concern is much less likely to suffer from shortage of capital, and is able to borrow (if necessary) more cheaply. (This is a genuine technological economy, and not merely a pecuniary one, in that the investment of capital in large-firm industries will tend to be pushed much further than in small-firm industries.) Fourthly, the large concern is able to engage in activities, the expense and riskiness of which would be prohibitive to the small firm; the most important of these being a research laboratory. The last two points, taken together, mean that the large-firm industries are much better adapted to take advantage of continuous technological improvement than small-firm industries. As against these advantages, the main disadvantage of this type of organisation (again from the point of view of productive efficiency) lies in the

---

[1] The economies of large-scale production and the economies of standardisation are not always kept distinct from one another, though the two are separate. There are certain economies which depend on the scale of the producing organisation, and others which depend on the output of a particular "product". There are reasons to believe that economies of the second type continue to be important long after economies of the first type are exhausted.

[2] Cf. ¶35, pp. 129-30.

diseconomies of large-scale management; though it is arguable that inefficiencies of management are more the consequence of rapid growth than of mere size; and that they are more important in the case of "vertical" than of "horizontal" expansion.[1]

33. There can be little doubt that on the side of efficiency, the advantages of the large-firm organisation of industry may be considerable. The main disadvantages of this type of economic organisation are in a different field; they are connected with the nature of the competitive conditions, the peculiar blend of competition and monopoly, which is associated with it. We have mentioned already[2] that the larger the size of, and the greater the goodwill attached to the typical firm in an industry, the greater is the degree of its "monopoly power", which means that the higher is the price it can charge without attracting new competitors into the field. In a purely competitive industry, where entry is completely free, the maximum price which "insiders" can charge without attracting "outsiders", and the minimum price which they require in order to continue to supply the same market, are approximately equal to each other. This, however, is not the case in markets that are imperfectly organised, and where, in consequence, goodwill or business connection is a significant element in trading. In such markets the freedom of entry is limited by the fact that there is a special cost to be incurred on entering the market—the cost of entry—which is not part of the costs of production of a going concern. If we denote the price which just fails to cover the costs of production[3] of potential new entrants by p and the costs of production (inclusive of normal profit) of the representative firm by c, then $p-c$ is the amount by which the selling price of the representative firm can exceed its own costs, and $\dfrac{p-c}{p}$ is the measure of the degree of its "monopoly power".[4]

34. It is true that if firms inside the trade competed with one another on the basis of price, this price-competition might drive

---

[1] The above arguments about the advantages of large-scale organisation referred to "horizontal" expansion. The economies of "vertical" expansion are largely pecuniary rather than technological in character.

[2] Cf. ¶25, pp. 118-19.

[3] Including, of course, a normal rate of profit under "cost".

[4] The definition of "monopoly power" here adopted is different, of course, from the more usual one based on elasticity of demand.

the price down to c (or even below it, to the level of prime costs) quite irrespective of p. But in an imperfect market price-competition between insiders is an exceptional state of affairs, not the rule. Even in a many-firm industry, firms do not usually compete by the crude method of trying to underbid each other.[1] Under conditions of oligopoly, it is even rarer; when it occurs (it is termed "cut-throat competition" by business-men) it is usually associated with some definite strategic objective—such as the elimination of a financially weak competitor, or as the prelude and inducement to amalgamation—and usually ends with amalgamation or agreement. It is no more a normal state of affairs than war is a normal state among nations. Hence we can assume that the prices ruling in an industry are normally set by the level of p, i.e. the threat of outside competition, and not by c, the costs of production applicable to "going concerns".

35. It would be wrong to suppose, however, that the difference $p-c$ is normally retained by the firms in the form of profit. In an industry that is not a pure monopoly but consists of a number of separate concerns, each of which is striving to obtain a growing share of the market, a considerable part, if not the whole, of the difference will tend to get taken up by the expenses incurred in order to enlarge the size of the market, the expenses consequent on "non-price competition", commonly referred to by economists as "selling costs". The distinguishing mark of "selling costs" is that they arise *in consequence* of the fact that the price is higher than the purely competitive price, and their magnitude will vary with this difference, i.e. it will depend on the magnitude of the obstacles facing outsiders. Selling costs exist with all kinds of market organisation (except with the perfect market which dispenses completely with goodwill). They arise, therefore, with "wholesalers' domination" just as much as with "manufacturers' domination". But it is only in the latter case that they become quantitatively important as a proportion of final price.[2] A further

---

[1] Cf. the quotation from Hawtrey, p. 123 above.
[2] According to the investigations of the Twentieth Century Fund in America, *Does Distribution Cost Too Much* (New York, 1939), pp. 194-5 and p. 345, approximately half the costs incurred by wholesalers can be put down as "selling costs". But since the wholesale merchants' margin is only some 13·5% of the final price, in markets where selling costs are mainly incurred in the wholesaling stage, the proportion of selling cost in final price must necessarily remain limited.

complication arises from the fact that the difference $p-c$ cannot be taken as given, irrespective of whether selling costs are incurred or not, or of how they are incurred. In so far as the services provided[1] in conjunction with these selling costs are such that they increase the manufacturer's goodwill and attach his customers more firmly to himself[2]—which they mostly are—the level of p is raised. Hence the incurring of selling costs may be regarded as partly "competitive" (i.e. aiming to enlarge the firm's share in the market) and partly "protective" (i.e. aiming to increase the firm's monopoly power), though these two kinds of effects may not always be clearly distinguishable from each other.[3] No generalisation seems possible as to how far p can be raised by the expenditure on selling costs, or how much of the difference $p-c$ will tend to be taken up by these outlays.[4] But it is fairly obvious that, as a proportion of the final price, these expenditures might become considerable.

A Digression on "Selling Costs"

36. The distinction between "selling costs" and "production costs" occupies such an important place in the modern theories of value that it is surprising that more effort has not been made by economists to get the theoretical basis of this distinction sufficiently clear. The first systematic treatment of selling costs in economic theory is Chamberlin's;[5] subsequent writers have elaborated the theory further, but without any significant change in the theoretical approach to the problem. The basis of Chamberlin's

---

[1] Cf. pp. 132-5.

[2] *I.e.*, they not only raise the demand curve, facing the individual firm, but also reduce its elasticity at any given price.

[3] "Protective" expenditures would exist, of course, even in an industry which is in the hands of a single concern, i.e. where internal competition is absent.

[4] The purely formal solution of this problem is that the entrepreneur, wishing to maximise his profits, will incur selling costs up to the point where the marginal selling outlay is equal both to the value of the increase in sales (less the marginal costs of production) and to the increase in the value of sales, attributable to this outlay. But this formal (and rather meaningless) proposition is further vitiated by the fact that the functions relating price and volume of sales to selling outlay both assume the price and selling outlays of competititors as given, whereas under conditions of oligopoly the entrepreneurs will take these reactions into account in varying degrees. The question, therefore, of how much the entrepreneur will spend on selling costs under conditions of oligopoly raises the same kind of problems of indeterminacy as the question of price in the theory of duopoly.

[5] *The Theory of Monopolistic Competition*, Cambridge, Mass., 1933, Chapters VI and VII.

distinction is that "selling costs are costs incurred in order to alter the position or shape of the demand curve for a product"[1] while "cost of production includes all expenses which must be met in order to provide the commodity or service, transport it to the buyer, and put it into his hands ready to satisfy his wants",[2] hence the distinction between the two kinds of costs is that "those made to adapt the product to the demand are costs of production; those made to adapt the demand to the product are costs of selling".[3]

The difficulty with this kind of definition is that it leaves the demarcation line between production costs and selling costs entirely a matter of subjective judgment as to what constitutes a "product". If "products" were merely thought of in the purely physical sense (as a certain quantity of "stuff"), *all* costs could be looked upon as "selling costs", since they all have the effect of "raising the demand curve" confronting them. Every lump of coal on its way from the bottom of a mine in Durham to a drawing-room in London is continuously "shifting its own demand curve" upwards or to the right as it travels along. If, on the other hand, a "product" were to be defined by market criteria (i.e. by the attitude of buyers), then all costs would be "production costs", since they all involve a change of "product", as defined by the preferences of the consumers. As between these extremes, the demarcation line as to where product-adaptation ends and demand-adaptation begins necessarily involves the arbitrary judgment of the investigator. No sensible distinction can be drawn, for example, between the entrepreneur's expenditure on advertising (which leaves the physical description of the thing sold unchanged), the expenditure on fancy packing or gift coupons, or the expenditure on "style" (such as the provision of a new bonnet on motor-cars), though some of these clearly must involve some change in the "utility" of the commodity to the consumer. It is this kind of difficulty which has led some economists to deny the validity of the distinction altogether. Thus Professor

---

[1] *Op. cit.*, p. 117.

[2] *Ibid.*, p. 123.

[3] *Ibid.*, p. 125. A more recent definition of selling costs, given in the chapter on Selling Costs in the National Bureau of Economic Research's *Cost Behaviour and Price Policy* (New York, 1943), does not seem to carry the matter any farther: "Selling costs are defined as costs incurred in the effort to obtain those sales which would not have been made without the impetus lent by the selling expenditure" (p. 193).

Knight: "In fact, the advertising, puffing or salesmanship necessary to create a demand for a commodity is causally indistinguishable from a utility inherent in the commodity itself."[1]

This arbitrariness in the distinction between selling costs and costs of production is only apparent, however; it is not really inherent in the subject, but merely the consequence of the (tacit) insistence of economists on looking upon a "product" as a single, indivisible whole, and in confining the analysis to the "single-product" firm. In fact, any "final product", sold to the final consumer, is the result of a greater or lesser number of separate operations and of services conjointly performed, so that it is more akin to a basket containing a bundle of commodities than to a single "unit". A motor-car, for example, as sold by the manufacturer, contains hundreds of parts and embodies hundreds of "improvements", all of which add to the cost, and increase its "utility" to the consumer in varying degrees. When, moreover, the consumer buys a motor-car of a certain make, from a particular dealer, he purchases for a single sum not only the car (as supplied by the manufacturer), but a miscellaneous collection of services as well, such as the assurance of quality as afforded by the reputation of the particular manufacturer; delivery from the factory to his house; the services of a salesman willing to spend hours explaining its merits and offering free demonstration; a certain amount of initial repairs, and guarantees of replacement of defective parts over a certain period; a certain satisfaction of the snob-instinct, as conveyed by particular advertising appeals, etc., etc. All of these undoubtedly add to the value of the car to the particular buyer (though in the case of certain of these services the addition might be very small), and in this sense improve the final "product". But they may not increase the value by nearly as much as the increase in the cost; and under a system of joint pricing (where the whole bundle of goods and services is sold together for a lump sum) the buyer has no means of selecting some of the services and refusing to take others. Since the joint price is given, and since each of the services provided is likely to have *some* value to the buyer, he will prefer having them to not having them—i.e. he will prefer a bundle which contains more of these to one which

[1] *Risk, Uncertainty and Profit*, Boston and New York, 1921, p. 339.

contains less, since in the former case he will get something for nothing. But this does not mean, of course, that he might not prefer to go without them, if the commodity could also be obtained without these services, at an appropriately lower price.[1]

37. It was argued in paragraph 3, p. 100, that in a purely competitive system all services which were, or could be, separately provided would be priced separately. This itself followed automatically from the assumption that the entry to every part of the market was perfectly free and unimpeded, so that if one seller refused to price distinct services or "improvements" separately, there would always be some others who did so.[2] It was also argued in paragraph 35, p. 129, that when there is restriction of entry and the selling price in consequence is higher than the cost of production, competition between insiders will tend to fill the gap by additional expenditures on product differentiation, quality improvements and ancillary services, aiming to attract customers from competitors. Hence "selling costs" are a phenomenon that emerges as a result of joint pricing. The definition which naturally suggests itself from this analysis is that "selling costs" are *the excess of the total expenditures actually incurred, at all stages of the chain of production and distribution, over the amount that would have been incurred, if all separate services performed in the course of the productive and distributive process had been priced separately.* This definition is free from the type of ambiguity mentioned above in that it does not make use of any arbitrary definition of a "product". It is based solely on the changes in expenditure entrepreneurs would find

---

[1] A prospective buyer of motor-cars would prefer, of course, to buy from a dealer who provided nice showrooms with leisurely salesmen having ample time at the customers' disposal, to buying from one who lacked these facilities. But if a dealer of the latter type could be found who sold the same at a 10% lower price, the buyer might easily prefer him.

[2] A certain amount of joint pricing would, of course, be inevitable under any system, simply because of the cumbrousness that pricing would involve if everything were priced separately and each particular customer could select any combination from almost infinite "bundles". But this is merely another way of saying that the economies (in time and bother) gained from a simpler system of pricing themselves introduce certain restrictions on competition; though in the absence of other causes of restriction these may not amount to very much. It shows, however, that the requirements of "perfectly free and unimpeded" competition are impossible of realisation in a world where the number of potential commodities (i.e. the number of distinct commodities and services that are "desired" by consumers and are potentially obtainable) is infinitely large and where, owing to the economies of large-scale operations and of standardisation, only a small fraction of these could actually be produced at any one time.

profitable under two different systems of pricing but in otherwise equal circumstances. The expenditure on services which would be performed equally under separate pricing must clearly be classed as "production costs", since here the value added by the performance must be higher than, or equal to, the cost. The expenditures on services which would not be provided under a régime of separate pricing are selling costs, though it does not follow, of course, that the value added by the performance is necessarily nil; only that it is less than its cost.

Thus selling costs can arise at all stages of the process of manufacture and distribution, in so far as the commodity manufactured and distributed embodies "features", or is sold in association with complementary services, the independent value of which (to the buyer) is less than the cost incurred in providing them. Thus, suppose that the difference between the manufacturers' "ex-factory" price and the retailers' delivered price of, *e.g.*, a motor-car is £100. This distributive cost of the motor-car covers a host of miscellaneous services to the buyer—delivery from the factory to the home; the opportunity to inspect and to test the article prior to purchase; the servicing of the car during an initial period, etc. If the total value of these services provided by the distributor to the buyer is £50 (in the sense that the buyer would have been willing to pay an additional £50 for these services, even if he had the choice of buying the car without them at the factory price) then £50 of the total cost of distribution will consist of "production costs", while the remaining £50 are "selling costs".

38. It follows from the above analysis that, under monopolistic competition, the investment of resources in any particular direction (i.e. in any particular "line") always tends to be pushed higher than would be profitable under pure competition, the extent varying with the importance of any particular feature as a selling point.[1] The extent of such additional expenditures is a measure of the element of non-price competition. Some form of

---

[1] It would appear that in certain directions it is pushed less far—e.g. in making commodities less durable, in order to increase the rate of replacement purchases. The latter, however, is properly attributable to the existence of imperfect knowledge, on behalf of the consumer, rather than to imperfect competition; the same tendency might operate in much the same way under pure competition, if the consumers are unable to estimate accurately the differences in the probable service-life of competing goods.

such excess expenditures involve changes in the specification of the things produced,[1] which under any existing accounting system would be classed under "costs of manufacture" and not "costs of selling".[2] It cannot, therefore, be expected that the full extent of selling costs incurred in particular commodities could be empirically determined. Nevertheless, certain approximations can be made. Apart from the selling costs incurred in the course of manufacture itself (the excess expenditures on quality and on more variety, "style" costs, costs of expensive package, etc.), which empirically probably could not be separated from the genuine costs of production, the selling costs incurred take, roughly, three forms: (*i*) manufacturers' selling cost in the narrower sense—the compensation and expenses of salesmen, the cost of various kinds of sales-promotion efforts such as free samples, demonstrations, gift coupons, etc.; (*ii*) advertising; (*iii*) the selling costs incurred in the wholesale and retail stages of distribution.[3] Advertising, on the above test, and for the reasons set out in paragraphs 7-9, may be classed almost wholly a selling cost, since the independent value conferred by the service of large-scale advertising must be small, relatively to the expenditures incurred.

39. According to an American estimate,[4] out of a total of 65·6

[1] One interesting conclusion which emerges as a result of this analysis is that under monopolistic competition the quality of the products offered tends to be higher than under a system where the market registers accurately the consumers' choice; the increase in quality being all the larger the higher the degree of monopoly. The business-men's frequent contention that large-scale advertising leads to offering a higher quality product is therefore supported by analysis, in so far as large-scale advertising also tends to raise the degree of monopoly power.

[2] In some ways analogous to selling costs (because they are also part of the "costs of competition", though it is better to treat them as a separate category) are costs deliberately incurred by the entrepreneur in order to raise the costs of competing firms and thus place them in a financially weaker position. This always presupposes that different firms in the same industry show wide differences in unit costs.

[3] The selling costs incurred in the retail stage of distribution are probably more important than those incurred in all the other stages; they take the form of the provision of extra convenience in shopping provided by a multiplicity of shops and a host of miscellaneous services provided free to customers. It is clear that manufacturers' price policies can only partially be held responsible for the growth of selling costs incurred in retail distribution and the decline of price competition among retailers: the growth of price-fixing Retail Trade Associations are probably equally important. Nevertheless, in the case of certain commodities—such as cigarettes, petrol or chocolate—it is fairly certain that the competition between manufacturers had the effect of raising retail margins and thus the number of retail outlets—i.e. the manufacturers induced retailers to push their own brands by the offer of higher margins.

[4] *Does Distribution Cost Too Much*, The Twentieth Century Fund, New York, 1939, pp. 118 *et seq.*

billion dollars' worth of goods sold to final buyers in 1929, 38·5 billions, or 59%, represented the cost of distribution,[1] and only 27·1 billion dollars, or 41%, the costs of manufacture. Out of the total distribution costs incurred by manufacturers, wholesalers and retailers, on the authors' estimate "at least 40% are accounted for by selling and promotional activities, in contrast to the physical task of handling, storing and delivering the goods".[2] Hence the aggregate selling costs incurred in America in 1929 (this excludes, however, the "selling costs" incurred in the course of manufacture itself) were estimated at 14·4 billion dollars, or 22% of the aggregate price paid by final buyers. Of this sum, advertising accounted, however, for only 2 billions, or about 14%. The share of advertising in total selling outlays is therefore relatively modest, even though the above global estimates understate its relative importance, for while selling costs are incurred with most commodities, appreciable amounts of advertising are only incurred in about half of them. Even so, advertising accounts for only 25–33% of the total selling cost of the commodities that are advertised.[3]

Issues Connected with Advertising

40. The conclusions which emerge from our analysis may be summarised as follows:

(1) Large-scale advertising is undoubtedly connected with the type of marketing organisation known as "manufacturers' brand domination". This type of organisation has also involved the

---

[1] This 38·5 billions is estimated to have been made up as follows:

	Billion Dollars	%
Retail Trade	12·6	32·7
Intermediary Trade (wholesale stage)	7·0	18·2
Manufacturers' distribution costs	9·1	23·6
Transportation	8·8	22·9
Other Costs	1·0	2·6
	38·5	100

Of these items, manufacturers' distribution cost is subject to the greatest error, as it was derived from a relatively small sample. The figures for retail and intermediary trade are based on the Census of Distribution. Part of advertising is included in "other costs".

[2] *Ibid.*, p. 298.

[3] Borden, *op. cit.*, pp. 61-7, prints a series of sample studies, by Dun and Bradstreet and others, leading to roughly the same conclusion.

emergence of a much greater degree of concentration of production among firms, and a higher degree of standardisation of the products, than are typical under the system of "wholesalers' domination" which preceded it. Though it does not necessarily follow that because large-scale advertising was instrumental in establishing this type of organisation, continued advertising on a large scale is necessary for its maintenance, there is a presumption that this is, in fact, the case.[1]

(2) The economic effects of advertising must be judged therefore in terms of the advantages of the manufacturers' oligopoly (as against the polypoly under wholesalers' domination), which it helped to create and maintain. The general presumption is that this type of marketing organisation is associated with relatively low production costs and relatively high selling costs (of which advertising is only one manifestation); judgment on its social advantages could only be reached, therefore, as a result of empirical investigations which would throw light on the relative magnitude of these two factors. While the extent of selling costs incurred under oligopoly could roughly be estimated, an estimate of the order of magnitude of the reduction in production costs resulting from a higher degree of concentration and standardisation could only be gained as a result of extensive studies. The most promising method for such an investigation would be to compare the long-term increase in productivity in industries which underwent the transformation to a manufacturers' oligopoly, and compare it with others which remained under "wholesalers' domination".

(3) Given the fact of the economies of large-scale production and standardisation, an efficient productive organisation exploiting these economies necessarily involves restriction on the freedom of choice and the freedom of competition (particularly on the freedom of entry). Large-scale advertising, at best, could be looked upon as one of the possible instruments for bringing about the necessary restriction on competition consistent with efficient

---

[1] In the United Kingdom before the war, 52% of all advertising expenditure (comprising the great bulk of all large-scale advertising) was undertaken by manufacturers; while advertising expenditure, as a percentage of selling price, was considerable, mostly in industries where the advertising was largely confined to 3-9 firms (cf. Kaldor and Silverman, *op. cit.*, pp. 10-11 and 35-6).

production. In judging its social effects, however, it would be necessary to explore possible alternative methods of securing a similar degree of concentration and standardisation in production which may not involve the same waste in the form of high selling costs.

"Retailers' Domination"

41. It remains to consider one other type of market organisation, which might combine, to some extent, the advantages of concentration with those of low selling costs—that of the "retailers' domination". Under this system the original functions of wholesalers are controlled by the retailers, rather than the manufacturers. So long as the size of individual retailing units is small, for the retailers to contact manufacturers directly (or vice versa) is a costly and inefficient method of clearing supply against demand. It requires a knowledge of the market which the individual retailer cannot possess; it involves making individual orders to manufacturers on much too small a scale; and it also involves carrying much greater stocks, in relation to turnover, by the community as a whole. This is no longer the case, however, with the co-operatives, the chain stores, or with mail order houses, whose characteristic features are that they cater for a national, rather than a local, market. Retail organisations of this kind conduct their own wholesaling, and acquire their own goodwill by establishing their own brands of merchandise. Though the rate of expansion of the co-operatives in Britain has declined for some years, the growth of chain stores and of special multiple shops seems to indicate that "retailers' domination" was gaining ground before the war. The same was true in the United States, where the competition of chain stores forced retailers to form their own co-operative wholesaling organisations (the so-called "retailer co-operatives"), while the independent wholesalers, in turn, attempted to protect themselves from threatened extinction by organising their retail customers on co-operative lines (the so-called "voluntary chains"). All three types of large-scale retailing present a potential threat to "manufacturers' domination"; the problem which needs to be explained is why this type of marketing organisation has not made more rapid progress.

42. There can be little doubt that selling costs are considerably

smaller under this kind of organisation. This is shown by the American Census figures,[1] which indicate that the costs of distribution, both at the wholesale and the retail stage, have been considerably lower in the case of chain stores than in the case of manufacturer-dominated distributive organisations, or with the independent wholesalers or retailers, despite the fact that the wages of chain-store employees were some 20% higher than those of corresponding employees of other shops. A third, and possibly even larger, source of economy arises from the fact that with commodities marketed under the distributors' brands the manufacturer is relieved of selling costs[2] and, consequently, the chain and mail order houses are able to secure extra discounts ("advertising allowances") from the manufacturers.[3] In the case of electric refrigerators, for example, the price of Sears Roebuck's brand in the U.S. was lower, for all models, than that of manufacturers' brands, by anything between 15-30%.[4] The distinguishing

---

[1] The U.S. Census of Distribution figures give the following results:
Operating Expenses of Various Types of Retailing Organisations as Percentage of Net Sales.

	1929	1935
Independent Retail Shops	25·6	28·4
Chain Stores (Sectional and National)	22·6	24·0
Manufacturers' Chain Stores	31·6	39·5
Mail Order Houses	25·6	26·2
State Liquor Stores	—	8·3
House-to-House Selling	46·0	45·7
Other Types	15·7	25·2
Average—All Types	24·8	27·5

Operating Expenses of Various Types of Wholesale Organisations, as Percentage of Net Sales.

	1929	1935
Wholesale Merchants	—	13·2
Manufacturers' Sales Branches	9·8	10·1
Chain Store Warehouses	4·3	4·1
Retailer-Co-operative Warehouses	—	5·9
Voluntary Group Wholesalers	—	8·9
Average—All Types	8·9	9·5

Information is also available, classified according to the kind of business, which shows that in certain trades the differences are much larger than that shown for all trades together. Thus in the case of drugs, wholesale merchants' costs were 16·6% of net sales, manufacturers' sales branches 28·4%, and chain store warehouses only 3%.

[2] The distributors' selling costs are included, of course, in the expenses shown above at the wholesale and retail stages.

[3] The Federal Trade Commission in the U.S. brought actions under the Robinson-Patman Act against Bird & Son and the Goodyear Tyre & Rubber Co. for selling to mail order houses at lower prices than to other customers. In both cases the respondents justified the lower price by the lower costs, which in one case amounted to between 10-19% of net sales, in the other between 11 and 23% of the retail price. (Quoted by Borden, *op. cit.*, pp. 467-8.)

[4] Quoted by T.N.E.C. Monograph No. 1, pp. 144-64. Borden (*op. cit.*, Chapter XX) has collected a fair amount of evidence from other trades, pointing in the same direction.

features of "retailers' domination" are, therefore: (*a*) that advertising and other selling expenses are low, because the manufacturer is relieved of them, while the retailers' advertising and other brand-promotional costs are much lower, and generally do not exceed a small percentage of the retail price; (*b*) there are other sources of economies in distribution costs, due to the chain-store type of organisation, notably a higher volume of turnover per store and a higher rate of stock-turn, both in the retail stage and in the wholesale stage.

43. The question whether these economies in distribution costs could be matched with a high degree of efficiency in production, if this system of marketing organisation became general, ultimately turns on whether the number of independent wholesaling units, existing side by side, would turn out to be large or small. If the functions of wholesaling could be concentrated in a few hands, there is no reason why the degree of concentration and standard-isation of production achieved should be any less (it might even be greater) than with manufacturers' oligopoly. The available empirical evidence certainly suggests that manufacturers' brand control, whatever its advantages on the production side, is generally associated with wasteful methods of distribution, and that there are strong inherent advantages in a system which separates the functions of wholesaling from that of manufacturing.

7

WELFARE PROPOSITIONS IN ECONOMICS[1]

In the December 1938 issue of the *Economic Journal* Professor Robbins returns to the question of the status of interpersonal comparisons of utility.[2] It is not the purpose of this note to question Professor Robbins' view regarding the scientific status of such comparisons; with this the present writer is in entire agreement. Its purpose is rather to examine the relevance of this whole question to what is commonly called "welfare economics". In previous discussions of this problem it has been rather too readily assumed, on both sides, that the scientific justification of such comparisons determines whether "economics as a science can say anything by way of prescription". The disputants have been concerned only with the status of the comparisons; they were—apparently—agreed that the status of prescriptions necessarily depends on the status of the comparisons.

This is clearly Mr. Harrod's view. He says: "Consider the Repeal of the Corn Laws. This tended to reduce the value of a specific factor of production—land. It can no doubt be shown that the gain to the community as a whole exceeded the loss to the landlords—*but only if individuals are treated in some sense as equal.* Otherwise how can the loss to some—and that there was a loss can hardly be denied—be compared with the general gain? If the incomparability of utility to different individuals is strictly pressed, not only are the prescriptions of the welfare school ruled out, but all prescriptions whatever. The economist as an adviser is completely stultified, and unless his speculations be regarded as of paramount aesthetic value, he had better be suppressed completely."[3] This view is endorsed by Professor Robbins: "All that I proposed to do was to make clear that the statement that social

---

[1] Originally published in *Economic Journal*, September, 1939.

[2] "Interpersonal Comparisons of Utility: A Comment", *Economic Journal*, December, 1938, pp. 635-91.

[3] "Scope and Method of Economics", *Economic Journal*, September, 1938, pp. 396-7. (Italics mine.)

wealth was increased [by free trade] itself involved an arbitrary element—that the proposition should run, *if* equal capacity for satisfaction on the part of the economic subjects be assumed, *then* social wealth can be said to be increased. Objective analysis of the effects of the repeal of duties only showed that consumers gained and landlords lost. That such an arbitrary element was involved was plain. It seemed no less plain, therefore, that, here as elsewhere, it should be explicitly recognised."[1]

It can be demonstrated, however, that in the classical argument for free trade no such arbitrary element is involved at all. The effects of the repeal of the Corn Laws could be summarised as follows: (i) it results in a reduction in the price of corn, so that the *same* money income will now represent a higher real income; (ii) it leads to a shift in the distribution of income, so that some people's (i.e. the landlord's) incomes (at any rate in money terms) will be lower than before, and other people's incomes (presumably those of other producers) will be higher. Since aggregate money income can be assumed to be unchanged, if the landlords' income is reduced, the income of other people must be correspondingly increased. It is only as a result of this consequential change in the distribution of income that there can be any loss of satisfactions to certain individuals, and hence any need to compare the gains of some with the losses of others. But it is always possible for the Government to ensure that the previous income-distribution should be maintained intact: by compensating the "landlords" for any loss of income and by providing the funds for such compensation by an extra tax on those whose incomes have been augmented. In this way, everybody is left as well off as before in his capacity as an income recipient; while everybody is better off than before in his capacity as a consumer. For there still remains the benefit of lower corn prices as a result of the repeal of the duty.

In all cases, therefore, where a certain policy leads to an increase in physical productivity, and thus of aggregate real income, the economist's case for the policy is quite unaffected by the question of the comparability of individual satisfactions; since in all such cases it is *possible* to make everybody better off than before, or at any rate to make some people better off without

[1] *Loc. cit.*, p. 638.

making anybody worse off. There is no need for the economist to prove—as indeed he never could prove—that as a result of the adoption of a certain measure nobody in the community is going to suffer. In order to establish his case, it is quite sufficient for him to show that even if all those who suffer as a result are fully compensated for their loss, the rest of the community will still be better off than before. Whether the landlords, in the free-trade case, should in fact be given compensation or not, is a political question on which the economist, *qua* economist, could hardly pronounce an opinion. The important fact is that, in the argument in favour of free trade, the fate of the landlords is wholly irrelevant: since the benefits of free trade are by no means destroyed even if the landlords are fully reimbursed for their losses.[1]

This argument lends justification to the procedure, adopted by Professor Pigou in *The Economics of Welfare*, of dividing "welfare economics" into two parts: the first relating to production, and the second to distribution. The first, and far the more important part, should include all those propositions for increasing social welfare which relate to the increase in aggregate production; all questions concerning the stimulation of employment, the equalisation of social net products, and the equalisation of prices with marginal costs, would fall under this heading. Here the economist is on sure ground; the scientific status of his prescriptions is unquestionable, provided that the basic postulate of economics, that each individual prefers more to less, a greater satisfaction to a lesser one, is granted. In the second part, concerning distribution, the economist should not be concerned with "prescriptions" at all, but with the relative advantages of different ways of carrying out certain political ends. For it is quite impossible to

[1] This principle, as the reader will observe, simply amounts to saying that there is no interpersonal comparison of satisfactions involved in judging any policy designed to increase the sum total of wealth just because any such policy *could* be carried out in a way as to secure unanimous consent. An increase in the money value of the national income (given prices) is not, however, necessarily a sufficient indication of this condition being fulfilled: for individuals might, as a result of a certain political action, sustain losses of a non-pecuniary kind—e.g. if workers derive satisfaction from their particular kind of work, and are obliged to change their employment, something more than their previous level of money income will be necessary to secure their previous level of enjoyment; and the same applies in cases where individuals feel that the carrying out of the policy involves an interference with their individual freedom. Only if the increase in total income is sufficient to compensate for such losses, and still leaves something over for the rest of the community, can it be ₋aid to be "justified" without resort to interpersonal comparisons.

K

decide on economic grounds what particular pattern of income-distribution maximises social welfare. If the postulate of equal capacity for satisfaction is employed as a criterion, the conclusion inescapably follows that welfare is necessarily greatest when there is complete equality; yet one certainly cannot exclude the possibility of everybody being happier when there is some degree of inequality than under a régime of necessary and complete equality. (Here I am not thinking so much of differences in the capacity for satisfactions between different individuals, but of the satisfactions that are derived from the prospect of improving one's income by one's own efforts—a prospect which is necessarily excluded when a régime of complete equality prevails.) And short of complete equality, how can the economist decide precisely how much inequality is desirable—i.e. how much secures the maximum total satisfaction? All that economics can, and should, do in this field, is to show, given the pattern of income-distribution desired, which is the most convenient way of bringing it about.

8

A NOTE ON TARIFFS AND THE TERMS OF TRADE[1]

1. In a paper on *The Terms of Trade* Dr. Benham raises the question whether the advantage accruing to a country through improvement in the terms of trade, consequent upon the imposition of a tariff, could compensate for the disadvantage arising on account of a smaller volume of trade.

It can be demonstrated that the introduction of a system of import duties will always improve the position of the country imposing it, provided that the rate of duty is below a certain critical level, and provided also that the introduction of the tariff does not lead to retaliation, in the form of the imposition of higher duties, by other countries.[2] It can also be shown that there is a particular rate of duty which makes the net advantage accruing from the tariff a maximum.[3]

2. Our demonstration is based on the Edgeworth barter diagram, and since the two parties in question here are two nations, and not two individuals, it employs the concept of "community indifference curves", of which it is necessary to say a few words. A "community indifference curve" is the locus of points representing a constant real income for the community as a whole. In so far as individuals' tastes differ or their money-incomes differ, or the distribution of incomes varies, positions representing a constant real income for the community as a whole do not imply an unchanged real income for each individual taken separately. Some individuals will be worse off (as between two such positions) and others better off. But the real income can nevertheless be regarded as constant for the community as a whole if, supposing that those who are worse off were exactly

---

[1] Originally published in *Economica*, November, 1940.
[2] We shall ignore here the possible disadvantages due to increased unemployment in the export trades.
[3] The argument which follows is of course not new. *Cf.* Bickerdike, "The Theory of Incipient Taxes", *Economic Journal*, December, 1906, and Edgeworth, *Collected Papers*, Vol. ii, pp. 340 ff. But the modern indifference curve technique permits a simple demonstration of it which it may be worth while to reproduce; and it also shows that the proposition is quite independent of any assumption as to a measurable utility function (with which at one time it was erroneously thought to be associated).

compensated for their loss at the expense of those who are better off, this redistribution of incomes would leave the real income of everyone the same as before. In other words in order that two situations, A and B, should represent constant total real income, it is necessary to suppose that, if all those who are better off in B than in A were taxed to the extent necessary to make them indifferent as between A and B, and those who are worse off in B than in A were subsidised by an amount which would make them indifferent as between A and B, the total amount of taxes to be imposed would be equal to the total amount of subsidies to be paid.[1, 2]

3. Let us now suppose that there are two countries, France and England, and two commodities, wine and coal. In the diagram on p. 149 we measure the amount of coal bought by France (and

[1] For a further discussion of this concept, *cf.* my note "Welfare Propositions in Economics and Interpersonal Comparisons of Utility", *Economic Journal*, September, 1939, [pp. 143-6 above] and Hicks, "The Foundations of Welfare Economics", *Economic Journal*, December, 1939.

[2] The derivation of the community indifference curve is as follows: Let us assume two commodities, a and b. Take an arbitrary Point, P_1, on the line R_1. Since along R_1

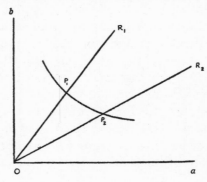

FIG. 1

the ratio $\frac{a}{b}$ is constant, it is clear that all points on R_1, to the right of P_1, represent real incomes higher than P_1, and all points on the left, lower real incomes. It follows, therefore, that there cannot be two points along R_1 which represent the *same* total real income. This must be equally true of any other line R_2 (representing a different ratio $\frac{a}{b}$). Hence there can be only one point (P_2) along R_2 where the real income is the same as at P_1. Finding these points for each of the radiuses R_3 . . . etc., and connecting up the corresponding points P_3 . . . etc., we obtain the community indifference curve representing the real income at P_1. The shape of this curve should be similar to the shape of an ordinary indifference curve.

sold by England) along Ox and the amount of wine bought by England (and sold by France) along Oy. The indifference curve IF_0 which passes through O then represents the level of real income of the French community in the absence of coal purchases from England, and the indifference curve IE_0 (passing through O) the real income of the English community deprived of French wine. OE and OF represent the two offer curves: the English

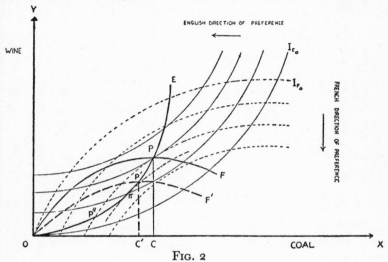

FIG. 2

demand curve for wine (and supply curve of coal) and the French demand curve for coal (and supply curve of wine). In the absence of import duties and transport costs, competitive equilibrium will be established at P with PC wine exchanged against OC coal, the French terms of trade being $\dfrac{OC}{PC}$.

If we now suppose that France imposes an import duty on coal, the French demand curve will be shifted (to OF'), in such a way that the difference in the height at any point between the old demand curve and the new represents the revenue of the French State (import duty × amount bought) in terms of wine. The resulting new equilibrium is at P', with $P'C'$ wine being exchanged against OC' coal. It is clear that the new position secures a higher real income for France so long as P' is to the right of P''—the point on the English demand curve which passes through the *same* French indifference curve as at P. The optimal rate of import duty is the one which secures equilibrium at π—this being the point on the English demand curve which is tangential to one of France's indifference curves (i.e. which therefore places France in the best position compatible with the English demand for wine). With the same reasoning it can also be shown that a subsidy on exports, by shifting the offer curve in the opposite direction, necessarily places the country in a worse position than before.

4. π is in fact the optimum monopoly position, and the corresponding price the optimum monopoly price—i.e. the price which would result in the absence of a tariff, if the French wine trade were in the hands of a monopolist who decided to exploit his monopoly power to the full. Our analysis shows, therefore, that the introduction of import duties can reproduce exactly the same effects as the introduction of monopoly. The extent to which it is possible to exploit the foreigner in this way depends on the country's monopoly power; i.e. the elasticity of foreign demand for its products, and the extent to which the foreign power desires, or is able, to retaliate. (Retaliation will improve the position of the exploited country, but it might leave both countries worse off than they were originally.) Provided that the elasticity of foreign demand is less than infinite there is always *some* rate of duty which it is advantageous to introduce in the absence of retaliation; and if the elasticity of the country's own demand for foreign products is markedly higher than the elasticity of foreign demand for its own products—an unusual case—this policy may be advantageous even if the "optimum degree of retaliation" of foreign countries is allowed for.

PART IV

THE THEORY OF CAPITAL

9

THE CONTROVERSY ON THE THEORY OF CAPITAL[1]

I

THE last few years have witnessed the emergence of a tremendous literature on the theory of capital and interest—stimulated, no doubt, by the urgency of finding the appropriate theoretical criteria for a policy designed to mitigate economic instability. A large part of this literature has been directly concerned with the question how far the concept of the "period of production" is relevant for an analysis of industrial fluctuations. Another part, digging deeper into the problem, dealt with the *prima facie* question how far traditional capital theory, formulated under the hypothesis of a stationary state, still retains its validity in essential features once this hypothesis is abandoned. These writings were mainly concerned with the problems of expectations, foresight, uncertainty. Finally, largely owing to the offensive launched by Professor F. H. Knight, there was a revival of the discussion on the fundamentals of capital theory itself, comparable in nature to the famous controversy between J. B. Clark and Böhm-Bawerk in the first decade of the century. In this controversy the problems introduced by dynamic changes were not so much in question as the legitimacy of the "investment period" theory of capital even within the narrow framework of static assumptions. Professor Knight's attack[2] has been taken up and supported by other writers,[3] has been frequently reiterated by Professor Knight

[1] Originally published in *Econometrica*, July, 1937.

[2] The following articles by Professor Knight deal mainly with this question: "Capital Production, Time and the Rate of Return", *Economic Essays in Honour of Gustav Cassel*, London, 1933, pp. 327-42; "Capital, Time and the Interest Rate", *Economica*, August, 1934, p. 257; "Professor Hayek and the Theory of Investment", *Economic Journal*, March, 1935, p. 77; "The Ricardian Theory of Production and Distribution", *The Canadian Journal of Economics and Political Science*, February, 1935; "The Theory of Investment Once More: Mr. Boulding and the Austrians", *Quarterly Journal of Economics*, November, 1935; "The Quantity of Capital and the Rate of Interest, Part I", *Journal of Political Economy*, August, 1936; "Part II", *ibid.*, October, 1936. (The last of these appeared too late for consideration in this paper.)

[3] The following authors could be regarded as supporting Knight's criticism in varying degrees: M. F. Joseph and K. Bode, "Bemerkungen zur Kapital und Zinstheorie", *Zeitschrift für Nationalökonomie*, Vol. 6, June, 1935; H. S. Ellis, "Die Bedeutung der Produktionsperiode für die Krisentheorie", *Zeitschrift für Nationalökonomie*,

himself and, on the Austrian side, has been answered by Professor F. Machlup and Professor F. A. von Hayek.[1] It is with this particular controversy that the present essay will be concerned.

The literature created by this discussion is already sufficient to fill volumes, and most of it makes very difficult and often tedious reading. Yet a perusal of the more recent publications does not suggest that much progress has been made towards mutual understanding. While Professor Knight's position and those of other critics is not entirely acceptable in the view of the present writer, it appears that on the Austrian side none of his chief points have yet been fully understood or effectively answered.

For this state of affairs, I think Professor Knight is partly responsible. A serious reading of his numerous articles on this particular subject does not make it easy to discover the essential points of departure. He makes so many points that one is apt to get lost among them, not knowing how to distinguish between the primary and secondary, the important and the unimportant; while the conclusions are frequently clothed in paradoxical sentences

Vol. 6, 1935; Nurkse, "The Schematic Representation of the Structure of Production", *Review of Economic Studies*, June, 1935.

The following articles, recently published, deal with more or less the same problems though they are not directly related to the issues of the present controversy: C. H. P. Gifford, "The Concept of the Length of the Period of Production", *Economic Journal*, December, 1933, p. 611; "The Period of Production under Continuous Input and Point Output in an Unprogressive Community", *Econometrica*, Vol. 3, April, 1935, p. 199; K. E. Boulding, "The Theory of a Single Investment", *Quarterly Journal of Economics*, Vol. 49, May, 1935, p. 475; "Time and Investment", *Economica*, May, 1936, p. 196; J. Marschak, "A Note on the Period of Production", *Economic Journal*, Vol. 44, March, 1934, p. 146; J. Marcus Fleming, "The Period of Production and Derived Concepts", *The Review of Economic Studies*, Vol. 3, October, 1935; A. Smithies, "The Austrian Theory of Capital in Relation to Partial Equilibrium Theory", *Quarterly Journal of Economics*, Vol. 50, November, 1935; V. Edelberg, "Elements of Capital Theory: A Note", *Economica*, August, 1936; Karl H. Stephans, "Zur neueren Kapitaltheorie", *Weltwirtschaftliches Archiv*, January, 1935; "Zur Problematik der Zinstheorie", *Zeitschrift für Nationalökonomie*, Vol. 7, 1936; Richard von Strigl, "Zeit und Produktion" *Zeitschrift für Nationalökonomie*, Vol. 6, 1935; E. Schneider, "Das Zeitmoment in der Theorie der Produktion, I", *Jahrbücher für Nationalökonomie und Statistik*, 1935; "II", *ibid.*, 1936; A. Mahr, "Das Zeitmoment in der Theorie des Produktivzinses", *Zeitschrift für Nationalökonomie*, Vol. 7, 1936; Carl Iversen, "Die Probleme des festen Realkapitals", *Zeitschrift für Nationalökonomie*, Vol. 7, 1936; O. Lange, "Interest in the Theory of Production", *Review of Economic Studies*, Vol. 4, June, 1936; H. Gaitskell, "Notes on the Period of Production," *Zeitschrift für Nationalökonomie*, Vol. 7, 1937.

[1] F. Machlup, "Professor Knight and the 'Period of Production'", *Journal of Political Economy*, Vol. 43, October, 1935, p. 577 (together with Professor Knight's comment), and a further Rejoinder, *ibid.*, December, 1935, p. 808; F. A. von Hayek, "The Mythology of Capital", *Quarterly Journal of Economics*, Vol. 50, February, 1936, p. 199. Reference should also be made to another article by Professor Hayek, dealing with earlier criticisms and a further elucidation of his views, "On the Relationship Between Investment and Output", *Economic Journal*, June, 1934, p. 207.

which are intended to challenge the mind but without a sufficient indication of where to turn in order to uncover those mental processes which must have led up to them.

The aim of the present article is to review the essential points in Professor Knight's argument, to examine them in the light of other criticisms which have been put forward and, finally to analyse to what extent and in what respects they destroy the validity of traditional theory. Since this reconstruction of Knight's views has involved some "filling in" of gaps in the printed argument at certain stages, it is not necessarily a "correct" version of his views; it should be considered as an interpretation rather than a summary; and it is possible that it will be repudiated by the author himself.

II

Professor Knight's criticism of the "Austrian" doctrine can, I think, be summarised under three headings: first, that it is impossible to distinguish between permanent and non-permanent resources (or "original" and "produced" means of production) or between the services of those resources; second, that it is irrelevant and, in many cases, impossible to distinguish—analytically or physically—between expenditures incurred in "maintaining" resources and those incurred in "replacing" them; third, that there is no necessary correlation between the "period of production" and the quantity of capital. Among these, perhaps, the second is most open to criticism and, at the same time, least important; whereas the third is certainly the most important and at the same time the most inadequately explained. But let us deal with each of these points in turn.

1. *Permanent versus Non-permanent Resources.*—Here Professor Knight makes use of two separate arguments. In the first place he sharply distinguishes between the services of resources and the resources themselves (the actual physical objects from which the services flow). The former, in his view, cannot be thought of except as a rate of flow in time: like light or electricity (but unlike water) they flow, but cannot exist as a stock, or have their use transferred to any other period. Just as one cannot "bottle up" sunshine—except in the sense of transferring its energy into some

other object, like oranges, which means "consuming" it by creating value in that object—to-day's labour hours cannot be deferred until to-morrow: they must be used immediately or lost. As regards the latter—pieces of land, labourers and machines—no distinction can be drawn between permanent and non-permanent resources, simply because permanent resources—apart from a few and insignificant exceptions—do not exist. It is essentially a fiction that there are "permanent" resources which exist without being maintained and whose services are therefore forthcoming at a rate independent of their price. This fiction is admissible in static or stationary-state analysis, where it does not affect the immediate issues involved; but it is inadmissible to treat it as a relevant *fact* upon which a theory may be built. That it is fiction and not fact is shown by the reflection that neither land nor labour services would continue to flow (from the same resources) without the application of current services for their maintenance. No type of natural resources truly possesses "indestructible powers"; the best that can be expected is that the flow of services can be kept up permanently by continued maintenance.[1] A piece of land can be kept permanently in good condition by careful husbandry; but its "consumption" (in the same sense that capital goods can be consumed) is certainly possible by reducing its value to nil through non-maintenance. In fact some types of resources (such as sources of coal and oil) cannot be kept intact however much is spent on their maintenance, though how long they last and the amount of services yielded may be influenced by expenditures on their upkeep.[2]

The point is equally obvious in the case of labour. The services flowing from a labourer cannot be forthcoming unless he is

---

[1] The most important exception to this is sunshine which—given static weather conditions—flows at even rate without anything being done to the sun. But since neither sunshine nor the sun can be made subject to human property rights and thus market valuation, this exception is irrelevant. It might be argued also that sheer area (involving exposure to light and rainfall and power to support structure) *is* an "original and indestructible power of the soil" in the Ricardian sense and the only one; but even here we must qualify in that the area may shrink in some cases (e.g. on river banks) without maintenance.

[2] Professor Knight would go further and say that such non-exhaustible resources can also be "maintained" permanently by creating resources whose services provide a substitute for them. This view is justified, only in so far as *perfect substitutes* can be found (which is by no means always the case; not all uses of coal can be equally replaced by water power).

given food nor can he be replaced after his death unless children are "maintained" until they reach the age when valuable services begin to flow from them (during their "construction period"). This way of looking at the matter would not sound so ridiculous but for the historical accident of the abolition of slavery. In a slave state, investment in human labour is in all respects identical with investment in machinery. And even in the non-slave state there is a minimum price necessary to maintain the labourer, while the Malthusian theory of reproduction applies, in certain countries and periods, to a considerable extent.

Even if the maintenance of labour does not proceed on strictly economic grounds in a world where everyone owns his own labour —since the preference for life over death cannot be expressed in marginal terms—maintained (and replaced) it must be; and therefore all resources (i.e. *all* scarce objects, including human beings) must have some input or maintenance stream in order to have a permanent output stream (both of which are, of course, to some extent variable). No distinction can be drawn along this line; and the criticism urged against Professor Knight,[1] that he regards capital as maintaining itself permanently without maintenance expenditure, misses its point. From one standpoint all resources are "permanent"—which merely implies that, if they are maintained, they are maintained; while from another standpoint, none are permanent—since none will remain unconsumed unless maintained. What matters is that no distinction can be drawn between permanent and non-permanent resources, whichever standpoint is adopted.[2]

Professor Knight's second argument in this connection refers

---

[1] Cf. Hayek, "The Mythology of Capital", *op. cit.*, p. 214. "The very concept of capital arises out of the fact that, where non-permanent resources are used in production, provision for replacement of the resources used up in production must be made, if the same income is to be enjoyed continually, and that in consequence part of the gross produce has to be devoted to their production." But are there any resources for which this is not true?

[2] Moreover, even if it were true that some resources are permanent (in the sense of requiring *no* maintenance) whilst others are not, this fact would not really be relevant from the point of view of capital theory. As will be shown below, "permanent resources" might very well be "capital goods", so long as they are augmentable in quantity; while there are various "non-permanent-goods" which are not part of capital (in the sense that they do not enter into the determination of the rate of interest) for the simple reason that their quantity cannot be augmented. In any case, the distinction between permanent and non-permanent goods cannot be used to demarcate capital from other resources.

to the analogous, but by no means identical, distinction between "original and "produced" factors. Even if the distinction between permanent and non-permanent resources is invalid, this latter distinction would still be valid, if it were true that the services of one set of resources—the "original factors"—produced another set of resources, the services of which—either by themselves, or with the aid of the services of the former—produced want-satisfying service flows. But there is no such one-way causation as is assumed by the Austrian theory. Resources are produced with the aid of the services of all kinds of resources; and it is even conceivable that the services of produced resources *by themselves alone* and without any aid from the services of "non-produced" resources, should produce an endless succession of further produced resources. (It is "conceivable", but I think Professor Knight will admit that such an eventuality is not very likely.)

I hope to show later on that the importance of this latter point has been rather exaggerated—at any rate if it still remains true that the services of produced resources always require the co-operation of the services of non-produced resources in further production. Professor Knight is quite right in insisting, however, that it destroys Böhm-Bawerk's concept of a "period of production". If the services of produced resources become embodied in further resources (and so on, in endless succession), there is no definite time lag between the investment of a "service unit" and the corresponding emergence of another service unit which is instantaneously destroyed by consumption. The "investment period" for certain services invested on a particular date (or, rather, for a small portion of those services) might be infinity. But this does not imply, in our view, that it is impossible to attribute an "average investment period" for the services *embodied* in a given stream of consumption goods.

It might be argued that the services of the resources *accruing at the present moment* might be regarded as "original factors" as against the services of resources accruing at any subsequent moment. Such a distinction, however, would be meaningless when applied to the time continuum of static equilibrium; and it is questionable whether the periods for which the services accruing at a single moment are invested, are in any way definite in the absence of stationary conditions. For the inputs of different dates jointly produce the outputs of different dates; and it is impossible to separate out the contribution to the output of different dates of the input of a single date.[1, 2] This is the chief objection against the concept of an "investment period of currently accruing services" (as against the investment period of the services embodied in a given stream of consumption goods) which Professor Hayek now regards as relevant.[3] Another (alternative) objection is that, in the absence of stationary conditions, this measure would be correlated with changes in the scale of new investment, rather than changes in the quantity of capital. It may easily remain constant while the quantity of capital is increasing if accumulation proceeds at a steady rate; while it could actually diminish if the rate of accumulation slowed down.

2. *Maintenance versus Replacement.*—Professor Knight argues in the second place that the maintenance expenditure (which we have seen is necessary for all resources) cannot be distinguished from expenditure incurred to replace worn-out capital goods. The usual distinction between replacement and maintenance is based on the idea that the former does (while the latter does not) bear a definite ratio to the service life of particular capital goods. This is best elucidated by an example. If the investment in a particular stock of houses is not maintained—the amortisation funds are not put aside year by year—the amount thus "released" will bear a mathematical relation to the service life of the houses (a relation varying with the rate of interest, but definite at any given rate).

[1] It is only under the assumption of stationary conditions, where both the output stream and the input stream are constant over time, that an investment period can be imputed to the input of a particular date; since in this case, this period will equal the investment period of the services *embodied* in the capital goods. Cf. also p. 167 below.

[2] This has already been stated by Wicksell, *Lectures on Political Economy*, English edition, Vol. I, London, 1934, p. 260. Wicksell was considering the analogous problem (or, rather, the same problem from the "other end", so to speak) whether the amount of labour disinvested by the "annual use" of a machine can be measured. ". . . fundamentally it is just as absurd to ask how much labour is invested in either one or the other annual use as to try to find out what part of the pasture goes into wool and what part into mutton. It is only at the margin of production that these quantities can be differentiated and have a concrete significance attached to them." Assuming variability at the margin, it is possible of course to determine by how much the output of various dates can be increased by a *marginal increment* of the input of a single date. But this does not imply, as Machlup appears to believe ("Professor Knight and the 'Period of Production' ", *op. cit.*, p. 587), that it is possible to evaluate the contribution of the input of a given period to the output of different future periods.

[3] "The Mythology of Capital", *op. cit.*, pp. 206, 218-19.

If, on the other hand, "maintenance expenditure" in the narrower sense is not incurred (the roof leakages are not stopped, etc.), the house may become immediately useless and the destruction in value caused thereby bears no relation to the amount "released". Now, in the case of many capital goods no definite "replacement" ever occurs; the maintenance may consist only in the periodic replacement of "individual bits"; but that type of replacement need bear no relation to the shortening of service life (or, rather, the reduction in the discounted value of future services) caused by a reduction in maintenance expenditure. A railway locomotive, for example— apart from changes in knowledge, causing technical obsolescence —is never entirely replaced although every single part of it might be exchanged in the course of time, as this becomes necessary. But the sum of such maintenance expenditures cannot be brought into any simple relation with the cost of the locomotive as a whole; and failure to incur such expenditure in any particular respect (e.g. the replacement of a piston) will not destroy *part* of the value of the locomotive; it will destroy its entire value.¹

Moreover, if "replacement" occurs regularly and continuously —and we shall see presently Professor Knight's reasons for regarding it as if it did—"replacement expenditure" becomes indistinguishable from "maintenance expenditure" in the narrower sense; and therefore, according to Professor Knight, *the two should be lumped together, and not treated separately*.² I am not

---

¹ This, I believe, is also the reason for the view, which most people found so puzzling, that the "investment period" of the services of resources must be either zero or infinity; i.e. zero for the services engaged in producing current output-streams (from existing capacity) and infinity for the services employed in creating new capacity. It does not imply a denial that capacity requires maintenance, but merely the view that no definite investment period can be attributed to the services employed in such maintenance for the simple reason that such expenditure is the absolute condition of the functioning of the capacity rather than the cause of a definite prolongation of its service life. In the above case of the locomotive, the labour engaged in building it remains invested for an infinite period, if the locomotive is kept in repair, but only for a very short period—perhaps a day—if the necessary repairs are not made good. Similarly with the labour engaged in making repairs. It is impossible to say by how much the service life of a locomotive is prolonged by the replacement of a worn-out piston. If it is not replaced, the future service life of the locomotive becomes zero, while if it is (and all other "pistons" are also replaced in the course of time) its lifetime might be infinity.

² Cf. especially "The Theory of Investment Once More: Mr. Boulding and the Austrians", *op. cit.*, p. 59: "the process of amortisation and replacement is precisely the continuance of an old life and not a new birth"; also "particularly with reference to increments of value, capital as capital, it seems truistical to say that if it is kept in existence there is no amortisation and replacement but only continuous maintenance".

sure that even so, with a little mental effort, it would not be possible to forge a criterion for an analytical distinction, but I certainly do not think it would be worth the trouble. As we shall see later on, the essential point of the "Austrian" theory of capital does not really depend upon the validity of this distinction.

3. *The Optimal Length of the Investment Period.*—None of the points mentioned so far affects the fundamental assumption of the Austrian theory: the law of roundaboutness. Now we come to the argument with which Professor Knight seeks to prove that this law, irrespective of whether it is true in reality or not, is irrelevant from the point of view of capital theory, for it cannot be shown that an increase in the quantity of capital in a community will necessarily imply the adoption of more "roundabout" processes.[1] In order to show that this argument is independent of the previous objections, we shall assume for the present that "maintenance" does consist of periodic replacement of capital goods, as the Austrian theory apparently assumes, and that capital goods are exclusively produced by the services of other resources, i.e. labour. Let us revert therefore to the traditional situation exemplified by a world where only houses are produced and only labour is required to build (or replace) such houses. The only consumption good will then be the services flowing from houses, i.e. "room-years"; and we might assume the co-existence of different types of room-years. We shall defer for a moment the question how the "degree of roundaboutness" is to be measured; under these assumptions it will obviously vary with the lifetime of the houses. The famous Jevons-Böhm-Bawerkian law is satisfied if we assume that for each particular type of house (i.e. a type of house is one which provides a given kind of room-year) it is always possible to increase service life in a given proportion by increasing the construction costs of the houses in a lesser proportion.

We shall make two further assumptions which, in my view, are also implicit in Knight's analysis. The first is that there is perfect competition and constant returns to scale (i.e. the production function is homogeneous in the first degree). The second is that investors have static foresight regarding the future, which implies

---

[1] I am indebted to Mr. Milton Friedman, of the National Resources Committee, Washington, for helping me to understand Knight's argument in this connection.

L

that they expect the continuance of the same prices in the future as are ruling at present.

Under these assumptions the "optimum degree of durability", i.e. the optimum length of service life of houses, will be the one which maximises the rate of return on a given quantity of investment. In the case of resources, such as houses, which are assumed to be periodically replaced, it is not immediately clear how this rate of return is obtained. It will obviously depend on the building cost of the houses (on the price of labour) and on the price of room-years; but it will also depend on the way amortisation is provided. The representative investor, in deciding upon the degree of durability he should adopt, will deduct from the expected annual (gross) income of the house a sum sufficient for its replacement when it falls due. The net return of the investment will thus depend on the annual amount of this deduction, i.e. the annual amortisation quota. It is only when the relative costs of amortisation of the different types of houses are known that it is possible to determine the optimal length of service life.

But the amount of this annual deduction, given the length of service life, will obviously depend on the rate of interest at which the amortisation quotas are accumulated. The higher this rate the lower the annual sum required to secure a given replacement fund at the end of a definite period; and the higher, in consequence, the rate of return on the investment itself. Now the rate of interest at which the amortisation quotas are accumulated can certainly not be higher than the rate of return on the investment, since this would imply the existence of an investment opportunity which is superior to the one in question, in which case that particular investment would never be adopted. For similar reasons, it cannot be lower than the rate of return, since this would imply that the amortisation quotas are invested in an investment opportunity which is inferior to the one in question, and the investor always has the choice of reinvesting his capital in the same uses in which it was originally invested. *Consequently the two must be equal to one another:* and this condition makes the rate of return on a particular type of investment uniquely determinate. *The real rate of return on a particular type of investment is therefore that rate which satisfies the condition that the rate at which the amortisation quotas are accumulated is identical with the yield of the investment itself.*[1] The optimum "degree of durability" is the one which maximises the rate of return, calculated in this manner.[2]

This can be elucidated by the following example. Let us assume that the same house (i.e. a house having 75 rooms, of exactly the same type, with each room earning 1 unit per annum) can be built in three different degrees of durability. The first costs 1,000 units to build and lasts thirty years. The second costs 1,100 units and lasts forty years. The third 1,200 units and lasts fifty years. We shall calculate first the net yield of the three houses by assuming that the amortisation quotas are accumulated at various "given" rates of interest, and second, we shall calculate the real rate of return for each type by assuming that the amortisation quotas are accumulated at the same rate as the "net yield" itself. The table on p. 164 shows the comparative rates of return under the two assumptions.

It is easily seen that for each type of house the net yield will be at its maximum at the "real rate of return". This is the return which the investment yields if the amortisation quotas are re-invested in the same use as the one represented by the original investment. This in turn implies that the investment—after a certain lapse of time, at any rate—is so arranged that the amount of capital invested in a given use is kept at an (approximately) steady and even level over time; this means, in real terms, that

---

[1] The real rate of return, as defined above, is necessarily the same as the one which equates the sum of the discounted *gross* returns of a house (with no deduction for amortisation) with its costs of reproduction. It is identical therefore with Professor Fisher's "rate of return over cost" (*The Theory of Interest*, pp. 155 ff.), Wicksell's "real" or "natural" rate, and the "internal rate of return" of Mr. Boulding. ("The Theory of the Single Investment", *op. cit.*, p. 479.) But it is only under the assumption of constant (value) returns to scale (from the point of view of the individual investor) that the optimal mode of investment can be determined by the condition that the real rate of return is maximised. Under conditions of diminishing returns to scale the determination of the optimal method of investment is more complicated and presupposes that the rate of interest is already known.

[2] This conclusion is true, irrespective of whether the output or input streams are uniform over time (as assumed in the text) or not. Whatever the time shape of output and input streams, there is only one rate of interest, corresponding to any given constellation of outputs and inputs, which makes the discounted value of all outputs minus the sum of the discounted values of all inputs (including the initial input, or construction cost), for any given date, equal to zero. And since all possible constellations of the time shapes of output and input streams are given by the production function, there will be (normally) only one possible time constellation of inputs and outputs which makes this "internal" rate a maximum. Cf. also Knight, "The Quantity of Capital and the Rate of Interest, Part I", *op. cit.*, p. 445.

the age distribution of houses of each type remains constant in successive periods of time. If individual houses last, e.g., 30 years, a "house investment" will consist of a series of 30 houses, varying in age between o and 29 years, one of which is replaced every year. The gains from the investment of a certain amount of capital are therefore only maximised if the time quantity of the investment is stabilised: unless it pays to do the latter it does not pay to undertake the investment at all. Such a "staggering" of capital is thus an indispensable condition of a state of equilibrium.[1]

Rates of Interest Used in Calculating Amortisation	Net Yield (%) of		
	Type I	Type II	Type III
%			
2	4·8	5·0	5·0
3	5·4	5·5	5·4
4	5·7	5·8	5·5
5	6·0	6·0	5·7
6	6·2	6·2	5·8
(7	6·4	6·3	6·0)*
Real Rate of Return	6·35	6·2	5·9

* At 7% none of the investments would be undertaken, since none would have a yield equal to that rate.

There need be no difficulty in arranging a maintenance scheme of this type, at any rate under the idealised conditions assumed in the theory. "Houses" may be big (too big for the individual investor to buy a series of 30 houses), but, if not houses, at any rate the ownership titles in those houses are divisible: and so it ought to be possible for anybody to arrange his investment in such a way as to keep the amount of the investment per unit of time constant. To achieve this end may be considered, therefore, as one of the functions of the capital market.[2] All that is necessary to assume is

[1] This has been stated by Wicksell and set out at length by Åkerman, *Realkapital und Kapitalzins*. Cf. also Wicksell, "Real Capital and Interest," *Lectures*, I, pp. 258 ff.
[2] Moreover, it is sufficient to assume that this is possible for *some* investors, since they, through the workings of competition, can prevent the others from investing anything at all in that particular type of investment.

that the indivisibilities do not go so far as to prevent the co-existence of a sufficient number of houses of each type and age.

This is the meaning of Professor Knight's repeated assertions that capital goods ought to be treated as if they were permanently and continually maintained, that capital is perpetual or a "permanent fund". Investing in 30 houses, one of which falls due for replacement and is *planned to be replaced* every year *ad infinitum*, is the same thing as investing in a house which lasts for ever, while a certain sum has to be paid out every year to keep it in repair. This sum can be looked upon as "maintenance cost"; it can also be looked upon as the contribution of the services of other resources needed to produce the room-year service which is instantaneously consumed.[1] Thus every investment should be regarded as the source of a certain output stream and the consumer of a certain input stream (both of which are, of course, to some extent variable), in addition to which it will have a certain "initial input" or construction cost. As Professor Knight has shown, in the case where these streams are constant over time, the relation of output value to input value determines the investment period (in his terminology, the turnover period).[2] Since the annual net income of the investment is merely the difference between the two and since, under our assumptions (i.e. constant returns to scale), every unit of capital in that investment is assumed to earn interest at the same rate, the relation between output value and input value will also determine the relation between "construction cost" and "annual maintenance cost". For investments which are continuously maintained at an even rate in time, the degree of roundaboutness can be measured by the ratio of the initial or

[1] This is also the meaning, I believe, underlying Knight's statements that "maintenance is merely a detail of administration", or that "capital is an integrated, organic conception". What it means is that, in a state of equilibrium, all capital, however durable or perishable are the individual capital goods of which it consists, must be regarded as a fund which is continuously maintained—it cannot be thought of otherwise—since its yield can only be maximised on this basis.

[2] "The Theory of Investment Once More", *op. cit.*, p. 55. According to Professor Knight, this turnover period has only meaning "provided it is taken as an accumulation period and not as a period of investment". I confess I do not understand the meaning of this distinction, since in the context output value and input value represent permanent time streams, while input is regarded as "provision for maintenance or as payments for the other agencies co-operating with the particular capital good . . . or as including elements of both" (*ibid.*, p. 56). The "period" clearly cannot refer merely to the time during which the capital stock is accumulated (which is the sense in which the term "accumulation period" is generally used).

construction cost to the annual maintenance cost (assuming that the expected future prices of productive services are the same as present prices).[1] The "law of roundaboutness" then simply says that it is always possible to reduce annual maintenance cost by increasing initial construction cost, in producing a given permanent output stream.

[If a is the value of the annual input, b the value of the annual output, i the rate of interest, t the average "investment period" sought, their relation will be given by the equation

$$a(1+i)^t = b \qquad \ldots (1)$$

The rate of interest in question, however, is the investment's "real rate of return" (calculated above, p. 164). If C is the value of current services needed to produce (or reproduce) an "investment" of balanced age-composition, capable of yielding an output stream b at an input stream a, then its value is given by

$$C = \frac{b-a}{i} \qquad \ldots (2)$$

Since the production of resources also takes a certain time, this construction cost will itself include an element of interest. This, however, causes no logical difficulty; for the construction cost (including interest) will still have a unique value if we impose the further condition that interest during construction must be identical with the interest earned on the investment itself. In other words, given the inputs of all dates (including the series of

[1] The "annual maintenance cost" of a resource (or good) includes the value of *all* services consumed in producing whatever is regarded as the output stream of that particular resource. It is determinate therefore only if the output stream of the particular good is regarded as given. Since, however, the resources themselves can only be unequivocally defined by their output streams, this problem ought to cause no difficulty. To elucidate our concept by an example: if the output stream of certain boot-manufacturing machines is regarded as a certain quantity of machine services per unit of time (assuming that these services are capable of physical measurement, in terms of machine-service-hours, like labour-hours), the "annual maintenance cost" or "input value" of those machines will consist of the expenditures—in the form of upkeep and replacement—continuously incurred in securing a permanent flow of these services. If, on the other hand, not "quantity of machine-service-hours, per unit of time" but "quantity of boots per unit of time" is regarded as the output stream of those particular machines, "the annual maintenance cost" will include, in addition to the above, also the cost of the services of the factors (labour, etc.) normally regarded as co-operating with the machines in producing the boots. The ratio of construction to maintenance cost—which, perhaps, should more properly be called *the ratio of the initial input to the annual input flow*, the former, as distinct from the latter, being a single expenditure which is incurred only once, at the beginning of the investment—will of course be different in the two cases: but so will the "investment period", if measured in any other manner.

initial inputs, representing "construction"), the outputs of all dates and the "real rate of return" on the investment, the value of C can be determined.

It can be shown that the ratio of "initial cost" (C) to "annual maintenance cost" (a) provides an *index* to the period of investment. This ratio will correspond with the period of investment only when the rate of interest approaches zero. Equation (1) can be expanded to

$$a\left(1 + ti + \frac{t(t-1)i^2}{1.2} + \frac{t(t-1)(t-2)i^3}{1.2.3} + \cdots \right) = b$$

This yields a rapidly converging series if both ti and i are appreciably less than unity (as would be the case, for example, if $i = \cdot05$ and $t = 10$). In that case the cubic and subsequent terms of the above series can be neglected. From (2) we have

$$b = Ci + a$$

$$\therefore \quad \frac{C}{a} = t + \frac{it}{2}(t-1) \qquad \qquad \cdots (3)$$

As is readily seen, the second term of this equation will be an appreciable magnitude in relation to the first term, so that $\frac{C}{a}$ will exceed t unless $i \longrightarrow 0$. However, for any given value of i, $\frac{C}{a}$ is uniquely related to t, and can thus serve as a rough index of t. Similarly, it can be shown that $\frac{C}{b}$ (the capital/output ratio) is also uniquely related to t for any given value of i (but will be smaller than t), and will approximate t (and $\frac{C}{a}$ of course) as $i \longrightarrow 0$.

In the case of our three types of house investments, for each case the invested capital is an integrated structure of balanced age-composition. The ratio of the invested capital (i.e. "initial cost") to "annual cost" will be for the three types, $19\cdot7$, $27\cdot8$ and 36 (approximately) when the lifetime of the individual houses comprising the investment is 30, 40 and 50 years respectively. The ratio of annual output to annual input will be $2\cdot25$, $2\cdot73$ and $3\cdot125$ and the rates of return $6\cdot35$, $6\cdot2$ and $5\cdot9\%$ respectively. Hence the value of t from equation (1) can be computed as $13\cdot1$,

16·7 and 19·9 years (approximately). The capital/output ratio $\left(\dfrac{C}{b}\right)$ will be 8·8, 10·2 and 11·5. It will be readily seen that the relationship of $\dfrac{C}{a}$ or $\dfrac{C}{b}$ to t, and the value of t itself, will vary with the rate of interest; and all three will approximate Böhm-Bawerk's definition of the "average period of production" (=half the lifetime of the houses) as the rate of interest approaches zero.

In the above the investment period, t, was *implicitly* defined as that particular period of time which satisfies the equation $a(1+i)^t=b$, when the values of a, b and i are independently given. An *explicit* definition must relate the "investment period" to the construction period and the service life of the individual items of equipment comprising the investment. Since this paper was originally written, D. G. Champernowne and R. F. Kahn,[1] and C. A. Blyth[2] have considered this problem from a different angle. It follows from their work (as well as that of Wicksell) that there is no generally valid formula for expressing the relationship between t and the service life of the individual items of equipment (which we may call T) but that in the case of "point-input continuous output" (i.e. in the case of our houses) writing r for the instantaneous rate of interest the relationship is given by the expression

$$t=-\frac{1}{r}\log_e\frac{e^{rT}-1}{rTe^{rT}}$$

The approximation for this when r is sufficiently small in relation to T so that $rT<2$ is

$$\frac{T}{2}-\frac{rT^2}{24}$$

Taking this approximation and substituting $ae^{rt}=b$ for equation (1) so that equation (3) becomes $\dfrac{C}{a}=t+\dfrac{rt^2}{2}$, we have

$$\frac{C}{a}=\frac{T}{2}-\frac{rT^2}{24}+\frac{r}{2}\left(\frac{T}{2}-\frac{rT^2}{24}\right)^2$$

[1] "The Value of Invested Capital", *Review of Economic Studies*, 1953-4, pp. 107-12.
[2] "The Theory of Capital and its Time-Measures", *Econometrica*, 1956, pp. 467-79.

Neglecting any term in which r is of the second- or higher-order, this becomes

$$\frac{C}{a} = \frac{T}{2} + \frac{rT^2}{12} \quad \text{or} \quad \frac{C}{Ta} = \frac{1}{2} + \frac{rT}{12} \quad \dots (4)$$

Equation (4) is the Champernowne-Kahn formula which gives the ratio of the value of capital to the replacement cost (Ta) of the whole stock of capital. It must be understood, however, that this formula yields a reasonable approximation only for particular constellations of values of r and T.][1]

Now, according to Professor Knight, the concept of the investment period, or "degree of roundaboutness", is without significance for capital theory; for "the average investment period and the quantity of capital may perfectly well be affected in opposite ways".[2] The argument, if I rightly understand it, could be summarised as follows: the optimum degree of roundaboutness, on any single investment, is the one which maximises the rate of return on that investment. A change in the quantity of capital could only lead to a shift in the optimum degree of roundaboutness by affecting the relative rates of return on different degrees of durability. It is usually assumed that this will be the case because an increase in the supply of capital will lead to a fall in the rate of interest. But in the case of "continuous maintenance" the *rate of return*, on any single investment, will be independent of the rate of interest. It is only by assuming that the amortisation quotas are accumulated at some "outside" rate of interest that this "internal rate" will be affected; in which case a given fall in the rate of interest would reduce the return from less "durable" investments to a greater extent. In the numerical example we have given above, the reduction in the interest rate to 4% would make Type II houses more profitable than either of the other two types. But this method of calculation is obviously mistaken since it overlooks the fact that, by reinvesting the amortisation quotas

[1] The above is an amended version of footnotes 20 and 21 of the original article, which did not contain the approximations for $\frac{C}{a}$ given in equations (3) and (4), and merely showed that if i is negligible $\frac{C}{a}$ approximated to t. In making these amendments, I am indebted to Dr. C. A. Blyth and Mr. Hugh Hudson.

[2] *Ibid.*, p. 45.

in the same uses, a much higher net return is obtained than by reinvesting them at the current interest rate outside. It is not true, therefore, that a fall in the interest rate would make it profitable to shift to more durable houses. In the above example, the least durable house (Type I) has the highest real rate of return— 6·35%—and so long as the price of room service and the rate of wages remain the same, this is the type that will be preferred, irrespective of how much the rate of interest might fall.

An increase in the quantity of capital, therefore, will not change the "degree of roundaboutness" involved on *already existing* investments; and there is no reason to suppose that this "degree of roundaboutness" will be higher on new investments than the average on already existing capital goods. What happens when the rate of interest falls is that investments whose real rate of return was lower than the previous interest rate become profitable. More houses will be built. But the houses which have only just become profitable on account of the lower rate of interest need not be "more durable houses"; they may be houses with a different quality of room service. It is the relation between net return and cost of construction which must be lower. But the kind of houses which have a lower net return may very well have a lower ratio of construction cost to maintenance cost and thus a lower "period of production". The two are not related to each other at all— durability, as Knight contends, is merely one of an "infinite number" of considerations that affect the net return of investments.

III

Before we proceed to a criticism of this argument, we might attempt to piece together these various aspects and give a general picture of the world as Professor Knight sees it. It consists of a collection of resources which, like heavenly bodies, emanate light and absorb light. All these resources have to be "maintained"; i.e. they all absorb a quantity of services at every unit period, which is the absolute condition of their continuing to radiate another stream of services, which is their "output". No distinction can be made between maintenance and replacement, or even between production for immediate consumption and production for "maintenance"—or future consumption—since all that we know is that during a certain period a certain quantity of all kinds of services have been "put in" (into each particular "resource" or "factor") and a certain other quantity of services has been "put out". It is impossible to say "how much" of the input served to produce the immediate output, and how much served to maintain the resource itself. And since, in a well-organised competitive world, for each particular resource both input stream and output stream must be constant, per unit of time (if the ruling prices are expected to remain in operation),[1] the question itself is meaningless. Looked at in one way, all production is "instantaneous"—if the input stream is regarded as "producing" the output stream. If the resources themselves are regarded as producing the output stream, all input is to be regarded as producing output in an indefinite future. The output stream of all resources in so far as they do not directly consist of consumption services and in so far as they are not actually creating some *additional* resource—must therefore be input or "maintenance cost" for some other resources. Even consumption can be looked upon as the input of the resources called "labourers". Not all consumption, of course, for on the one hand labourers' consumption falls short of total consumption by the consumption of the owners of other resources— on the other hand, the labourers' consumption must itself include the net return from the investment of owning themselves. This difference (property owners' consumption plus the difference between labourers' income and maintenance cost) can be regarded as the "net return" from the whole system. It is precisely the extent to which all inputs fail to cancel out all outputs.

In a growing system some of the service stream (of all types of resources) will also be engaged in producing further resources. To the extent that such services are obtained by reducing the input-stream of other resources—and this is the only way of obtaining them if a world of "full employment" is contemplated—these other resources will, for the period of construction of the new

---

[1] I believe this assumption underlies the whole of Knight's analysis. When he mentions "perfect foresight" he uses this word in a different sense from the one in which Professor Hayek uses the term. Professor Knight, I believe, merely implies that the markets are sufficiently perfect to adjust themselves immediately to any given change—they are "Walrasian" markets. It is "perfect foresight" only under the static assumption that no further changes occur in the future.

resources, be "undermaintained"—their input stream will be temporarily reduced. Not all the resources "lent" will be repatriated, of course, at the end of the construction period. Some of them will permanently remain with the new resources, as their permanent input flow. This deficiency, however, will be more than offset by the output stream from the new resources, which directly or indirectly will also help to maintain the old ones.[1]

As the quantity of capital is increasing, the rate of return falls, since this implies the adoption of progressively inferior investment opportunities. It is at the margin of investment that the rate of interest is determined; capital quantity itself is a "marginal concept". Accumulation implies the conversion of current income into additional streams of permanent income; it implies an increase in "resources" in general, in the capacity to produce output streams, and in this sense *every* addition to the stock of capital should be considered as a permanent improvement. Accumulation requires abstinence (in the sense that abstaining from a part of the current product is the price of creating an additional output stream) but there is no "waiting period" involved in the maintenance of a given stock of resources[2] and, since the services of all resources equally contribute to the creation and maintenance of each other, no definite meaning can be attached to the term of an investment period itself. This concept is in any case *irrelevant*; for

[1] The whole situation is analogous to the case of a hydroelectric plant, which lends part of its water power for the construction of another plant. Once the new plant is constructed, the old plant's power will no longer be required except for "maintenance" which is a small proportion of the construction cost and, if I rightly interpret Professor Knight, could easily be less than the additional net output of the new plant.

[2] Among Austrian theorists, the "waiting period" is sometimes measured by the extent to which current consumption has to be reduced (below some technical maximum) in order to permit the maintenance of the existing stock of capital, i.e. in order to secure the continuance of the same rate of consumption permanently. Now it is perfectly true that at any time, given the technical composition of the system, the rate of consumption could be stepped up a certain extent if all productive services were devoted to producing for immediate consumption—given the length of time for which the increased rate of consumption-output is supposed to last. But the extent to which this can be done will depend on the type of capital goods used as well as on their quantity; and it is quite possible that with an increase in capital, the possibility of expanding consumption by not maintaining capital goods should decrease rather than increase. In any case, the extent to which this can be done will certainly have no relation to the *value* of capital in terms of current income, except in those simple cases where the capital consists exclusively of circulating capital, physically homogeneous with the final product. (E.g. if capital consisted of the stock of grain annually reinvested—in the form of seed and advances to labour—the quantity of consumption could be expanded in precisely the same ratio as the value of the capital stock in terms of the annual product.)

even under the most favourable assumptions it could not be substantiated that an increase in capital will necessarily imply the adoption of "lengthier" processes.

I am not sure whether this brief picture does justice to Professor Knight's views. But if it is a correct interpretation of his theory, it fails to account for a number of factors which it is the fundamental task of a theory of capital to explain. In the first place, it does not explain how the rate of return, on different investments, is kept at a level of equality. Under the conditions postulated, the rate of return should correspond in equilibrium to the current rate of interest not only on the marginal unit of investment, but on all units. It can be argued that "inframarginal" investments will earn rents which, in terms of money costs, will equalise this difference; but then the question still arises: why should "rents", if they arise, not be eliminated by competition? In the second place (and this is closely linked up with the first) it does not really explain why an increase in capital should lead to a fall in interest. To say that resort must be had to inferior investment opportunities does not in itself meet the problem. Diminishing returns necessarily presuppose the existence of some "fixed factor" as their cause; and there is no room for such "fixed factors" if we regard, as Professor Knight apparently regards, capital accumulation as an increase in the quantity of resources in general. In the last place, this theory contributes little to an explanation as to how *interest as a distributive share* is determined, along with other distributive shares. The great merit of the Austrian capital theory —at any rate of Wicksell's version of this theory—is that it explains the interrelation between wages and interest; and thus makes it possible to extend the general marginal productivity theory so as to include capital. So far as this problem is concerned, the critics of the traditional theory can hardly be said to have offered an alternative explanation.

We shall attempt to demonstrate in the following that the crucial argument concerning the irrelevance of the "law of roundaboutness" ignores the all-important effect of a change in the quantity of capital on price relationships; and that an interpretation can be given to the theory which allows it to survive most of the other criticisms that have been brought forward.

Finally we shall endeavour to show that the "law of roundabout-ness" itself is merely a derivation from the general law of non-proportional returns; while the Austrian view of capital merely implies an attempt to measure the quantity of variable resources by the average productivity of the services of "fixed" resources, which is possible so long as the latter are homogeneous in kind and the composition of the final output stream can be considered as given.

IV

1. In the first place, let us go back for a moment to the question of the definition of resources. Here Professor Knight appears to have overlooked one distinction which survives the strictures levelled against the traditional classification. Even if all resources require to be maintained and the services of all resources con-tribute to the production of new resources, it is still not true that *all* kinds of resources can be *produced*. It is not possible to produce "land"; and, in a capitalist economy which no longer knows the institution of slavery, it is not even possible to "produce" labour. The quantity of labour, through a change in the birth rate, can certainly be increased, but to regard this quantity as being a function of saving or the rate of interest is turning an analogy into a falsehood.

If the services of producible resources provided "perfect substi-tutes"[1] for the services of the non-producible resources this difference would not constitute a "relevant economic fact"—the prices of the services of non-producible resources would be entirely governed by the services of produced resources. In reality, however, the services of capital goods provide merely an imperfect substitute to services of labour; the one can be substituted against the other in any sort of production only at continuously increasing marginal rates of substitution. Thus even if the distinction between "permanent" and "non-permanent" resources or between "original" and "produced" resources is untenable or irrelevant, there is still a distinction to be drawn between "producible" and "non-producible" (or rather, "augmentable" and "non-augment-able") resources.

[1] In the sense of their having infinite "elasticities of substitution" with the services of the other resources, i.e. that this rate of substitution did not vary with the pro-portions in which they were combined.

Given this distinction, we must immediately make note of another factor, which in this paper has so far been left in the background: that in a position of equilibrium, assuming perfect competition, the value of producible resources must always correspond to their cost of reproduction (to the value of the quantity of services needed to produce another "identical" resource). The value of non-producible resources, on the other hand, need not conform to any such criterion simply because they have no costs of reproduction.

Now, what Professor Knight's own theory has not explained— or at any rate the present interpretation of his theory has not explained so far—is the problem, how this correspondence between the value of producible resources and their costs of reproduction is achieved, or if achieved, how this correspondence is again re-established, once equilibrium has been for any reason disturbed. A fall in the rate of interest, e.g., will raise the discounted value of *all* future income streams, and thus the present value of all resources whose ownership can be bought and sold (that is to say, all resources except labour). Moreover, if it is assumed that all resources are "continuously" maintained, it must raise the market value of all investments in the same proportion. If their value was previously equal to their costs of reproduction, they will now exceed these costs by the proportion which the fall in the rate of interest bears to the new rate of interest. How will this correspondence be re-established?

2. In order to analyse the interrelation of different factors let us return to the simplest hypothetical situation, where the stock of capital consists of houses which are built exclusively by labour, while "room-years" represent the only kind of consumption good. In order to avoid monetary complications which are not relevant in the present discussion, we might also assume that "room-years" serve as a *numéraire* in terms of which debts are contracted, wages are paid and property is valued. In this society "savings" imply a desire to convert current income ("room-years") into "houses"— in other words, an increased desire for "holding" houses. If this increased demand can be satisfied by an increased supply (when e.g. unemployed labour is available for additional house building) there need be no change in the value of houses in consequence.

But if *all* the labour is already engaged in building (or rather "replacing") houses, it is the value of houses that will rise (which is merely another way of saying that the rate of interest, in terms of room-years, will fall); and, as the value of houses rises, wages will rise. For the value of existing houses cannot be higher than their costs of reproduction, and a rise in costs of reproduction must imply a rise in wages.

Alternatively one might say that saving first leads to a fall in the room-year rate of interest (which is "determined" in the annuity market), this creates the rise in the value of houses, which in turn increases wages. The rise in wages increases construction costs; but it will also reduce the value of houses (i.e. below their new level, which they reached after the fall in interest). For the rise in wages, by raising expected future wages, increases maintenance costs, relatively to gross incomes (input values relatively to output values) and thus reduces the "net incomes" on the basis of which capital values are calculated. Thus, while costs of construction rise, capital values fall, and "somewhere in the middle" they again meet, thus bringing the movement to an end. In either case, it is the change in wages which brings the real rate of return on individual investments into equality with the rate of interest.

It would seem to follow from this that in this society "savings" merely resulted in a transference of income from the capitalists to the labourers.[1] There would be no increase in aggregate real income; and (save for changes in relative demand arising out of changes in distribution) there would be no changes in composition. In particular, it is difficult to see how investment opportunities which were previously ultramarginal (which were previously not adopted because their real rate of return was lower than the prevailing interest rate) would, as a result of savings, become inframarginal. For the rise in wages would have offset the effect of the reduction of interest; and in the new situation, they would still be below the margin of profitability. Continued

---

[1] This transference would not be temporary, but permanent (even if "savings" were temporary). For it would be financed, so to speak, out of two sources: first, the increase in the supply of capital, coming from the savers; second, the reduction in interest (in the return on investments) which the increase in the supply of capital creates (and which would thus be shared equally by all capitalists). The reduction in the interest rate, following upon a given increase in capital, would be precisely such as would enable the same transference of real income per time unit permanently as the volume of savings (per time unit) which was originally responsible for it.

capital accumulation in such circumstances would merely lead to the complete expropriation of the capitalists, by reducing the rate of interest to zero and making the value of annual labour input identical with the value of room-year output.[1]

3. But fortunately for the capitalists this will not be so—not even under our rigid assumptions. For the rise in wages in terms of house-room creates something which by itself tends to check the tendency of the level of wages to rise and the income from capital to fall. It necessarily increases the optimum degree of round-aboutness.

Let us return to our numerical example of the three types of houses and see how their respective rates of return will be affected by varying increases in wages. Since the rise in wages must always be such as to equalise the rate of interest with the real rate of return, this will also show the level of wages corresponding to different rates of interest (represented by the italicised figures):

Increase in Wages %	Real Rate of Return (%) of		
	Type I	Type II	Type III
0	*6·35*	6·2	5·9
10	5·42	*5·45*	5·24
20	4·65	*4·83*	4·68
50	2·69	3·29	*3·37*

We can see from this that not only does Type II become the most profitable investment if the increase in wages is 10%, but the differences in profitability, expressed as a percentage,

---

[1] This sounds rather like a rehabilitation of the classical theory of the Wages Fund —which in a sense it is meant to be. If conditions were postulated under which an increase in the supply of capital would *not* lead to an increase in aggregate real income (when e.g. the technical coefficients between "capital" and labour—the services of produced and non-produced resources—were fixed and the quantity of labour given) the supply of capital would determine—in a linear fashion—the rate of wages. There is no reason to assume that in such a society the rate of interest will be necessarily zero—it will be determined at the point where the demand for "annuities" (in exchange for current income) is equal to its supply. (The rate would be zero only if at any positive rate the demand for annuities exceeded the supply.) The rate of interest thus determined will determine the level of wages and the share of labour in the product.

M

continuously increase with every increase in wages.[1] Assuming that there is a continuous range of alternatives and not merely three distinct types of durability there must be a shift in the optimum ratio of construction cost to maintenance cost (or input volume to output volume) as soon as the price of input units rises relatively to the price of output units. This shift can be thought of as being brought about (for the "representative enterprise") either by a reduction to present "output" with a view to increasing the future rate of output (the input stream remaining the same) or a reduction in present output with a view to reducing future rate of input; or, finally—since the input flow is subject to diminishing returns in terms of output flow—simply a reduction in the permanent rate of input which is followed by a less-than-proportionate reduction of the permanent rate of output. In all of these cases there will be a reduction in the permanent input flow per unit of output flow; which in turn will have three different consequences. In the first place, it damps down the fall in the value of investments, brought about by a rise in wages, since the increase in maintenance cost will no longer be proportionate to the increase in wages. In the second place, it increases the "costs of reproduction" of house investments more than in proportion to the increase in wages (since maintenance costs can only be reduced by increasing construction cost) and thus closes more rapidly the "gap" between the value of investments and the costs of reproduction, caused by a given increase in the supply of capital. (In other words, it closes the gap with a smaller increase in wage rates than otherwise.) All this can also be expressed by saying that the existence of Type II houses as an alternative to Type I houses prevents both the rate of interest from falling, and the level of wages from rising, so much—following upon a given percentage increase in "free capital"—as they would have fallen, or risen, had Type II houses not been available as an alternative. In the third place, it creates

---

[1] In the above example, the changes appear numerically slight (relatively to the changes in wage rates), but this is only because the maintenance costs, in the examples shown, were already very low in relation to the construction cost. Generally speaking, the numerical change in relative profitability for a given increase in wages will be greater, the higher is the ratio of maintenance cost to construction cost (the influence on relative profitability of changes in the interest rate in the case of "discontinuous maintenance" will be *per contra* the more noticeable the lower is this ratio) and greater the higher is the real rate of interest. With continued increases in wages, the differences generally increase in a diminishing proportion.

an increase in the permanent supply of house room, which otherwise could not have taken place, as a result of a fall in the interest rate.[1] If in the above example we further assume that there is only a single kind of house room in existence (that given in the example) the changeover to Type II investments from Type I investments will ultimately have increased the volume of available room-years in the ratio of $100(273-225)/225$, i.e. by $20·88\%$. This, divided by the quantitative increase in the investment period, which is involved in this changeover, should give the "marginal productivity of waiting" according to the Jevons' formula, to which the rate of interest must correspond at the point where the two types of investments are equally profitable.[2]

Thus, given the available quantity of labour and the productivity function of capital (the extent to which maintenance cost per unit of output can be reduced by a minute increase in the ratio of construction cost over maintenance cost), the rate of interest determines the relative price of labour service and consumption service. This price ratio in turn determines the "average investment period", i.e. the degree of roundaboutness which maximises the yield of investments. Alternatively, the increase in the supply of capital determines the extent to which the degree of roundaboutness will be changed by changing the ratio of the price of input units relatively to output units, which in turn determines the rate of interest, since in equilibrium the rate of interest must be equal to the "real rate of return" on investments.

All this is merely a simplified and somewhat loose account of the Wicksellian version of the Austrian theory, first put forward in the

---

[1] Furthermore if we assume that the "degree of roundaboutness" for different types of room-years is different, the rise in wages will change their relative rates of return. For a given rise in wages will affect the rate of return all the more the higher is the ratio of annual maintenance cost to construction cost. The re-establishment of equilibrium (i.e. equalisation of the rates of return) will then require, in addition, a relative fall in the prices of the services of more "durable" resources and a relative expansion of their supply.

[2] The two types of investments become (approximately) equally profitable at a wage increase of 6% at which both yield $5·8\%$. At this rate the "compound investment period" (calculated according to the formula on page 166 above) will be $14·73$ years for Type I and $17·85$ years for Type II. The net increase will therefore be $3·42$ years and the "marginal productivity of waiting" $20·8/3·42=6·2\%$, i.e. approximately the same as the rate of interest. (An exact equality could only result if very small changes were contemplated.) Since, however, in these cases, the "investment period" (in terms of years) can only be evaluated if the rate of interest appropriate to the situation is already known, the concept of the "marginal productivity of waiting" does not seem to be particularly helpful.

Über Wert, Kapital und Rente, and later in the *Lectures on Political Economy*,[1] and adapted to the case where all capital is "permanently and continuously" maintained. It differs from the Böhm-Bawerkian theory chiefly through the analysis that for the individual entrepreneur the optimal investment period is determined by the production function and the existing price relationships (which are given to him); while the supply of capital "determines" the investment period by determining the ratio of output prices to input prices (i.e. of a unit of consumption service to a unit of labour service).[2]

V

So far we have merely attempted to vindicate the traditional capital theory under the simple assumption that the capital of the world consists of houses produced exclusively by labour; that there is perfect competition, static foresight and the absence of uncertainty. The real world—for the purpose of the present discussion—differs from this, apart from the last three assumptions, in three important respects: (i) that the maintenance of capital does not have the character of "replacement" of units at definite intervals but rather that of continuous repairs; (ii) that the services of labour are not all invested in capital but partly co-operate with the services of capital goods in producing consumption services, i.e. the labour force itself is divided, to use Wicksell's expression, between "free" and "invested" labour; (iii) that capital goods are not produced exclusively by the services of labour but also by the services of other capital goods, i.e. the services of capital goods themselves help to produce (or "maintain") each other. How far do these facts modify our results?

(i) The first of these points can be treated briefly. Whether "maintenance expenditure" consists of definite replacement of physical units or merely of repairs, the ratio of initial cost to

---

[1] Cf. *Lectures*, Vol. I, Part II, Sect. D, "An Alternative Treatment of the Problems of Interest and Distribution", also Appendix 21, "Real Capital and Interest". Cf. also Wicksell's *Finanztheoretische Untersuchungen*, pp. 22-41.

[2] Cf., e.g., Wicksell, *Finanztheoretische Untersuchungen*, p. 33 (my translation): "Given the general postulate of Böhm-Bawerk's theory [i.e. the law of roundaboutness] one would think at first that the capitalist always aimed at a steadily longer investment period of his capital—at any rate once the loss of interest during the transition period can be neglected. This, however, will by no means be the case; for any given level of wages, there is always an optimal length of the investment period."

annual maintenance cost will still provide a measure of the "degree of roundaboutness"; and so long as it is still possible to reduce the annual maintenance charge, of a given service stream, by increasing the initial construction cost, it will still be true that the price ratio between output units and input units will determine the optimum relation between construction cost and maintenance cost which, in turn, will determine the rate of interest. It will not be possible, of course, to associate a definite "investment period" with the input of any *particular* period; but this, as we have seen, is hardly legitimate in any case, unless the whole contribution of the input of a particular period accrues at some given date in the future (as, e.g., with the storage of wine), which is only true in certain specific cases.

(ii) The second point is more serious. It affects our previous analysis in two ways: (*a*) In the first place, it is clear that if a part of the labour supply is co-operating with existing equipment in producing current output, simultaneously with savings a certain quantity of labour will be "released" for employment in new construction. If instead of houses we had taken the less unreal example of machines co-operating with labour in producing bread, it would have been at once obvious that savings would not merely increase the demand for "holding" machines, but would also reduce the demand for bread. Corresponding to the increase in the demand for labour in machine-making, there would be a released demand for labour in the making of bread.[1] If machines are produced exclusively by labour, while "bread" is produced partly by labour and partly by machines, there will still be an increase in the *aggregate* demand for labour. But if "labour" and "machines" co-operate in the same way in producing new resources as in producing final output—and this is what Professor Knight's first point really amounts to—there need be no net increase, as far as

[1] The reason why this has been apparently overlooked (by the classics and in Wicksell's treatment, cf. esp. *Lectures, op. cit.*, pp. 148-9) is due to the assumption that what is saved is the product of past labour and not of current labour, so that the current demand for labour is independent of current consumption; depending only on the current supply of capital. (This is the meaning, e.g., of Mill's statement that the "demand for commodities is *not* a demand for labour".) This again is true if (*a*) the unit of account is fixed in terms of the final product, so that changes in current consumption do not affect the profitability of investment *via* price expectations; (*b*) all labour is "invested labour"—as, e.g., in the case of an agricultural community, whose labour requirements consist mainly in sowing seed for the following harvest.

the *creation* of new capital goods is concerned, either in the demand for labour services or in the demand for machine services. There could thus be an increase in the number of machines even without a rise in wages. It would be wrong to conclude, however, that this would invalidate our previous conclusions. For once the new machines are in existence and "saving" correspondingly ceases, they will require some additional labour for their maintenance and operation which they can only get by reducing the quantity of labour employed in combination with the previously existing resources. This in turn (if machine services are merely an imperfect substitute for labour services) will increase the price of labour services, relatively to other services (which is merely another way of explaining that the relative increase in "other services" increases the relative scarcity of labour services), it will reduce the quantity of labour input per unit of bread output (by reducing either the labour embodied in, or the labour co-operating with, a unit of machine service, or both), which in turn implies an extension of the degree of roundaboutness and a fall in the rate of interest. It still remains true that it is the rise in wages, in terms of final output, which causes the fall in the rate of return—a fall which would be more severe if it were not possible to offset partly the effect of the rise in wages by extending the degree of roundaboutness.

(*b*) This brings us to the next point in this connection: the question of durability. We have already mentioned earlier[1] that the input stream (and thus the ratio of initial input to annual input) of resources will depend on how one defines the "output stream" of resources. In the example just given, either the "quantity of machine services per unit of time", or the "quantity of bread per unit of time" can be regarded as the output stream of the machines. In the first case the "input stream" will consist only of expenditures incurred in the upkeep and replacement of the machines (Wicksell's "invested labour"). In the second case it will include, in addition to the above, also the labour normally regarded as co-operating with the machines in producing the bread. According as the first view is taken or the second, we shall have two different measures of the "degree of roundaboutness".

---

[1] Cf. p. 166, note, above.

Only the first of these can be regarded as an index of the *durability* of capital goods. But only the second will be necessarily correlated with the quantity of capital.

It is only in so far as the proportion of invested labour to co-operating labour remains constant when the aggregate quantity of capital changes that the degree of roundaboutness will necessarily increase in both senses. And although this follows from Wicksell's analysis of the problem[1] there seems to be no reason why it should be the case if the possibility of a change in the *character* of the machines is taken into account.[2] An increase in the quantity of capital available might even lead to the introduction of *less durable* rather than more durable equipment, if only this equipment is more "automatic" (in the sense of requiring less labour to operate it) than the previous equipment. It is not true therefore (except in the special case, like houses, where all the labour used is invested labour) that the increase in the quantity of capital will *necessarily* lead to an increase in "average durability", or that it will lead to the making of "goods of still greater

[1] Cf. *Lectures*, Appendix 2, pp. 278 ff., esp. 287-8.

[2] Wicksell's argument could be summarised as follows: Let us suppose that in the beginning the increase in capital only leads to an increase in the number of machines of the same type as those already in use. This will imply that the amount of invested labour increases and the amount of "free" labour is reduced; which in turn will necessarily raise wages and reduce the price of the services of machines. The rise in wages, as we have seen before, makes it profitable to extend the lifetime of machines, which in turn will imply a reversal of this process: the amount of free labour will increase and the amount of invested labour will be reduced. On Wicksell's assumption this must continue until both regain their former proportion. Meanwhile "the labourers lose part of, but not all of, their recent increases in wages and the capital goods regain part of, but not all, the value they have just lost". (*Ibid.*, p. 288.)

It is quite possible, however, that as a result of the rise in wages, it becomes profitable to introduce not more durable but more automatic—and even less durable!—machines and in consequence there will be a further increase, rather than a reduction, in the amount of invested labour. It is often thought that machines which are both *more* efficient and *less* durable will be preferred irrespective of the quantity of capital. That this is not the case, can best be elucidated by a simple example. Let us assume, e.g., that bread can be manufactured by two different processes. The first involves machines which require an initial expenditure of 1,000 units of labour and an annual maintenance expenditure of 10 units (per 100 units of bread, per year). These machines will need in addition 50 units of labour to operate them. The second involves machines which require an initial expenditure of 1,500 units and an annual maintenance expenditure of 40 units; but these machines being much more "automatic" only require 10 units of labour to operate them (per 100 units of bread, per year). The ratio of initial cost to annual maintenance cost in the *first* sense will be 1,000/10, 1,500/40 respectively, in the two cases. In the second sense, it will be 1,000/60, and 1,500/50 respectively. Now, if the price of labour in terms of bread is unity, obviously the first of these methods is preferable to the second—since it will yield a return of 4% while the second yields only 3·3%. If, however, the price of labour rises, say by 50%, the second method will become preferable to the first; since in that case, the yield on the first method will be reduced to 0·66% while the yield on the second only to 1·1%.

durability in place of those produced before".[1] It *could* imply the opposite of these things. It must necessarily increase the "degree of roundaboutness" involved in producing final output (if co-operating labour and invested labour are taken together); but this is *not* the same thing (except in the special case where the amount of co-operating labour is zero) as an increase in the average durability of capital goods.

(iii) The last point—although it is the one most frequently emphasised by other critics[2]—does not, in our view, affect the theory any more than it has already been affected by previous considerations. It is perfectly true that at no stage of the production process is labour exclusively employed—the services of different types of resources contribute to the "maintenance" (or production) of each other; the output stream of resource A might be the input stream of some other resource B, whose output stream in turn forms part of the input of A. But this does not imply that this "circularity" in production is complete: this would only be the case if consumption itself could be regarded as part of the system's "input".[3] Now all "outputs" (of resources other than labour) which are *not* consumption services must be simultaneously inputs in some other resource. Similarly, all inputs, in so far as they do not consist of labour service, must be the outputs of some other resource. Therefore all outputs which are not consumption service and all inputs which are not labour service, exactly cancel each other out, if the input streams and output streams of individual resources are added together.[4] By defining the "net output" of resources as the volume of consumption we thereby also necessarily define their "net input" as the quantity of labour.[5] So long as the quantity of annual labour service

---

[1] Machlup, "Professor Knight and the 'Period of Production'", *op. cit.*, p. 590; and Hayek, "The Mythology of Capital", *op. cit.*, p. 213.

[2] Cf. Joseph and Bode, "Bemerkungen zur Zinstheorie", *op. cit.*; Nurkse, "The Schematic Representation of the Structure of Production", *op. cit.*

[3] It is possible, of course, to regard that part of the labourers' consumption which is necessary to maintain this productive capacity intact, as the "input" of labour as a factor of production. But only in a slave state would this magnitude have an economic significance.

[4] Cf. also the "analysis of interactions" in Fisher's *Theory of Interest*, pp. 18-22.

[5] This really follows from selecting "labour" as being distinct from other resources, in which case the input of *all* resources other than labour will consist of labour service. It would also be possible to regard some other factor—"land"—in the same way: in which case the input of all resources (including labour under this head) would consist

remains constant with variations in the quantity of capital, and so long as the quantity of no other type of services remains constant, there will be a unique correlation between the rate of interest and the amount of labour input per unit of final output— or, if you like, the rate of interest and the average investment period of the services of labour. For, as I hope to show in the next section, the "investment period" of a factor necessarily varies with its average productivity, once it is assumed that the factors themselves have a cost of production and not only the final products.

VI

For a proper understanding of the nature of capital and interest one ought to start by analysing the conditions of equilibrium in a society where *all* goods are capital goods, i.e. where "original" or non-augmentable resources do not exist at all. It is rather unfortunate that, following Böhm-Bawerk and his school, we have been generally accustomed to start with a more specialised set-up, with the picture of Robinson Crusoe engaged in net-making. This Crusoe-approach makes it unnecessarily difficult to single out features which are merely the property of a special case from the demonstration of general principles. Had the analysis started with the "general case"—by imagining a society where *all* resources are produced and the services of all resources co-operate in producing further resources—a great deal of the controversies concerning the theory of capital might not have arisen. As we shall see, it will be much easier to get back from this world to Böhm-Bawerk's world than to make the journey in the opposite direction.

Let us imagine, then, a society where "machines" and "slaves" are the only scarce resources, whose services are required equally for the production of each other and for the production of bread.[1]

exclusively of land service. The reason for regarding "labour" as distinct, is twofold: (a) that it is the ownership of labour which is non-alienable and in consequence has no capital value; (b) that it is the quantity of labour service which can be regarded as a constant with respect to "saving". Cf. also the next section, below.

[1] I.e. there is a production function for machines, whose variables are machine service and slave-labour service, a similar one for slaves, and yet another for bread. If we strictly adhered to the terms of our example, it should be added that the services of machines and of slave labour are directly required only for the production of machines and of bread. Only bread is required for the production of slaves. But bread in turn represents a certain quantity of machine services plus labour services, combined; so that we can say that the services of both resources are needed for the production of both resources.

The owners of slaves and machines (the entrepreneurs) will, under these assumptions, have essentially three degrees of freedom: (1) they can vary the proportions in which the services of machines and slaves are combined in the production of bread; (2) they can vary the proportions in which the machines and slaves themselves are produced, or reproduced; (3) they can decide how much of the "net output" of any period (i.e. the quantity of bread production compatible with maintaining the stock of slaves and machines intact) should be set aside to increase the permanent stream of bread output in the future.

Assuming perfect competition and constant returns to scale, the entrepreneurs will (individually) combine the two factors in such proportions as to maximise the output of a given outlay; and they will tend to produce the factors themselves in such proportions as would maximise the rate of return on a given investment (all in terms of "bread"). Assuming that the law of diminishing productivity operates throughout (i.e. that there is an increasing marginal rate of substitution between machine services and slave-labour services, in the production of bread, machines and slaves) the problem will have a unique solution. Given the cost function of machines, slaves and bread, there will be only one proportion between machines and slaves which will maximise the yield of capital: the proportion at which the value of both machines and slaves (calculated by discounting at the same rate their expected net income) is equal to their respective costs of reproduction.[1] It is this yield which in turn will determine the rate of interest. (All this can also be expressed by saying that the yield on capital will be maximised when the real rates of return, on machine investments and slave investments, are equalised.) This rate will represent at the same time the system's "maximum rate of growth": the rate at which the stock of resources would increase, per unit of time, if consumption were reduced to zero and the

---

[1] If there is a relative increase in the number of machines, and a consequent fall in the yield of machine investments, this would not imply an equivalent fall in the yield of "capital"—as it does in our own society—since the fall in the yield of machines would be largely offset by the corresponding increase in the yield of slaves. But on account of the law of diminishing returns it could never be so offset *entirely* (and vice versa if there is a relative increase in the number of slaves). Thus there will be only one ratio of investment in the two factors which equalises the real rates of return on these two types of investment and this will necessarily be also the arrangement which maximises the return per unit of bread.

services of all productive resources were devoted exclusively to their own production.

Thus both factors will yield a "net product"—i.e. the specific productivity of their services will be greater than the costs of production of these services—and the rate of return merely denotes the size of this excess, per unit of time, as a percentage of the cost. Since this "real productivity", and thus the real rate of return, on any resource will depend upon the relative scarcity of the services of that resource, and since the proportions of the factors are variable, investment will tend to get distributed in such proportions as would equalise the rate of return on all lines of investment.[1] Once this proportion is achieved, capital accumulation or decumulation (in the absence of a change in technical knowledge) will leave the rate of interest unaffected. How rapidly capital will be accumulated will depend, of course, on the rate at which people are willing to save at the given rate of interest; but no amount of capital accumulation could change this rate.[2]

In this society there will be two distinct "investment periods" which cannot be combined for the purposes of an average, since they are alternative ways of describing a single situation. We might either represent the entire bread output as the product of machines whose input consists of slave-labour service; or we might represent the entire bread output as the product of slaves whose input consists of machine-service. The average investment

---

[1] It would necessarily be true therefore of a slave state that both capital and labour yield a positive rate of return, irrespective of the extent of accumulation (unless there is some third "fixed" factor, like land, in relation to which both become less productive, by an increase in their quantity). But it will normally be true even in a non-slave state that the rate of return will be positive on both "machines" and labour (though the latter, owing to the inalienability of the ownership of labour, can only be calculated on rather arbitrary criteria) although, of course, there will no longer be forces operative which tend to make them *equal*. But the rate of return, on one or the other, could fall to zero in "extreme cases": (1) when the quantity of labour has increased, by multiplication, to the extent that the marginal productivity of labour has been brought down to the labourers' subsistence level (the "stationary state" of Ricardo and the classics); (2) when the quantity of material resources has increased, by accumulation, to the extent that the marginal productivity of the services of capital goods has been brought down to the level of their "maintenance costs" (the stationary state of Professor Schumpeter). There seems to be no reason to assume that in the real world forces are operative which will inevitably draw the system either to the one or to the other "extreme" of stationariness.

[2] If this rate is such that people are willing to save at that rate (and this desire, in the absence of a change in psychology, could only be strengthened by continued accumulation) our society would resemble the "expanding universe"; it could never become stationary.

period of the services of slave labour will depend on the ratio of the value of the entire labour input (of all machines) to that of the entire bread output. The average investment period of the services of machines will depend on the ratio of the value of the entire machine-service input (of all slaves)[1] to that of the entire bread output. Since both refer to the same bread output, an average between the two is completely meaningless. Both of these investment periods will, of course, remain unaffected by changes in the amount of capital.

If we now assume that, for some reason, the number of slaves is "held constant", when capital is accumulated, the increase in capital can only take the form of an increase in machines. Then the investment period of *labour* will rise, and the real rate of return on *machines* will fall. (Correspondingly, the investment period of machine services will *fall*, and the rate of return on slave labour will *rise*, but not to the same extent.) This "lengthening" of the investment period for slave labour can take various forms. (1) There might be an increase in the number of the *same* machines, and a substitution of machine services for labour services, in the production of bread; this will imply a reduction in the amount of co-operating labour, and an increase in the amount of invested labour, per unit of bread. (2) There might be an increase in the durability of machines, in which case the proportion of invested to co-operating labour can remain the same. (3) There might be a change in the "degree of automatism" of the machines (with or without a change in durability), in which case again the proportion of invested labour is increased and the proportion of co-operating labour reduced. All three cases imply a reduction in current labour input, and an increase in "initial input", per unit of bread output. If we now further assume that the slaves are liberated and in consequence only machines are regarded as "capital", the rate of interest will be determined by the yield of machines only; and we have then arrived at the Austrian theory of capital.

---

[1] The "machine-service input" of slave capital takes two different forms. (1) The services of machines directly co-operate with labour in producing bread. (2) Bread is also required for the maintenance of labour (which must be deducted from the "net output" of bread) and this maintenance bread also represents a certain quantity of machine service. (The same is true the other way round, of course.)

It follows from this analysis that the *Senior-Jevons-Böhm-Bawerkian law of roundaboutness is merely a roundabout way of expressing the law of non-proportional returns*. Once it it is realised that the only difference between "produced" and "non-produced" resources lies in the fact that the one can be augmented by economic disposition and the other cannot, it is clear that the ultimate reason why the rate of interest is falling with an increase in capital is precisely the same as the reason why rents are rising (or wages falling) with an increase in labour. A relative increase in the number of slaves, in the case where "land" and "slave labour" are the only scarce resources, could just as well be said to imply an increase in the "investment period" of the services of land, as a reduction of the marginal productivity of the services of labour; while the material content of the Austrian theory of capital could be equally well expressed by saying that capital accumulation leads to a reduction in the marginal productivity of the services of those factors whose quantity can be augmented by such accumulation, as by saying that it increases the investment period of the services of those resources whose quantity remains constant.

The purpose of the "investment period" approach is to reduce the production function to two variables, substituting "waiting" for the services of all produced (or variable) factors, with interest as the price of "waiting". In this way—and only in this way—can *capital as capital* be treated as a factor of production, commensurate with "labour". This, however, can only be done so long as the services of the "fixed" factors can themselves be regarded as homogeneous, or at any rate sufficiently homogeneous to leave their relative scarcity unaffected by changes in the amount of the services of other resources. In the above example machine services and labour services were the only scarce factors. This enables us, by regarding the quantity of labour as constant, to measure changes in the amount of machine services available by changes in the "investment period" of the services of labour. Had we assumed three factors, say the services of machines, labour and land, among which only the services of machines could be increased in quantity by capital accumulation, neither the investment period of the services of land, nor the investment period of the services of labour would have afforded an unambiguous measure of the amount of machine capital. A combined "invest-ment period" of the services of these "original", or rather constant, resources, on the other hand, would have been possible only if the services of machines were assumed to be an "independent good" relatively to the services of land and labour, i.e. if the marginal productivity-ratio between land services and labour services depended only on the relative amounts of land service and labour service, but not on the quantity of machines.[1]

Further consideration shows, moreover, that the same objection which can be brought up as regards the non-homogeneity of the services of fixed resources also applies as to the non-homogeneity of final products. So far we have treated consumption goods—"bread" —as if they were a homogeneous entity, or if not homogeneous, at any rate something the composition of which can be regarded as given. It is obvious, however, that except in the special case where all consumption goods contain the services of fixed resources in the same proportions, an increase in the quantity of capital will lead to a change in the relative prices of different types of con-sumption goods, and thus to a change in the composition of the consumption stream. In that case it will no longer be legitimate to speak of the degree of roundaboutness involved in producing a unit of "final output", since we no longer have an unambiguous measure of that unit. Nor can one ascertain (once allowance is made for the "circularity" in production) the degree of round-aboutness for each kind of consumption good, taken separately. For the contributions of the services of produced resources are diffused between different industries; and this renders it im-possible to impute a definite proportion of the aggregate stream of "labour" to a single kind of consumption good.[2]

So far we have conducted our analysis under purely static assumptions, and found that even under these assumptions the investment-period concept leads into difficulties once allowance is made for the fact that both the relative prices of different kinds

---

[1] This defect of the Austrian capital theory was first pointed out by F. X. Weiss, "Produktionsumwege und Kapitalzins", *Zeitschrift für Volkswirtschaft und Sozialpolitik*, 1921.

[2] It is only in cases where (as in our world of houses) the input stream of each single capital good consists exclusively of labour, or where the services of all capital goods are completely specific (i.e. they only contribute to the production of one final good) that the "investment periods" for individual commodities can be *separately* evaluated.

of labour (and land) and the relative prices of different kinds of consumption goods might change as a result of a change in the quantity of capital. It is not proposed here to examine the further difficulties that emerge once the static assumptions are, in one respect or another, relaxed; nor even to enquire how far the methods of "comparative statics" are legitimate for dealing with problems of capital accumulation. There can be no doubt that for an analysis of dynamic problems—and especially of the *par excellence* dynamic problem of the trade cycle—the investment-period concept could hardly be of any use. At the same time we hope that we have succeeded in demonstrating that the real objections against the "Austrian" capital theory relate to the *measurability* of the investment period, rather than to its *relevance*. It can be argued on many grounds (some of them emphasised by Knight, some already emphasised by earlier writers, such as Professor Fisher) that the "investment period" ceases to be a quantitatively measurable magnitude once one departs from the level of abstraction of Böhm-Bawerk's and Wicksell's writings. But this is a very different thing from maintaining—as Professor Knight maintained in various articles—that the investment-period concept is also wholly irrelevant, i.e. that even if conditions are postulated under which it can be measured, it will have no correlation with the quantity of capital and the rate of interest. In so far as it is possible to give an index to the "degree of round-aboutness", it can also be shown that an increase in capital, if associated with a lower interest rate, will necessarily imply the adoption of more roundabout processes.

ADDENDUM: A REJOINDER TO PROFESSOR KNIGHT[1]

PROFESSOR F. H. KNIGHT has done me the honour of writing a detailed reply[2] to a paper of mine[3] containing certain criticisms of his views and published in an earlier number of *Econometrica*. I do not propose to write a detailed rejoinder to his paper; especially since it contains much with which I agree and the

---

[1] Originally published in *Econometrica*, Vol. 6, April, 1938.
[2] "On the Theory of Capital: In Reply to Mr. Kaldor", *Econometrica*, Vol. 6, January, 1938, pp. 63-82.
[3] "Annual Survey of Economic Theory: The Recent Controversy on the Theory of Capital", *Econometrica*, Vol. 5, July, 1937, pp. 201-33 [pp. 153-91 above].

statements with which I do not agree are often so closely inter-
woven with those with which I do that it would tax the reader's
patience too much to attempt to disentangle them. Instead, I shall
try to make clear the issues between us, as I see them, by setting
out a brief résumé of my own position and comparing it with
Professor Knight's. As the reader will observe, apart from a
number of minor points, our difference lies in a single major issue.

I

1. The purpose of the Austrian or "time period" theory of
capital was to show that "capital" is a distinct factor of production, which can be measured in homogeneous units, both in the
production of particular goods and in the economic system as a
whole; that the price of this factor is the rate of interest; and that
both capital and interest can thus be brought into the framework
of production and distribution theory on the same plane as
"labour" and "land". (Some economists might, perhaps, disagree
with this statement as to the purpose of traditional capital theory.
But if this is *not* what the theory was aiming at, what was its
purpose?) It rested on two premises. First, the assumption that it
is possible to make a "valid general distinction" between capital
goods and other productive resources. Second, the attempted
demonstration that, with the aid of the concept of the "investment
period", the heterogeneous mass of capital goods can be reduced
to homogeneity, and thus "capital" can be treated as a quantity
per se. Professor Knight rejects both these premises. But since the
criticisms on the second count are more numerous, and more
difficult to deal with, they may be considered first.

2. It is best to begin by clarifying certain points of methodology.
(1) The question whether the "investment period" is something
"quantitatively definable" is distinct from the question whether
it can also be regarded as a measure of the quantity of capital, as
a factor of production—in other words, the question whether the
concept has *meaning* should be kept rigidly separate from the
question whether it is *relevant*. Examination of the second question
presupposes that the first can be answered in the affirmative. (2)
The question whether a definite investment period can be associated
with a *single investment*[1] is distinct from the question whether
an "investment period" can be defined for the *economic system as a*

[1] A "single investment" is here thought of, not as some concrete capital good, but
as something which produces a definite kind of output stream.

whole. It is possible that one of these questions can be answered positively, but not the other. (3) The question whether the investment period can be determined *under stationary conditions* (i.e. in "the stationary state") is distinct from the question whether it can also be determined in the absence of stationariness. Traditional capital theory (both by the Austrians and Wicksell) was elaborated under the postulate of the stationary state; while some of Professor Knight's strictures against the theory[1] clearly arise owing to the absence of stationary conditions. In my view, even if the investment-period theory were found to be a tenable explanation of the nature of capital in the stationary state, it could not be regarded as such for a society which is in a *process of change*;[2] and, this being the case, the question whether the theory is at all applicable for the real world depends on whether the method of *comparative statics* (which treats change as a result, and not as a process) is applicable to problems of capital accumulation. In traditional theory changes in the quantity of "capital" were dealt with merely by comparing different stationary states.[3]

3. In my paper I was first of all anxious to prove that, provided the investment-period concept is quantitatively definable, it is *relevant*, i.e. it will show a correlation with capital quantity. Hence I postulated artificial conditions, under which the meaning of the concept was not in question, in order to show that accumulation (=saving) will lead to a lengthening of this period. The reason for this procedure was the belief, gathered from Professor Knight's earlier articles, that his chief objections against the Austrian theory concerned the *relevance* of the investment-period concept, and not only its meaning or "reality": at any rate, this is how I interpreted his statement that "the average investment period and the quantity of capital may perfectly well be affected in

---

[1] Cf. *op. cit.*, p. 67: "One might in theory compute the 'investment period' for a national economy or for the world, but only after the close of its history in either case, or after its entire future history became predictable in quantitative detail." In the stationary state there is no such problem; the history of one day is the same as the history of any other day.

[2] The objections against the "investment period" concept under dynamic conditions cannot be gone into here in detail. It should suffice to repeat what was already stated in my previous paper (cf. *op. cit.*, p. 207) [p. 159 above], that even if such a concept were definable, it would measure changes in the scale of new investment and not changes in the quantity of capital.

[3] If one takes into account that certain types of equipment are extremely durable, and also indivisible and highly specialised—so that only one or a few units of them are needed—the extreme unreality of this approach in connection with the capital problem becomes at once apparent. It is only for "short-run analysis"—where the amount of existing equipment can be taken as given—that the method of "comparative statics" is at all realistic.

N

opposite ways".[1] This statement presupposes that the concept is meaningful; if it has no meaning it is impossible to make any statement about its behaviour. The question of relevance would then not arise.[2] Hence the sections in my paper which Professor Knight prefers "simply to pass over" were devoted to a disproof of the proposition that the "average investment period and the quantity of capital can be affected in opposite ways".

I now realise that I may have been fighting windmills; Professor Knight agrees that the Böhm-Bawerkian theory is valid under the conditions which it postulates, and hence the investment-period concept is not irrelevant, in this sense. He merely insists that the accumulation of capital will not necessarily involve the production of instruments which have a longer construction period, or which last longer, or both. It may do so (or probably will do so) but it may not. This, as I have tried to show in my paper,[3] is perfectly true but not relevant. The average construction period plus the average durability of capital goods merely indicate the average investment period involved in producing *the services of these instruments* and not (or not necessarily) the average investment period of *consumption services*. It is quite possible that the former should be reduced, when the latter is lengthened; when, e.g., capital accumulation implies the introduction of more "automatic" machines, which reduce the amount of "co-operating labour" per unit of output. It is only in cases (such as houses) where the instruments produce consumption services "by themselves", without the aid of co-operating labour, that the two concepts become identical; and, in this case, average durability, or average construction period, or both must become longer, when accumulation takes place.[4]

[1] "The Theory of Investment Once More: Mr. Boulding and the Austrians", *Quarterly Journal of Economics*, Vol. 50, November, 1935, p. 45.

[2] Even if the theory is found to be wrong because the conditions necessary to validate the investment-period concept do not obtain in the real world, it is important to know whether the things Böhm-Bawerk and his followers were talking about are at all relevant to the problem or not. If they are found to be irrelevant, the whole theory deserves more severe condemnation; it would not even be a "wrong track" in the Jevonian sense, but pure nonsense; and its examination sheer waste of time.

[3] *Ibid.*, pp. 226-7 [pp. 183-4 above].

[4] On p. 67 Professor Knight admits that the investment-period theory "can be modified and so stated as to be valid where capital and non-capital agencies co-operate in the creation of final product". On p. 73, however, he says that the only investment period to which he is able to attach meaning is "either some variant of the Jevons-Böhm-Bawerk-Wicksell average construction period and/or average durability, for all the capital items in a system considered individually, or one of these figures computed for the system as a whole, considered as a single investment". The second

It is only more recent writers, Professors Machlup and Hayek, who asserted that the accumulation of capital necessarily involves greater "average durability". This of course is wrong; so far as I am aware, neither Böhm-Bawerk nor Wicksell meant to assert it; nor does its denial constitute any sort of disproof of the "Austrian" theory.

4. We can now turn to the more important question whether the concept is meaningful, i.e. whether the investment period is "quantitatively definable".

(i) In the first place, difficulties arise—what has come to be called the "compound-interest problem"—as soon as we take cognisance of the fact that instruments take time to produce and wear out gradually, i.e. that there is no single, definite time-lag between "input" and the resultant "output". It is only when growing turnips (which are planted on one day and fully consumed on one day) that the intervening time-lag is something entirely unambiguous. In slightly more realistic cases (such as houses which are produced entirely by labour and "free goods" but which take, say, two years to produce and twenty years to wear out) the investment period involves the calculation of an *average* time-lag; and this average will be necessarily somewhat arbitrary; it will partly depend on the rate of interest ruling.[1] In my view—and I think this is also Professor Knight's view—this difficulty, taken by itself, would not be so very serious. Although it does make it impossible to determine what will be *the* investment period, it does not make it impossible to give an "index measurement" to it, i.e. to represent its variations by means of an index. And except for the calculation of the rate of interest as "the marginal productivity of waiting" which I do *not* consider an essential part of the theory,[2] there is no need for a quantitative

statement, I think, is inconsistent with the first. If the investment-period concept can also be extended to the case where capital goods co-operate with labour in the creation of the final product, the investment period will be something different from the average construction period and the average durability of instruments; nor will it necessarily vary in the same direction as the latter.

[1] This problem is not new; Wicksell was already well aware of it, cf. *Lectures*, Vol. I, English ed., p. 260. Cf. also my article, *op. cit.*, p. 206 [p. 159 above].

[2] It is often mistakenly supposed that the entrepreneur, in order to determine his optimum production plan, needs to know the "marginal productivity of waiting" in the Jevonian sense; since, in order to maximise his profits, he must push the application of "capital" up to the point where the rate of interest becomes equal to this marginal productivity (in the same way as the application of "labour" is pushed to the point where the marginal productivity of labour becomes equal to the wage rate). This, of course, is fallacious and is due to a mistaken conception of the nature of capital and interest. The optimum production plan is the one which maximises the rate of return on the investment: this can be determined without any reference to the investment period or its marginal productivity.

measurement of the investment period: an index of "capital intensivity" is all we want.[1]

(ii) In the second place, there is the further difficulty which Professor Knight brought to light, that maintenance often takes the form of necessary repairs, rather than of replacement; these repairs are a condition for the *functioning* of the equipment itself, so that it is impossible to impute any "investment period" to the input represented by such repairs.

". . . it is incorrect to speak of a time period or degree of round-aboutness unless the capital could be economically disinvested and the flow of final product kept up over the interval measured by this quotient [i.e. the investment period]. This is rarely if ever approximately the case for a single item, and for society as a whole the whole notion is fantastic."[2]

I agree with the latter part of this statement and also with the former part as far as the concept of a "time period" is concerned, but not as far as the "degree of roundaboutness" is concerned. It is impossible to speak of an "investment period" when the

[1] I misinterpreted Professor Knight's basic equation $a(1+i)^t=b$. Professor Knight was thinking of an investment that is perpetual without maintenance, in which case a, in my terminology, is zero and both indices register infinity. (In his terminology a is the rate of input *during construction*, while b is the rate of output *plus* the value of the regained consumption, a. The value of a in his terminology will not be equal to the value of a in my terminology, except in special cases; while t in his terminology stands for the construction period—the investment period being infinite—in my terminology t is the investment period, and not the accumulation or construction period; these two again only being equal in special cases.) Of course, if one assumes a case where the investment is perpetual without maintenance, the investment period necessarily becomes infinite: and, in order to examine the investment-period theory, one certainly should not start by making any such assumption unless one wants to condemn it wholesale at the start, in which case any further analysis of the problem becomes wholly superfluous. And when Professor Knight goes on to say that "neither of these pictures is typical of reality" (p. 71), I leave it to the reader to decide which of these two cases is more "typical" of reality: the case of investments which are perpetual without maintenance, or of investments which are only perpetual when they are maintained.

I should also like to add that *my* use of the basic equation $a(1+i)^t=b$ does not presuppose that individual capital items are produced by an initial application of factors, extending over a negligible interval, subsequently growing without any further input, and are consumed instantly when "mature" (Knight, footnote 12, p. 71). All that the equation presupposes is that it is possible to "build up" an integrated structure of capital goods (whatever the shape of the input stream or the output stream of individual capital items) which enables the output stream and the input stream, for the *structure as a whole*, to be constant; and that the input stream consists of non-capital services.

Professor Knight agrees that either of these two indices could serve as an "index of capital intensivity" (p. 73), but denies that an index of capital intensivity is also an index to the investment period. On this see below.

[2] Footnote 10, p. 69.

maintenance of capital goods is a condition of the current functioning of capital goods. But as I have tried to show, so long as it is still possible to vary the rate of necessary maintenance expenditure, per unit of output, by varying the initial construction expenditure, it is still possible to make production more or less "capitalistic" or "roundabout"; and the *degree of roundaboutness* (measured by the same sort of index as the investment period would be measured by) fulfils exactly the same rôle in this case as the investment period fulfilled in the previous case. There will still be a correlation, in comparing different stationary states, between the rate of interest ruling and the degree of roundaboutness adopted; and the mechanism described in Section IV in my paper, by which saving, in a barter economy, leads to an increase in the degree of roundaboutness, a lowering of the rate of interest and an increase in the flow of final product, will still be the same mechanism.

I am not sure whether the difference here between Professor Knight and myself is more than a quarrel over words. Professor Knight admits that, *so long as* a distinction can be made between capital goods and other resources, the concept of the "degree of capital intensivity" is valid; and the concepts of the "degree of roundaboutness" and of the "degree of capital intensivity" are, as far as I can see, exactly the same thing. We both agree, further, that, if capital cannot be "economically disinvested", the concept of an investment period is invalid; no matter how much (or how little) has to be spent on "maintaining" the stock of capital. We appear to differ as to the importance of the notion of the investment period itself, *within the traditional theoretical framework*. The virtue of this concept, in my view, is solely derived from its supposed ability to reduce the existing stock of capital to a homogeneous quantity. If it is impossible to measure capital in terms of an investment period, but *it is* possible to do so in some other way, the investment-period concept goes, and is replaced by this something else, but otherwise the theory remains pretty much as it was. It would be just as true (or more true) to say that the investment period gives, in certain cases, an index to the degree of capital intensity, as to say that the degree of capital intensity, in certain cases, is an index to the investment period. Fundamentally, both these concepts attempt to do no more than to measure the quantity of capital by measuring the ratio of the stock of capital goods to other factors; it is the validity of this "ratio" which is important and not the validity of the "investment period", which is merely one of several ways of measuring it.

Thus in cases where the investment period, though measurable, does not indicate the degree of capital intensity at all, it is the latter concept which is relevant (for the determination of the quantity of capital and the rate of interest) while the former is quite irrelevant. According to Professor Knight, I leave it

"a mystery as to why capitalistic intensivity should be regarded as corresponding in any way with any investment period, or as to what is meant by the degree of roundaboutness for which the ratio is said to be an index. The ratio would apparently have the same meaning in a system in which both machines and slaves lasted for ever, and regardless of their origin or what might be known about their past history."[1]

In a society where all capital instruments lasted for ever, without maintenance, the investment period of current labour would be zero under stationary conditions—irrespective of the number of such capital instruments. Yet there would be a productivity rate of interest (the size of the additional consumption stream that can be obtained by the sacrifice of a given amount of current consumption) and what this rate will be will depend on the degree of capital intensity. (If one wants to *define* capital simply as the investment period, as some Austrian die-hards would, one would have to say that in such a society the amount of capital is always zero in stationary equilibrium; but having said so, one would be no better off than before. Having relegated the term "capital" to some mystic entity, which has no relevance to economic problems, one would have to turn to some other concept and invent a different name in order to consider the problems of interest, investment and savings.)

If, on the other hand, capital instruments do *not* last for ever (which is, after all, the basic assumption on which Austria proceeded and one which—I hope Professor Knight will concede—is not entirely devoid of reality) the index of capital intensivity will always register the same kind of movements as the investment period (provided, of course, that the type of capital goods in existence is not such as to render the measurement of the investment period impossible). Hence, where the investment period is a definable concept, it provides a good index to the degree of

[1] *Op. cit.*, p. 73.

capital intensivity. (A rather cumbrous index perhaps, for its calculation will by no means be easy in all but the simplest cases.)

(iii) Lastly, there is the "brute fact" emphasised by Knight, that capital goods are not produced by the services of other factors, as is apparently assumed by the Austrians, but that the services of different kinds of capital goods co-operate in producing and reproducing each other. This certainly invalidates the concept of the degree of roundaboutness or capital intensivity when applied to a *single investment* (i.e. in the production of a single kind of consumption good).[1] But, as I have attempted to demonstrate in Section V, paragraph (iii) and Section VI of my paper—a demonstration which, as far as I can see, was not criticised nor refuted—it would not invalidate the concept for the *system as a whole*, if the latter concept were not deficient *on other grounds*, i.e. on account of the fact that both the services of non-augmentable resources and consumption services are heterogeneous; and their relative prices are altered by a change in the stock of capital goods.[2] It is only in so far as changes in these relative prices are absent or can be ignored—as for small changes in the stock of capital goods perhaps they can—that we can say how the quantity of capital has been affected, when the amount, or composition, of the stock of capital goods has been changed.[3] For these reasons, it is these latter facts—the heterogeneity of non-capital agencies and of final products—which are the ultimate objections to the traditional view of treating capital as a quantity. This is not to deny the importance of the so-called "circularity argument" (that capital goods produce other capital goods, and so on, in endless succession), but I think the difficulties thereby raised could be

[1] It does not invalidate the concept of "capital intensivity" for a single firm, or accounting unit, as Professor Knight admits. But it makes it impossible to "lump together" a series of accounting units in such a way that these *together* should only buy non-capital services and only sell consumption services.

[2] Professor Knight affirms the first (the heterogeneity of non-capital resources) and rejects the second (the heterogeneity of consumption services) of these facts as relevant in this connection (footnote 9, p. 69). I confess I do not understand his argument at all. To regard the "quantity of exchange of value of final products as established by perfect competition among sellers and consumers" (footnote 4, p. 64) as given, is only possible if the change in question does not affect the *relative* marginal costs of final products which it normally will. If, on the other hand, small changes are contemplated and these consequential changes in relative scarcities are so small that they can be ignored, they can be ignored with the same justification on the factor side as on the product side. In neither case is there any difference. Cf. also p. 203 note 3 below.

[3] Hence the problem of how to determine *when* the quantity of capital remains intact when its composition changes, on account of a change in relative demands for different consumption goods, is only soluble when the change does not affect the relative prices (i.e. when marginal costs are constant).

surmounted, in viewing a closed system as a whole, if factors other than capital goods were homogeneous in kind and the composition of the final output stream could be considered as given.

II

5. So far we have argued on the basis that a valid general distinction can be drawn which marks off capital goods from other productive instruments. This, Professor Knight, in the latter part of his article (Section IV), categorically denies; and regards the falsity of this assumption "as the ultimate and crucial fallacy in the time-period theory of capital".[1] To this question we must now turn.

In my article I argued (i) that the distinction between capital goods and other goods is the distinction between augmentable resources and non-augmentable resources;[2] (ii) that in a society where all resources are augmentable, the rate of interest is uniquely determined from the productive functions, and it is *independent of the extent of accumulation* and is equal to the maximum rate of expansion of the system;[3] (iii) hence the postulate of non-augmentable resources is necessary in order to explain diminishing returns to capital accumulation.[4]

6. As far as I can make out, Professor Knight would not deny that, in so far as a distinction *can* be drawn, it is the criterion of "augmentability" which is relevant.[5] Nor does he argue that the distinction ought to be drawn on some other basis.[6] What Professor Knight denies is simply that such a distinction *can* be drawn;

---

[1] Knight, *op. cit.*, p. 74

[2] Kaldor, *op. cit.*, Section IV, p. 218 [p. 174 above].

[3] *Ibid.*, Section VI, p. 228 [p. 186 above].

[4] *Ibid.*, p. 231 [p. 188 above].

[5] The distinction between augmentable or non-augmentable resources comes close to Böhm-Bawerk's distinction between "original" and "produced" resources, except that it is free from certain implications associated with the latter. In particular, it is not contended that "produced" resources are created from "original" resources, or that "original" resources are necessarily a "gift of nature", and have not been "produced" in some sense, in the past, or even that the original resources are necessarily physically non-augmentable, like mineral resources. The quantity of labour is certainly "augmentable", in a physical sense, yet labour will be a non-augmentable factor if saving does *not* lead to an increase in the available labour supply. The sole criterion is augmentability via capital accumulation.

[6] Professor Hayek has recently adopted a different definition. ("Einleitung zu einer Kapitaltheorie", *Zeitschrift für Nationalökonomie*, Vol. 8, No. 1.) He regards capital as the stock of "non-permanent goods" or "wasting assets" and he includes only such goods in this category which can be made to yield their services through any space of time (as, e.g., a stock of coal, as against a dwelling house, which lasts a certain number of years even if it is continuously used at maximum capacity; wasting assets are goods

in other words, he denies the existence of non-augmentable resources. All resources, according to him, are augmentable to a *certain degree*; hence all resources are capital goods.[1]

There can be no doubt that most resources *as defined and differentiated by the market*, are augmentable to a certain degree. Land can be improved by fertilisation, the supply of skilled labour can be increased by more training, the amount of hydro-electric power can be augmented by the utilisation of yet unexploited waterfalls. Coal available for consumption in large cities can be increased at will by sinking more shafts into the earth and improving transport facilities. But all this is beside the point. Coal in the drawing-room is not the same resource as coal in the earth, any more than the house is the same resource as the bricks out of which it is made. In all these cases augmentation is only possible at *increasing* cost, and it is only possible up to a point; for in all these cases production embodies an *invariable element*, which cannot be augmented at all. Analytically, at any rate, we must distinguish between hydro-electric plants and mere waterfalls; and it is pertinent to enquire whether more electric power means more plants and more waterfalls or whether it merely means more plants combined with a given number of waterfalls. In the one case the stream of services can be expanded at constant cost; in the other case, at increasing cost.

7. The important question is not so much whether non-augmentable resources do, in fact, exist or not, but whether diminishing returns *could* exist in the absence of such resources. On this cardinal question Professor Knight returns an unqualified affirmative:

with *vorwegnehmbare Erträgnisse*). This definition would include under "capital" such non-augmentable resources as minerals and would exclude a large part of what is commonly known as "fixed capital". A definition, of course, is a matter of convenience; it all depends on the purpose it is intended for. There can be no doubt that this definition of capital is not relevant for the determination of the productivity rate of interest.

[1] Knight, *op. cit.*, pp. 74-8. Similarly he denies that "rent" and "interest" can be treated as different shares, coming from different sources. "If any fact of economic life is beyond dispute, the fact that the productivity of capital represents the yield of concrete instruments of some sort surely comes in this category. The yield is rent when it is referred to the agency as a quantity of capital, or simply to the capital invested or embodied in it" (p. 74). All shares, of course, the share of labour not excluded, represent the yield of some concrete agency. The reason for differentiating between rent and interest as distributive shares is the fact that the yield of different kinds of resources is differently affected by changes in the rate of interest. Capital accumulation, if it leads to a reduction of the interest rate, will also lead to a reduction of the net yield (per unit) of those resources which are augmentable; but it will *increase* the net yield of non-augmentable resources. In a world where the rate of interest is zero the yield of capital goods, viewed as "concrete things", must also be zero; but this surely does not imply that no income will accrue to "land" or no wages to "labour"!

"Mr. Kaldor is (I say) clearly and egregiously wrong in holding that diminishing returns from capital implies changes in proportions between capital as a 'factor of production' and (an) other co-ordinate 'factor(s)'. It is the cornerstone of his argument, and a cardinal error of the whole time-period conception."[1]

Professor Knight does not examine the argument in Section VI of my paper showing that if everything is augmentable, the rate of interest can be derived from the production functions of the different resources and this rate will be independent of the quantity of capital. Instead, he puts forward, as far as I see, three arguments to disprove this proposition.

In the first place he argues that additions to the stock of capital (even if wants and technology are stationary) would never take the same form as units of the previously existing stock.

"In most cases, neither the cost nor the possibility of exact reduplication is in question in determining capital yield or quantity. The reason is simply that *reduplication is not what would happen* [my italics], not the form that capital growth would take, under most circumstances in real life, given perfect freedom of choice—even apart from new inventions or changes in wants. In an extreme case, such as a hydro-electric plant or a railway system, the very notion of physical (Mr. Kaldor says 'identical'—p. 219) [p. 175 above] reduplication is absurd."[2]

It is indeed absurd to assume that by saving, one could or would duplicate the Niagara electricity works or the railway that is alleged to run between Atchison, Topeka, and Santa Fé. But the fact that human ingenuity and thrift are not as yet capable of duplicating such agencies as the Niagara waterfalls or the area known as the United States is surely not irrelevant in this connection. "Reduplication is not what would happen"—but why? If capital accumulation takes the form of creating a resource *B*,

[1] Knight, *op. cit.*, p. 78. Actually I nowhere argued that the change in proportion involved is between "capital as a factor of production" and "other factors" (this statement would have begged all the questions as to the nature of capital). What I did argue was that "diminishing returns must always presuppose the existence of some fixed factor as the cause", hence diminishing returns to accumulation must imply a change in the proportion between different types of (concrete) resources. As is obvious from the context, however, this is how Professor Knight in fact interpreted the statement.

[2] Knight, *op. cit.*, p. 78.

and not another unit of an already existing resource A, this must imply that B is expected to yield more than a second unit of A; and since, in accordance with the assumption of diminishing returns, B actually yields less than the first unit of A has yielded, the yield of the second unit of A must be still less than that of the first unit of A. If A could be expanded at constant cost, the production of B would never be resorted to. Or has Professor Knight thrown overboard the assumption that investors want to maximise their pecuniary return?

Professor Knight's second argument seeks for an explanation of these diminishing returns in the realm of consumers' demand.

"It is true that non-reduplicability of existing agencies is a factor in the diminishing returns from investment; but it is a relatively small factor, and operates in different cases in widely different degrees. The main fact lies much deeper, in the nature of products and their 'utility', in relation to economic growth. . . ."[1]

"When the income of an individual increases, in units of fluid purchasing power which he is free to spend as he pleases in a given price situation, he will normally wish only within narrow limits to increase his consumption of products previously purchased. Much more he will wish to add new products to his consumption budget: but again, he will not stop with this, but will to a considerable extent reduce the expenditure on products previously used."[2]

There are two answers to this argument. In the first place, one could argue that these effects will be of the "second order of smalls" and should therefore be ignored in the first approximation. For the increase in income arises *on account* of the accumulation of capital; it will therefore be small *in relation to the investment* and thus the effect of this small increase in income on the productivity of this investment, through its effect on the relative demands for the different products, will be still smaller.[3] Secondly, even if these

---

[1] *Ibid.*, p. 80. [2] *Ibid.*

[3] In footnote 4, p. 64, as already noted, Professor Knight himself argues that the heterogeneity of final products "should be rejected as a factor playing any rôle in the theory of capital"; maintains that in relation to small changes, the exchange value of final products should be taken as given, and criticises me for not doing so. Yet there is no inconsistency in my own position. I was arguing that an increase in capital will affect the relative prices of consumption goods by affecting *relative costs*; while Professor Knight considers the effect on *relative demands*. The effects on relative costs, of course, are of a different order of magnitude from the effects on relative demands.

effects are not negligible, they do not prove the *existence of diminishing returns*. In fact the argument could be used equally to show that there will be increasing returns from investment. It all depends on whether the products for which the demand has relatively increased require more or less of the factors which can be created by investment, than the average of all products. In the first case, the marginal rate of return from investment will rise, in the second case it will fall. If these products contain "capital goods" neither more nor less than in the average proportion, the change in relative demands will leave the rate of return unaffected.[1]

But the crux of the whole matter is perhaps found in the third argument:

> "Even if increased production took the form of increasing the output of identical goods and services, without change in proportions, and if these were produced by use of the same productive agencies in the same proportions, all agencies being freely augmentable, investment would still be subject to diminishing returns [in the absence of technical improvements] because of the *diminishing utility of total economic income to the individual* [italics mine]."[2]

Now whatever may be said as to the previous arguments, there can be no doubt that this last argument is wrong.[3] The components of the rate of return are *products sacrificed* on the one hand and *products obtained* on the other (both measured in terms of purchasing power, i.e. in terms of one of the products serving as a standard of value); and the diminishing marginal utility of products could just as little affect their value *in terms of products* as a fall in the marginal utility of bread could affect the value of bread in terms of bread. Diminishing marginal utility of total income may be

---

[1] This is not to deny, of course, the importance of the question raised by Professor Knight that changes in the economic system are "qualitative" and not only "quantitative"; and that it is impossible to regard the number of different goods produced, or even the number of different factors of production as a *datum*. Here I am merely concerned to show that the "qualitative" character of economic changes, however important this may be in a different context, cannot be adduced as an explanation why investment opportunities are limited, i.e. why there are diminishing returns to capital accumulation.

[2] Knight, *op. cit.*, p. 80.

[3] On reading proof of this *Rejoinder*, Professor Knight asks that notation be made of his agreement that this third argument is wrong. He stands by the conclusion, and the first two arguments, and others which might be given, but his reasoning as quoted is untenable.—EDITOR.

an important factor in determining *the rate of capital accumulation*; but for the determination of the rate of return on investment it is wholly irrelevant.

The proposition that the existence of diminishing returns always presupposes the existence of some "fixed factor" as their cause, and that diminishing returns are entirely a matter of changes in proportions of factors, has never been more clearly or persuasively argued than by Professor Knight himself in his earlier writings.[1] It is a proposition on which, ultimately, not only Böhm-Bawerk and the Austrian theory of capital, but our whole inheritance of Ricardian economics, the whole theory of production and distribution, as we know it and teach it, rests. If Professor Knight could convince me that it is wrong, if he could be as persuasive in arguing against the proposition as he was in its favour, I should willingly admit that his recent attack on traditional capital theory had succeeded not merely in eliminating some ill-begotten formulations, but that it had destroyed the whole structure, burying everybody under the ruins. But until a convincing demonstration is forthcoming, I shall remain stubbornly old-fashioned on this point; I shall continue to believe in the Theory of Production, and proclaim the old Knight as against the new!

8. I shall look forward with interest to the new edition of *Risk, Uncertainty and Profit* where that "incubus on economic analysis", the notion of a factor of production, is "summarily eliminated".

---

[1] See especially *Risk, Uncertainty and Profit*, pp. 97 ff., and that brilliant essay "Fallacies in the Interpretation of Social Cost", *Quarterly Journal of Economics*, Vol. 38, 1924, reprinted in *The Ethics of Competition*, p. 217.

Part V

THE THEORY OF DISTRIBUTION

10

ALTERNATIVE THEORIES OF DISTRIBUTION[1]

ACCORDING to the Preface of Ricardo's *Principles*, the discovery of the laws which regulate distributive shares is the "principal problem in Political Economy". The purpose of this paper is to present a bird's-eye view of the various theoretical attempts, since Ricardo, at solving this "principal problem". Though all attempts at classification in such a vast field are necessarily to some extent arbitrary, and subjective to the writer, in terms of broad classification, one should, I think, distinguish between four main strands of thought, some of which contain important sub-groups. The first of these is the Ricardian, or Classical Theory, the second the Marxian, the third the Neo-Classical or Marginalist Theory and the fourth the Keynesian. The inclusion of a separate "Keynesian" theory in this context may cause surprise. An attempt will be made to show, however, that the specifically Keynesian apparatus of thought could be applied to the problem of distribution, rather than to the problem of the general level of production; that there is evidence that in its early stages, Keynes' own thinking tended to develop in this direction—only to be diverted from it with the discovery (made some time between the publication of the *Treatise on Money* and the *General Theory*) that inflationary and deflationary tendencies could best be analysed in terms of the resulting changes in output and employment, rather than in their effects on prices.

The compression of a whole army of distinguished writers, and schools of thought, between Ricardo and Keynes (Marx aside) under the term of Neo-Classical or Marginalist Theory is harder to justify. For apart from the marginalists proper, the group would have to include such "non-marginalists" or quasi-marginalists (from the point of view of distribution theory) as the Walrasians and the neo-Walrasians,[2] as well as the imperfect competitionists,

[1] Originally published in the *Review of Economic Studies*, Vol. XXIII, No. 2, 1955-6.
[2] By the term "neo-Walrasians" I mean the American "linear programming" and "activity analysis" schools, as well as the general equilibrium model of von Neumann

who though marginalist, do not necessarily hold with the principle of Marginal Productivity. But as I shall hope to show, there are important aspects which all these theories have in common,[1] and which justifies bringing them under one broad umbrella.

Ricardo prefaced his statement by a reference to the historical fact that "in different stages of society the proportions of the whole produce of the earth which will be allotted to each of these (three) classes under the names of rent, profit and wages will be essentially *different*".[2] To-day, a writer on the problem of distribution, would almost be inclined to say the opposite—that "in different stages of (capitalist) society the proportions of the national income allotted to wages, profits, etc., are *essentially similar*". The famous "historical constancy" of the share of wages in the national income and the similarity of these shares in different capitalist economies, such as the U.S. and the U.K.—was of course an unsuspected feature of capitalism in Ricardo's day. But to the extent that recent empirical research tends to contradict Ricardo's assumption about the variability of relative shares, it makes the question of what determines these shares, more, rather than less, intriguing. In fact no hypothesis as regards the forces determining distributive shares could be intellectually satisfying unless it succeeded in accounting for the relative stability of these shares in the advanced capitalist economies over the last 100 years or so, despite the phenomenal changes in the techniques of production, in the accumulation of capital relative to labour and in real income per head.

Ricardo's concern in the problem of distribution was not due, or not only due, to the interest in the question of distributive shares *per se*, but to the belief that the theory of distribution held the key to an understanding of the whole mechanism of the economic system—of the forces governing the rate of progress, of the ultimate incidence of taxation, of the effects of protection, and so on. It was

(*Review of Economic Studies*, 1945-6, Vol. XIII (1)) whose technique shows certain affinities with Walras even though their basic assumptions (in particular that of the "circularity" of the production process) are quite different. From the point of view of distribution theory, however, the approach only yields a solution (in the shape of an equilibrium interest rate) on the assumption of constant real wages (due to an infinitely elastic supply curve of labour); it shows therefore more affinity with the classical models than with the neo-classical theories.

[1] With the possible exception of the "neo-Walrasian" group referred to above.
[2] Preface (my italics).

through "the laws which regulate distributive shares" that he was hoping to build what in present-day parlance we would call "a simple macro-economic model".[1] In this respect, if no other, the Ricardian and the "Keynesian" theories are analogous.[2] With the neo-Classical or Marginalist theories, on the other hand, the problem of distribution is merely one aspect of the general pricing process; it has no particular theoretical significance apart from the importance of the question *per se*. Nor do these theories yield a "macro-economic model" of the kind that exhibits the reaction-mechanism of the system through the choice of a strictly limited number of dependent and independent variables.

I. THE RICARDIAN THEORY

Ricardo's theory was based on two separate principles which we may term the "marginal principle" and the "surplus principle" respectively. The "marginal principle" serves to explain the share of rent, and the "surplus principle" the division of the residue between wages and profits. To explain the Ricardian model, we must first divide the economy into two broad branches, agricul-ture and industry and then show how, on Ricardo's assumptions, the forces operating in agriculture serve to determine distribution in industry.

The agricultural side of the picture can be exhibited in terms of a simple diagram (Fig. 1), where Oy measures quantities of "corn" (standing for all agricultural produce) and Ox the amount of labour employed in agriculture. At a given state of knowledge and in a given natural environment the curve p—Ap represents the product per unit of labour and the curve p—Mp the marginal product of labour. The existence of these two *separate* curves is a consequence of a declining tendency in the average product curve—i.e. of the assumption of diminishing returns. Corn-output

---

[1] "Political Economy", he told Malthus, "you think is an enquiry into the nature and causes of wealth—I think it should rather be called an enquiry into the laws which determine the division of the produce of industry amongst the classes who concur in its formation. No law can be laid down respecting quantity, but a tolerably correct one can be laid down respecting proportions. Every day I am more satisfied that the former enquiry is vain and delusive, and the latter only the true object of the science." (Letter dated 9 October, 1820, *Works* (Sraffa edition), Vol. VIII, pp. 278-9.)

[2] And so of course is the Marxian: but then the Marxian theory is really only a simplified version of Ricardo, clothed in a different garb.

is thus uniquely determined when the quantity of labour is given:[1] for any given working force, OM, total output is represented by the rectangle $OCDM$. Rent is the difference between the product of labour on "marginal" land and the product on average land, or (allowing for the intensive, as well as the extensive, margin) the difference between average and marginal labour productivity which depends on the elasticity of the $p—Ap$ curve, i.e. the extent to which diminishing returns operate.

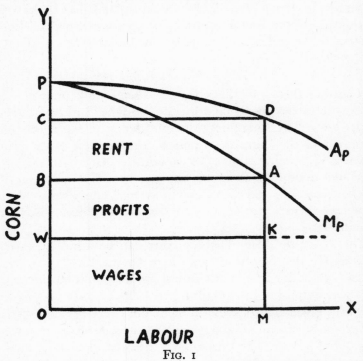

FIG. 1

The marginal product of labour (or, in classical parlance, the "produce-minus-rent") is not however equal to the wage, but to the sum of wages and profits. The rate of wages is determined quite independently of marginal productivity by the supply price of labour which Ricardo assumed to be constant in terms of corn.

[1] This abstracts from variations in output per head due to the use of more or less fixed capital relative to labour—otherwise the curves could not be uniquely drawn, relative to a given state of technical knowledge. As between fixed capital and labour therefore the model assumes fixed coefficients; as between labour and and, variable coefficients.

In modern parlance, the Ricardian hypothesis implies an infinitely elastic supply curve of labour at the given supply price, OW.[1] The demand for labour is not determined however by the $p—Mp$ curve, but by the accumulation of capital which determines how many labourers can find employment at the wage rate OW. Hence the equilibrium position is not indicated by the point of intersection between the $p—Mp$ curve and the supply curve of labour, but by the aggregate demand for labour in terms of corn —the "wages fund".[2] As capital accumulates, the labour force will grow, so that any addition to the total wage fund, through capital accumulation—the *agricultural* wages fund is indicated by the area $OWKM$—will tend to be a horizontal addition (pushing the vertical line KM to the right) and not a vertical one (pushing the horizontal line WK upwards).[3]

For any given M, profits are thus a residue, arising from the

[1] The basis of this assumption is the Malthusian theory of population, according to which numbers will increase (indefinitely) when wages are above, and decrease (indefinitely) when they are below, the "subsistence level". In Ricardo's hands this doctrine had lost its sharp focus on a biologically determined quantum of subsistence to which the supply price of labour must be tied; he emphasised that habits of restraint engendered in a civilised environment can permanently secure for labour higher standards of living than the bare minimum for survival. Yet he retained the important operative principle that in any given social and cultural environment there is a *"natural* rate of wages" at which alone population could remain stationary and from which wages can only deviate temporarily. The hypothesis of an infinitely elastic supply curve of labour thus did not necessarily imply that this supply price must be equal to the bare minimum of subsistence. Yet this assumption was inconsistent with another (implied) feature of his model discussed below, that wages are not only *fixed* in terms of "corn" but are entirely (or almost entirely) *spent* on corn.

[2] Total wages depend on—and are "paid out of"—capital simply because production takes time, and the labourers (unlike the landlords) not being in the position to afford to wait, have their wages "advanced" to them by the capitalists. This is true of fixed as well as circulating capital but since, with the former, the turnover period is relatively long, only a small part of annual wages is paid out of fixed capital; the amount of circulating capital was therefore treated as the proper "wages fund". Despite his analysis of the effect of changes in wages on the amount of fixed capital used relative to labour, i.e. on the proportions of fixed and circulating capital employed in production (Professor Hayek's celebrated "Ricardo effect"), for the purpose of his distribution theory this ratio should be taken as given, irrespective of the rate of profit.

[3] The feature which the modern mind may find most difficult to swallow is not that capital accumulation should lead to a rise in population but that the reaction should be taken as something so swift as to ignore the intervening stage, where the increase in the wages fund should raise the rate of wages rather than the numbers employed. The adjustment of population to changes in the demand for labour would normally be treated as a slow long-run effect whereas changes in the demand for labour (caused by capital accumulation) may be swift or sudden. Ricardo, however, conceived the economy as one which proceeds at a more or less steady rate of growth in time, with the accumulation of capital going on at a (more or less constant) rate; while he conceded that *changes* in the rate of capital accumulation will temporarily raise or lower wages, he assumed that the rate of population growth itself is adapted to a certain rate of capital accumulation which had been going on for some time.

difference between the marginal product of labour and the rate of wages. The resulting ratio, $\dfrac{\text{Profits}}{\text{Wages}}$ determines the rate of profit % on the capital employed; it is moreover *equal* to that ratio, on the assumption that the capital is turned over once a year, so that the capital employed is equal to the annual wages-bill. (This latter proposition, however, is merely a simplification, and not an essential part of the story.)

In a state of equilibrium, the money-rate of profit % earned on capital must be the same in industry and in agriculture, otherwise capital would move from one form of employment to the other. But it is the peculiarity of agriculture that the money-rate of profit in that industry cannot diverge from the rate of profit measured in terms of that industry's own product, i.e. the corn-rate of profit. This is because in agriculture both the input (the wage outlay) and the output consist of the same commodity, "corn". In manufacturing industry on the other hand, input and output consist of heterogeneous commodities—the cost per man is fixed in corn, while the product per man, in a given state of technical knowledge, is fixed in terms of manufactured goods. Hence the only way equality in the rate of profit in money terms can be attained as between the two branches is through the prices of industrial goods becoming dearer or cheaper in terms of agricultural products. The money-rate of profit in manufacturing industry therefore depends on the corn-rate of profit in agriculture;[1] the latter, on the other hand, is entirely a matter of the margin of cultivation, which in turn is a reflection (in a closed economy and in a given state of technical knowledge) of the extent of capital accumulation. Thus "diminishing fertility of the soil", as James Mill put it, "is the great and ultimately only necessary cause of a fall in profit".

To make the whole structure logically consistent it is necessary to suppose, not only that wages are fixed in terms of "corn" but that they are entirely spent on "corn", for otherwise any change in the relation between industrial and agricultural prices will

---

[1] The analytical basis for this conclusion, given above, was never, as Sraffa remarks, stated by Ricardo in any of his extant letters and papers though there is evidence from Malthus's remarks that he must have formulated it either in a lost paper on the Profits of Capital or in conversation (cf. *Works*, Vol. I, Introduction, p. xxxi).

alter real wages (in terms of commodities in general) so that the size of the "surplus", and the rate of profit on capital generally is no longer derivable from the "corn-rate of profit"—the relationship between the product of labour and the cost of labour working on marginal land. Assuming that agricultural products ("corn") are wage-goods and manufactured products are non-wage-goods (i.e. ignoring that *some* agricultural products are consumed by capitalists, and *some* non-agricultural products by wage-earners), the whole corn-output (the area *OCDM* in the diagram) can be taken as the annual wages fund, of which *OWKM* is employed in agriculture and *WCDK* in the rest of the economy. Any increase in *OWKM* (caused, e.g., by protection to agriculture) must necessarily lower the rate of profit (which is the source of all accumulation) and thus slow down the rate of growth.[1] Similarly all taxes, other than those levied on land, must ultimately fall on, and be paid out of, profits, and thus slow down the rate of accumulation. Taxation and agricultural protection thus tend to accelerate the tendency (which is in any case inevitable—unless *continued* technical progress manages to shift the p—Ap and p—Mp curves to the right sufficiently to suspend altogether the operation of the Law of Diminishing Returns) to that ultimate state of gloom, the Stationary State, where accumulation ceases simply because "profits are so low as not to afford [the capitalists more than] an adequate compensation for their trouble and the risk which they must necessarily encounter in employing their capital productively".[2]

II. The Marxian Theory

The Marxian theory is essentially an adaptation of Ricardo's "surplus theory". The main analytical differences are : (1) that Marx paid no attention to (and did not believe in) the Law of Diminishing Returns, and hence made no analytical distinction between rent and profits; (2) that Marx regarded the supply price of labour (the "cost of reproduction" of labour) as being fixed,

---

[1] The evil of agricultural protection is thus not only that income is reduced through the transfer of labour to less productive employments, but that owing to the reduction in the rate of profit, industrial prices fall in terms of agricultural prices; income is thus transferred from the classes which use their wealth productively to classes which use it unproductively.

[2] Ricardo, *Principles*, p. 122 (Sraffa Edition).

not in terms of "corn", but of commodities in general. Hence he regarded the share of profits (including rent) in output as determined simply by the surplus of the product per unit of labour over the supply price (or cost) of labour—or the surplus of production to the consumption necessary for production.[1]

There are important differences also as between Marx and Ricardo in two other respects. The first of these concerns the reasons for wages being tied to the subsistence level. In Marx's theory this is ensured through the fact that at any one time the supply of labour—the number of workers seeking wage-employment—tends to exceed the demand for labour. The existence of an unemployed fringe—the "reserve army" of labour—prevents wages from rising above the minimum that must be paid to enable the labourers to perform the work. Marx assumed that as capitalist enterprise progresses at the expense of pre-capitalistic enterprise more labourers are released through the disappearance of the non-capitalist or handicraft units than are absorbed in the capitalist sector, owing to the difference in productivity per head between the two sectors. As long as the growth of capitalist enterprise is at the cost of a shrinkage of pre-capitalist enterprise the increase in the supply of wage labour will thus tend to run ahead of the increase in the demand for wage labour.

Sooner or later, however, the demand for labour resulting from accumulation by capitalist enterprise will run ahead of the increase in supply; at that stage labour becomes scarce, wages rise, profits are wiped out and capitalism is faced with a "crisis". (The crisis in itself slows down the rate of accumulation and reduces the demand for labour at any given state of accumulation by increasing the "organic composition of capital", so that the "reserve army" will sooner or later be re-created.)

The second important difference relates to the motives behind capital accumulation. For Ricardo this was simply to be explained by the lure of a high rate of profit. Capitalists accumulate voluntarily so long as the rate of profit exceeds the minimum "necessary compensation" for the risks and trouble encountered in the

---

[1] Ricardo himself abandoned in the *Principles* the idea that wages *consist* of corn (to the exclusion of manufactures), but whether he also abandoned the idea that the agricultural surplus is critical to the whole distribution process through the fixity of wages in terms of *corn only* is not clear. (Cf. Sraffa, *op. cit.*, pp. xxxii–xxxiii.)

productive employment of capital. For Marx, however, accumulation by capitalist enterprise is not a matter of choice but a necessity, due to competition among the capitalists themselves. This in turn was explained by the existence of economies of large-scale production (together with the implicit assumption that the amount of capital employed by any particular capitalist is governed by his own accumulation). Given the fact that the larger the scale of operations the more efficient the business, each capitalist is forced to increase the size of his business through the re-investment of his profits if he is not to fall behind in the competitive struggle.

It is only at a later stage, when the increasing concentration of production in the hands of the more successful enterprises removes the competitive necessity for accumulation—the stage of "monopoly capitalism"—that in the Marxian scheme there is room for economic crises, not on account of an excessive increase in the demand for labour following on accumulation, but on account of an insufficiency of effective demand—the failure of markets resulting from the inability of the capitalists either to spend or to invest the full amounts of profits (which Marx called the problem of "realising surplus value").

Marx has also taken over from Ricardo, and the classical economists generally, the idea of a falling rate of profit with the progressive accumulation of capital. But whereas with the classicists this was firmly grounded on the Law of Diminishing Returns, Marx, having discarded that law, had no firm base for it. His own explanation is based on the assumed increase in the ratio of fixed to circulating capital (in Marxian terminology, "constant" to "variable" capital) with the progress of capitalism; but as several authors have pointed out,[1] the law of the falling rate of profit cannot really be derived from the law of the "increasing organic composition" of capital. Since Marx assumes that the supply price of labour remains unchanged in terms of commodities when the organic composition of capital, and hence output per head, rises, there is no more reason to assume that an increase in "organic composition" will yield a lower rate of profit than a higher rate. For even if output per man were assumed to increase more slowly than ("constant" plus "variable") capital per man, the "surplus

[1] Cf., in particular, Joan Robinson, *An Essay in Marxian Economics*, pp. 75-82.

value" per man (the excess of output per man over the costs of reproduction of labour) will necessarily increase faster than output per man, and may thus secure a rising rate of profit even if there is diminishing productivity to successive additions to fixed capital per unit of labour.

While some of Marx's predictions—such as the increasing concentration of production in the hands of large enterprises—proved accurate, his most important thesis, the steady worsening of the living conditions of the working classes—"the immiseration of the proletariat"[1]—has been contradicted by experience, in both the "competitive" and "monopoly" stages of capitalism. On the Marxian model the share of wages in output must necessarily fall with every increase in output per head. The theory can only allow for a rise of wages in terms of commodities as a result of the collective organisation of the working classes which forces the capitalists to reduce the degree of exploitation and to surrender to the workers some of the "surplus value".[2] This hypothesis, how-ever, will only yield a constant share of wages on the extremely far-fetched assumption that the rate of increase in the bargaining strength of labour, due to the growth of collective organisation, precisely keeps pace with the rate of increase in output per head.

III. THE NEO-CLASSICAL THEORIES

(A) *Marginal Productivity*

While Marx's theory thus derives from Ricardo's surplus principle, neo-classical value and distribution theory derives from another part of the Ricardian model: the "marginal principle" introduced for the explanation of rent (which explains why both Marx and Marshall are able to claim Ricardo as their precursor). The difference between Ricardo and the neo-classics is (1) that whereas Ricardo employed the "principle of substitution" (or

---

[1] It is not clear, in terms of Marx's own theoretical model, why such a progressive immiseration should take place—since the costs of reproduction of labour appear to set an *absolute* limit to the extent to which labour can be exploited. Some parts of *Das Kapital* could, however, be construed as suggesting that wages can be driven below the (long run) reproduction cost of labour, at the cost of a (long run) shrinkage in the labour force: and with the increasing organic composition of capital, and the rise of monopolies, the demand for labour may show an equally declining tendency.

[2] Marx himself would have conceived a reduction in the "degree of exploitation" in terms of a reduction in the length of the working day rather than a rise in real wages per day. In fact both have occurred side by side.

rather, the principle of "limited substitutability"—which is the basic assumption underlying all marginal analysis) only as regards the use of labour relative to land, in neo-classical theory this doctrine was formalised and generalised, and assumed to hold true of any factor, in relation to any other;[1] (2) whereas Ricardo employed the principle for showing that a "fixed" factor will earn a surplus, determined by the gap between the average and marginal product of the variable factor, neo-classical theory concentrated on the reverse aspect—i.e. that any factor variable in supply will obtain a remuneration which, under competitive conditions, must correspond to its marginal product. Thus if the total supply of *all* factors (and not only land) is being taken as given, independently of price, and all are assumed to be limited substitutes to one another, the share-out of the whole produce can be regarded as being determined by the marginal rates of substitution between them. Thus in terms of our diagram, if we assumed that along Ox we measure the quantity of any particular factor of production, x, the quantities of all the others being taken as fixed, p—Mp will exhibit the marginal productivity function of the variable factor. If the actual employment of that factor is taken to be M, AM will represent its demand price per unit, and the rectangle $OBAM$ its share in the total produce. Since this principle could be applied to any factor, it must be true of all (including, as Walras and Wicksell have shown, the factors owned by the entrepreneur himself) hence the rectangle $BCDA$ must be sufficient, and only just sufficient, for remunerating all other factors but x on the basis of their respective marginal productivities. This, as Wicksteed has shown,[2] requires the assumption that the production function is homogeneous of the first degree

---

[1] As well as of any particular commodity in the sphere of consumption. The utility theory of value is really Ricardian rent-theory applied to consumption demand. In fact, as Walras has shown, limited substitutability in consumption might in itself be sufficient to determine distributive shares, provided that the proportions in which the different factors are used are different in different industries. His solution of the problem of distribution, based on "fixed coefficients" of production (intended only as a first approximation) is subject, however, to various snags since the solution of his equations may yield negative prices for the factors as well as positive ones and it cannot be determined beforehand whether this will be the case or not. If the solution of the equations yields negative prices the factors in question have to be excluded as "free goods"; and the operation (if necessary) successively repeated until only factors with positive prices are left. Also, it is necessary to suppose that the number of different "factors" is no greater than the number of different "products", otherwise the solution is indeterminate.   [2] *The Co-ordination of the Laws of Distribution* (1894)

for all variables taken together—an assumption which he himself regarded as little more than a tautology, if "factors of production" are appropriately defined.[1] From the point of view of the theory, however, the *appropriate* definition of factors involves the elimination of intermediate products and their conversion into "ultimate" or "original" factors, since only on this definition can one assume the properties of divisibility and variability of coefficients. When factors are thus defined, the assumption of constant returns to scale is by no means a tautology; it is a restrictive assumption, which may be regarded, however, as being co-extensive with other restrictive assumptions implied by the theory—i.e. the universal rule of perfect competition, and the absence of external economies and diseconomies.

The basic difficulty with the whole approach does not lie, however, in this so-called "adding-up problem" but in the very meaning of "capital" as a factor of production.[2] Whilst land can be measured in acres-per-year and labour in man-hours, capital (as distinct from "capital goods") cannot be measured in terms of physical units.[3] To evaluate the marginal product of labour it is necessary to isolate two situations containing identical "capital" but two different quantities of labour, or identical amounts of labour, and two differing quantities of "capital", in precise numerical relationship.[4]

[1] *The Co-ordination of the Laws of Distribution* (1894), p. 53. "We must regard every kind and quality of labour that can be distinguished from other kinds and qualities as a separate factor; and in the same way, every kind of land will be taken as a separate factor. Still more important is it to insist that instead of speaking of so many £'s worth of capital we shall speak of so many ploughs, so many tons of manure, and so many horses or footpounds of power. Each of these may be scheduled in its own unit." Under these conditions it is true to say that "doubling all factors will double the product", but since these "factors" are indivisible in varying degrees, it does not mean that the production function is a linear and homogeneous one in relation to incremental variations of output. Also a change in output may be associated with the introduction of *new* factors of production.

[2] For a general equilibrium system, capital goods cannot be regarded as factors of production *per se* (in the manner suggested by Wicksteed), otherwise the same things are simultaneously treated as the parameters and the unknowns of the system.

[3] Measurement in terms of value (as so many £'s of "capital") already assumes a certain rate of interest, on the basis of which services accruing in different periods in the future, or costs incurred at different dates in the past, are brought to a measure of equivalence.

[4] The product of the "marginal shepherd" is the difference in terms of numbers of sheep, between 10 shepherds using 10 crooks and 11 shepherds using 11 slightly inferior crooks, the term "slightly inferior" being taken to mean that the 11 crooks in the one case represent precisely the same amount of "capital" as the 10 crooks in the other case. (Cf. also Robertson, "Wage Grumbles", in *Economic Fragments*, 1931).

Marshall, without going into the matter in any detail, had shown in several passages that he was dimly aware of this; and in carefully re-defining marginal productivity so as to mean "marginal *net* productivity" (*net* after deduction of all associated expenses on other "factors") he shied away from the task of putting forward a general theory of distribution altogether.[1]

In fact, in so far as we can speak of a "Marshallian" theory of distribution at all, it is in the sense of a "short period" theory, which regards profits as the "quasi-rents" earned on the use of capital goods of various kinds, the supply of which can be treated as given for the time being, as a heritage of the past. The doctrine of the "quasi-rent" assimilates capital as a factor of production to Ricardian land: the separate *kinds* of capital goods being treated as so many different kinds of "land". Here the problem of the measurement of capital as a factor of production does not arise: since, strictly speaking, no kind of change or reorganisation in the stock of intermediate products is permitted in connection with a change in the level or composition of production. It was this aspect of Marshall which, consciously or sub-consciously, provided the "model" for most of the post-Marshallian Cambridge theorising. Prices are equal to, or determined by, marginal prime costs; profits are determined by the difference between marginal and average prime costs; prime costs, for the system as a whole, are labour costs (since raw-material costs, for a closed economy at any rate, disappear if all branches of industry are taken together); ultimately therefore the division of output between profits and wages is a matter depending on the existence of diminishing returns to labour, as more labour is used in conjunction with a *given* capital equipment; and is determined by the elasticity of labour's average productivity curve which fixes the share of quasi-rents.

Marshall himself would have disagreed with the use of the quasi-rent doctrine as a distribution theory, holding that distributive

---

[1] "The doctrine that the earnings of a worker tend to be equal to the net product of his work, has by itself no real meaning; since in order to estimate the net product, we have to take for granted all the expenses of production of the commodity on which he works, other than his own wages." Similarly, the doctrine that the marginal efficiency of capital will tend to equal the rate of interest "cannot be made into a theory of interest, any more than a theory of wages, without reasoning in a circle". (Cf. *Principles*, 8th edition, Book VI, Chapter I, paras. 7-8.)

shares in the short period are determined by long-period forces.[1] Clearly even if one were to hold strictly to the assumption that "profit margins" are the outcome of short-period profit-maximisation, this "short-period" approach does not really get us anywhere: for the extent to which diminishing returns operate for labour in conjunction with the capital equipment available to-day is itself a function of the price-relationships which have ruled in the past because these have determined the quantities of each of the kinds of equipment available. The theory does not therefore really amount to more than saying that the prices of to-day are derived from the prices of yesterday—a proposition which is the more true and the more trivial the shorter the "day" is conceived to be, in terms of chronological time.

For the true neo-classical attempt to solve the general problem of distribution we must go to Wicksell who thought that by integrating the Austrian approach to capital with Walrasian equilibrium theory he could provide a general solution, treating capital as a two-dimensional quantity, the product of time and labour. The "time" in this case is the investment period or waiting period separating the application of "original" factors from the emergence of the final product, and the marginal productivity of capital the added product resulting from an extension of "time". This attempt, again, came to grief (as Wicksell himself came near to acknowledging late in life):[2] (i) owing to the impossibility of measuring that period in terms of an "average" of some kind;[3] (ii) owing to the impossibility of combining the investment periods of different "original" factors in a single measure.[4]

In fact the whole approach which regards the share of wages and of profits in output as being determined by the marginal rate of substitution between Capital and Labour—with its corollary,

[1] Cf., in particular, *Principles*, 8th edition, Book V, Chapters V and VI, and Book VI, Chapter VIII, para. 4.

[2] Cf. the concluding passage of his posthumous contribution to the Wieser Festschrift. *Die Wirtschaftstheorie der Gegenwart* (1928), Vol. III, pp. 208-9; also his "Analysis of Åkerman's Problem", reprinted in *Lectures*, Vol. I, p. 270.

[3] Since owing to compound interest, the weights to be used in the calculation of the average will themselves be dependent on the rate of interest.

[4] For a more extended treatment cf. my articles on capital theory in *Econometrica*, April, 1937, and May, 1938 [pp. 153-205 above]; also Joan Robinson, "The Production Function in the Theory of Capital", *Review of Economic Studies*, Vol. XXI (1953-4), p. 81, and "Comment" by D. G. Champernowne, *ibid.*, p. 112.

that the constancy of relative shares is evidence of a unit-Elasticity of Substitution between Capital and Labour[1]—is hardly acceptable to present-day economists. Its inadequacy becomes evident as soon as it is realised that the "marginal rate of substitution" between Capital and Labour—as distinct from the marginal rate of substitution between labour and land—can only be determined once the rate of profit and the rate of wages are already known. The same technical alternatives might yield very different "marginal rates of substitution" according as the ratio of profits to wages is one thing or another. The theory asserts, in effect, that the rate of interest in the capital market (and the associated wage rate in the labour market) is determined by the condition that at any lower interest rate (and higher wage rate) capital would be invested in such "labour-saving" forms as would provide insufficient employment to the available labour; whilst at any higher rate, capital would be invested in forms that offered more places of employment than could be filled with the available labour.

Quite apart from all conceptual difficulties, the theory focuses attention on a relatively unimportant feature of a growing economy. For accumulation does not take the form of "deepening" the structure of capital (at a given state of knowledge) but rather in keeping pace with technical progress and the growth in the labour force. It is difficult to swallow a theory which says, in effect, that wages and profits are what they are for otherwise there would be too much deepening or too little deepening (the capital/output ratios would be either too large or too small) to be consistent with simultaneous equilibrium in the savings-investment market and in the labour market.

(B) The "Degree of Monopoly" Theories of Distribution

Monopoly profit was always regarded as a distinct form of revenue in neo-classical theory, though not one of any great quantitative importance since the mass of commodities was thought of as being produced under competitive conditions. But the modern theories of imperfect competition emphasise that monopoly profit is not an isolated feature. Profits in general

---

[1] Cf. Hicks, *The Theory of Wages* (1932), Chapter VI, passim.

contain an *element* of monopoly revenue—an element that is best defined as the excess of the actual profit margin in output over what the profit margin would have been under perfectly competitive conditions. Under Marshallian "short-period" assumptions the perfectly-competitive profit margin is given by the excess of marginal cost over average prime costs. The additional monopoly element is indicated by the excess of price over marginal cost. The former, as we have seen, is a derivative of the elasticity of labour's productivity curve where capital equipment of all kinds is treated as given. The latter is a derivative of the elasticity of demand facing the individual firm. The novel feature of imperfect competition theories is to have shown that the increase of profit margins due to this element of monopoly need not imply a corresponding excess in the rates of profit on capital over the competitive rate; through the generation of excess capacity (i.e. the tendency of demand curves to become "tangential" to the cost curves) the latter may approach a "competitive" or "normal" rate (as a result of the consequential rise in the capital/output ratio) even if the former is above the competitive level.

Kalecki[1] built on this a simplified theory of distribution, where the share of profits in output is shown to be determined by the elasticity of demand alone. This was based on the hypothesis that in the short period, labour and capital equipment are largely "limitational" and not "substitutional" factors, with the result that the short-period prime cost-curve is a reverse L-shaped one (prime costs being constant up to full capacity output). In that case marginal costs are equal to average prime costs; the ratio of price to prime costs (and hence, in a closed economy, the ratio of gross profits to wages) is thus entirely accounted for by the elasticity of the firm's demand curve.

On closer inspection, however, the elasticity of the demand curve facing the individual firm turned out to be no less of a broken reed than its counterpart, the elasticity of substitution between factors. There is no evidence that firms in imperfect markets set their prices by reference to the elasticity of their

[1] The original version appeared in *Econometrica*, April, 1938. Subsequent versions appeared in *Essays in the Theory of Economic Fluctuations* (1938), Chapter I, *Studies in Economic Dynamics* (1943), Chapter I, and *Theory of Dynamic Economics* (1954) Part I.

sales-function, or that short-period pricing is the outcome of any deliberate attempt to maximise profits by reference to an independent revenue and a cost function. Indeed the very notion of a demand curve for the products of a single firm is illegitimate if the prices charged by different firms cannot be assumed to be independent of each other.[1]

In the later versions of his theory Kalecki abandoned the link between the "degree of monopoly" and the elasticity of demand, and was content with a purely tautological approach according to which the ratio of price to prime costs was *defined* simply as the "degree of monopoly". Propositions based on implicit definitions of this kind make of course no assertion about reality and possess no explanatory value. Unless the "degree of monopoly" can be defined in terms of market relationships of some kind (as, for example, in terms of the cross-elasticities of demand for the products of the different firms)[2] and an attempt is made to demonstrate how these market relationships determine the relation between prices and costs, the theory does not provide a hypothesis which could be affirmed or refuted.

There is no need, of course, to follow Kalecki in the attempt to lend spurious precision to the doctrine through implicit theorising —a vice which afflicts all theories which we grouped together as "neo-classical" in varying degrees. Fundamentally, the proposition that the distribution of income between wages and profits depends on market structures, on the strength or weakness of the forces of competition, is not a tautological one; it asserts *something* about reality (which may in principle be proved false) even if that "something" cannot be given a logically precise formulation. Just as the positive content of the marginal productivity theory can be summed up by the statement that the rate of profit on capital (and the margin of profit in output) is governed by the need to prevent the capital/output ratio from being either too

[1] The theory of the "kinked" demand curve is in fact no more than a recognition of the fact that the demand curve of the firm (in the sense required for the purpose of deriving price from the postulate of profit maximisation) is non-existent. Since the position of the "kink" *depends* on the price, it cannot *determine* the price; it thus leaves the profit margin completely undetermined.

[2] The "cross-elasticities" of demand indicate the degree of interdependence of the markets of different firms and are thus inversely related to monopoly power in the usual sense of the word.

large or too small, the positive content of the "degree of monopoly" theory can be summed up in the sentence that "profit margins are what they are because the forces of competition prevent them from being higher than they are and are not powerful enough to make them lower than they are". Unfortunately neither of these statements gets us very far.

Dissatisfaction with the tautological character and the formalism of the "marginal revenue-equals-marginal cost" type of price theory led to the formulation of the "full cost" theories of pricing,[1] according to which producers in imperfect markets set their prices independently of the character of demand, and solely on the basis of their long-run costs of production (including the "normal" rate of profit on their own capital). If these theories asserted no more than that prices in manufacturing industry are *not* determined by the criterion of short-run profit-maximisation, and that profit margins can be fairly insensitive to short-period variations in demand[2] (the impact effect of changes in demand being on the rate of production, rather than on prices), they would provide a healthy antidote to a great deal of facile theorising. When, however, they go beyond this and assert that prices are determined quite independently of demand, they in effect destroy existing price theory without putting anything else in its place. Quite apart from the fact that a "full cost" theory is quite unable

[1] Cf. Hall and Hitch, *Oxford Economic Papers*, 1939; P. W. S. Andrews, *Manufacturing Business* (1949).

[2] This, I believe, was the intention of the original Hall-Hitch article. Cf. Marshall, *Principles*, Book VI, Chapter VIII, paragraph 4: "We see then that there is no general tendency of profits on the turnover to equality; but there may be, and as a matter of fact there is, in each trade and in every branch of each trade, a more or less definite rate of profits on the turnover which is regarded as a 'fair' or normal rate. Of course these rates are always changing in consequence of changes in the methods of trade; which are generally begun by individuals who desire to do a larger trade at a lower rate of profit on the turnover than has been customary, but at a larger rate of profit per annum on their capital. If however there happens to be no great change of this kind going on, the traditions of the trade that a certain rate of profit on the turnover should be charged for a particular class of work are of great practical service to those in the trade. Such traditions are the outcome of much experience tending to show that, if that rate is charged, a proper allowance will be made for all the costs (supplementary as well as prime) incurred for that particular purpose, and in addition the normal rate of profits per annum in that class of business will be afforded. If they charge a price which gives much less than this rate of profit on the turnover they can hardly prosper; and if they charge much more they are in danger of losing their custom, since others can afford to undersell them. This is the 'fair' rate of profit on the turnover, which an honest man is expected to charge for making goods to order, when no price has been agreed on beforehand; and it is the rate which a court of law will allow in case a dispute should arise between buyer and seller." Cf. also Kahn, *Economic Journal*, 1952, p. 119.

to explain why some firms should be more successful in earning profits than others, the level of the "normal profit" on which the full cost calculations are supposed to be based is left quite undetermined. The very fact that these full cost theories should have received such widespread and serious consideration as an alternative explanation of the pricing process is an indication of the sad state of vagueness and confusion into which the neo-classical value theory had fallen.

IV. The Keynesian Theory

Keynes, as far as I know, was never interested in the problem of distribution as such. One may nevertheless christen a particular theory of distribution as "Keynesian" if it can be shown to be an application of the specifically Keynesian apparatus of thought and if evidence can be adduced that at some stage in the development of his ideas, Keynes came near to formulating such a theory.[1] The principle of the Multiplier (which in some ways was anticipated in the *Treatise* but without a clear view of its implications) could be alternatively applied to a determination of the relation between prices and wages, if the level of output and employment is taken as given, or the determination of the level of employment, if distribution (i.e. the relation between prices and wages) is taken as given. The reason why the multiplier-analysis has not been

[1] I am referring to the well-known passage on profits being likened to a "widow's cruse" in the *Treatise on Money*, Vol. I, p. 139. "If entrepreneurs choose to spend a portion of their profits on consumption (and there is, of course, nothing to prevent them from doing this) the effect is to *increase* the profits on the sale of liquid consumption goods by an amount exactly equal to the amount of profits which have been thus expended. . . . Thus, however much of their profits entrepreneurs spend on consumption, the increment of wealth belonging to entrepreneurs remains the same as before. Thus profits, as a source of capital increment for entrepreneurs, are a widow's cruse which remains undepleted however much of them may be devoted to riotous living. When on the other hand, entrepreneurs are making losses, and seek to recoup these losses by curtailing their normal expenditure on consumption, i.e. by saving more, the cruse becomes a Danaid jar which can never be filled up; for the effect of this reduced expenditure is to inflict on the producers of consumption-goods a loss of an equal amount. Thus the diminution of their wealth as a class is as great, in spite of their savings, as it was before." This passage, I think, contains the true seed of the ideas developed in the *General Theory*—as well as showing the length of the road that had to be traversed before arriving at the conceptual framework presented in the latter work. The fact that "profits", "savings" etc. were all defined here in a special sense that was later discarded, and that the argument specifically refers to expenditure on consumption goods, rather than entrepreneurial expenditure in general, should not blind us to the fact that here Keynes regards entrepreneurial incomes as being the resultant of their expenditure decisions, rather than the other way round—which is perhaps the most important difference between "Keynesian" and "pre-Keynesian" habits of thought.

developed as a distribution theory is precisely because it was invented for the purpose of an employment theory—to explain why an economic system can remain in equilibrium in a state of under-employment (or of a general under-utilisation of resources), where the classical properties of scarcity-economics are inapplicable. And its use for the one appears to exclude its use for the other.[1] If we assume that the balance of savings and investment is brought about through variations in the relationship of prices and costs, we are not only bereft of a principle for explaining variations in output and employment, but the whole idea of separate "aggregate" demand and supply functions—the principle of "effective demand"—falls to the ground; we are back to Say's Law, where output as a whole is limited by available resources, and a fall in effective demand for one kind of commodity (in real terms) generates compensating increases in effective demand (again in real terms) for others. Yet these two uses of the Multiplier principle are not as incompatible as would appear at first sight: the Keynesian technique, as I hope to show, can be used for both purposes, provided the one is conceived as a short-run theory and the other as a long-run theory—or rather, the one is used in the framework of a static model, and the other in the framework of a dynamic growth model.[2]

We shall assume, to begin with, a state of full employment (we shall show later the conditions under which a state of full employment will *result* from our model) so that total output or income (Y) is given. Income may be divided into two broad categories,

[1] Although this application of Keynesian theory has been implicit in several discussions of the problem of inflation. (Cf. e.g. A. J. Brown, *The Great Inflation*, Macmillan, 1955.)

[2] I first thought of using the Multiplier technique for purposes of a distribution theory when I attempted to analyse the ultimate incidence of profits taxation under full employment conditions in a paper prepared for the Royal Commission on Taxation in 1951. The further development of these ideas, and particularly their relationship to a dynamic theory of growth, owes a great deal to discussions with Mrs. Robinson, whose forthcoming book, *The Accumulation of Capital*, contains a systematic exploration of this field. I should also like to mention here that I owe a great deal of stimulus to a paper by Kalecki, "A Theory of Profits" (*Economic Journal*, June-September, 1942) whose approach is in some ways reminiscent of the "widows' cruse" of Keynes' *Treatise* even though Kalecki uses the technique, not for an explanation of the share of profits in output, but for showing why the *level* of output and its fluctuations is peculiarly dependent on entrepreneurial behaviour. (In doing so, he uses the restrictive assumption that savings are entirely supplied out of profits.) I have also been helped by Mr. Harry Johnson and Mr. Robin Marris, both in the working out of the formulae and in general discussion.

Wages and Profits (W and P), where the wage-category comprises not only manual labour but salaries as well, and Profits the income of property owners generally, and not only of entrepreneurs; the important difference between them being in the marginal propensities to consume (or save), wage-earners' marginal savings being small in relation to those of capitalists.[1]

Writing S_w and S_p, for aggregate savings out of Wages and Profits, we have the following income identities:

$$Y \equiv W+P$$
$$I \equiv S$$
$$S \equiv S_w+S_p.$$

Taking investment as given, and assuming simple proportional savings functions $S_w=s_w W$ and $S_p=s_p P$, we obtain:

$$I = s_p P+s_w W=s_p P+s_w(Y-P)=(s_p-s_w)P+s_w Y$$

Whence

$$\frac{I}{Y}=(s_p-s_w)\frac{P}{Y}+s_w \qquad \dots \text{(1)}$$

and

$$\frac{P}{Y} = \frac{1}{s_p-s_w}\frac{I}{Y}-\frac{s_w}{s_p-s_w} \qquad \dots \text{(2)}$$

Thus, given the wage-earners' and the capitalists' propensities to save, the share of profits in income depends simply on the ratio of investment to output.

The interpretative value of the model (as distinct from the formal validity of the equations, or identities) depends on the "Keynesian" hypothesis that investment, or rather, the ratio of investment to output, can be treated as an independent variable, invariant with respect to changes in the two savings propensities s_p and s_w. (We shall see later that this assumption can only be true within certain limits, and outside those limits the theory ceases to hold.) This, together with the assumption of "full employment", also implies that the level of prices in relation to the level of money wages is determined by demand: a rise in investment, and thus in total demand, will raise prices and profit

---

[1] This may be assumed independently of any skewness in the distribution of property, simply as a consequence of the fact that the bulk of profits accrues in the form of company profits and a high proportion of companies' marginal profits is put to reserve.

margins, and thus reduce real consumption, whilst a fall in investment, and thus in total demand, causes a fall in prices (relatively
to the wage level) and thereby generates a compensating rise in
real consumption. Assuming flexible prices (or rather flexible
profit margins) the system is thus stable at full employment.

The model operates only if the two savings propensities differ
and the marginal propensity to save from profits exceeds that
from wages, i.e. if:

and
$$s_p \neq s_w$$
$$s_p > s_w$$

The latter is the stability condition. For if $s_p < s_w$, a fall in
prices would cause a fall in demand and thus generate a further
fall in prices, and equally, a rise in prices would be cumulative.
The degree of stability of the system depends on the *difference* of
the marginal propensities, i.e. on $1/(s_p-s_w)$ which may be
defined as the "coefficient of sensitivity of income distribution",
since it indicates the change in the share of profits in income
which follows upon a change in the share of investment in output.

If the difference between the marginal propensities is small, the
coefficient will be large, and small changes in I/Y (the investment/
output relationship) will cause relatively large changes in income
distribution P/Y; and vice versa.

In the limiting case where $s_w=0$, the amount of profits is equal
to the sum of investment and capitalist consumption, i.e.:

$$P = \frac{1}{s_p} I.$$

This is the assumption implicit in Keynes' parable about the
widow's cruse—where a rise in entrepreneurial consumption
raises their total profit by an *identical* amount—and of Mr.
Kalecki's theory of profits which can be paraphrased by saying
that "capitalists earn what they spend, and workers spend what
they earn".

This model (i.e. the "special case" where $s_w=0$) in a sense is
the precise opposite of the Ricardian (or Marxian) one—here
wages (not profits) are a residue, profits being governed by the
propensity to invest and the capitalists' propensity to consume,
which represent a kind of "prior charge" on the national output.

Whereas in the Ricardian model the ultimate incidence of all taxes (other than taxes on rent) falls on profits, here the incidence of all taxes, taxes on income and profits as well as on commodities, falls on wages.[1] Assuming however that I/Y and s_p remain constant over time, the share of wages will also remain constant —i.e. real wages will increase automatically, year by year, with the increase in output per man.

If s_w is positive the picture is more complicated. Total profits will be reduced by the amount of workers' savings, S_w; on the other hand, the sensitivity of profits to changes in the level of investment will be greater, total profits rising (or falling) by a greater amount than the change in investment, owing to the consequential reduction (or increase) in workers' savings.[2]

The critical assumption is that the investment/output ratio is an independent variable. Following Harrod, we can describe the determinants of the investment/output ratio in terms of the rate of growth of output capacity (G) and the capital/output ratio, v:

$$\frac{I}{Y} = Gv \qquad \qquad \ldots \ (3)$$

In a state of continuous full employment G must be equal to the rate of growth of the "full employment ceiling", i.e. the sum of the rate of technical progress and the growth in working population (Harrod's "natural rate of growth"). For Harrods' second equation:

$$\frac{I}{Y} = s$$

we can now substitute equation (1) above:

[1] The ultimate incidence of taxes can only fall on profits (in this model) in so far as they increase s_p, the propensity to save out of *net* income after tax. Income and profits taxes, through the "double taxation" of savings, have of course the opposite effect: they reduce s_p, and thereby make the share of *net* profits in income larger than it would be in the absence of taxation. On the other hand, discriminatory taxes on dividend distribution, or dividend limitation, by keeping down both dividends and capital gains, have the effect of raising s_p. (All this applies, of course, on the assumption that the Government *spends* the proceeds of the tax—i.e. that it aims at a balanced budget. Taxes which go to augment the budget surplus will lower the share of profits in much the same way as an increase in workers' savings.)

[2] Thus if $s_p = 50\%$, $s_w = 10\%$, $I/Y = 20\%$, P/Y will be 25%; but a rise in I/Y to 21% would raise P/Y to $27 \cdot 5\%$. If on the other hand $s_w = 0$, with $s_p = 50\%$, P/Y would become 40%, but an increase in I/Y to 21% would only increase P/Y to 42%. The above formulae assume that average and marginal propensities are identical. Introducing constant terms in the consumption functions alters the relationship between P/Y and I/Y, and would reduce the *elasticity* of P/Y with respect to changes in I/Y.

$$\frac{I}{Y} = (s_p - s_w)\frac{P}{Y} + s_w.$$

Hence the "warranted" and the "natural" rates of growth are not independent of one another; if profit margins are flexible, the former will adjust itself to the latter through a consequential change in P/Y.

This does not mean that there will be an *inherent* tendency to a smooth rate of growth in a capitalist economy, only that the causes of cyclical movements lie elsewhere—not in the lack of an adjustment mechanism between s and Gv. As I have attempted to demonstrate elsewhere[1] the causes of cyclical movements should be sought in a disharmony between the entrepreneurs' *desired* growth rate (as influenced by the degree of optimism and the volatility of expectations) which governs the rate of increase of output capacity (G), and the natural growth rate (dependent on technical progress and the growth of the working population) which governs the rate of growth in output over longer periods (let us call this G'). It is the excess of G over G'—not the excess of s over $G'v$—which causes periodic breakdowns in the investment process through the growth in output capacity outrunning the growth in production.[2]

Problems of the trade cycle however lie outside the scope of this paper; and having described a model which shows the distribution of income to be determined by the Keynesian investment-savings mechanism, we must now examine its limitations. The model, as I emphasised earlier, shows the share of profits P/Y, the rate of profit on capital P/vY, and the real wage rate W/L,[3] as functions of I/Y which in turn is determined independently of P/Y or W/L. There are four different reasons why this may not be true, or be true only within a certain range.

(1) The first is that the real wage cannot fall below a certain

<hr>

[1] *Economic Journal*, March, 1954, pp. 53-71. [See my *Essays on Economic Stability and Growth*, pp. 213-32.]

[2] I/Y will therefore tend to equal Gv, not $G'v$. It may be assumed that, taking very long periods, G is largely governed by G' but over shorter periods the two are quite distinct, moreover; G' itself is not independent of G, since technical progress and population growth are both stimulated by the degree of pressure on the "full employment ceiling", which depends on G. The elasticity of response of G' to G is not infinite however: hence the greater G, the greater will be G' (the *actual* trend-rate of growth of the economy over successive cycles) but the greater also the ratio G/G' which measures the strength of cyclical forces.   [3] Where $L=$labour force.

subsistence minimum. Hence P/Y can only attain its indicated value, if the resulting real wage exceeds this minimum rate, w'. Hence the model is subject to the restriction $W/L \geqslant w'$, which we may write in the form:

$$\frac{P}{Y} \leqslant \frac{Y - w'L}{Y} \qquad \ldots \; (4)$$

(2) The second is that the indicated share of profits cannot be below the level which yields the minimum rate of profit necessary to induce capitalists to invest their capital, and which we may call the risk "premium rate", r. Hence the restriction:

$$\frac{P}{vY} > r \qquad \ldots \; (5)$$

(3) The third is that apart from a minimum rate of profit on capital there may be a certain minimum rate of profit on turnover —due to imperfections of competition, collusive agreements between traders, etc., and which we may call m, the "degree of monopoly" rate. Hence the restriction:

$$\frac{P}{Y} \geqslant m \qquad \ldots \; (6)$$

It is clear that equations (5) and (6) describe *alternative* restrictions, of which the higher will apply.

(4) The fourth is that the capital/output ratio, v, should not in itself be influenced by the rate of profit, for if it is, the investment/output ratio Gv will itself be dependent on the rate of profit. A certain degree of dependence follows inevitably from the consideration, mentioned earlier, that the value of particular capital goods in terms of final consumption goods will vary with the rate of profit,[1] so that, even with a *given technique*, v will not be independent of P/Y. (We shall ignore this point.) There is the further complication that the relation P/Y may affect v through making more or less "labour-saving" techniques profitable. In other words, at any given wage-price relationship, the producers will adopt the technique which maximises the rate of profit on capital, P/vY; this will affect (at a given G) I/Y, and hence P/Y. Hence any rise in P/Y will reduce v, and thus I/Y, and conversely,

[1] Cf. p. 220 above. In fact the whole of the Keynesian and post-Keynesian analysis dodges the problem of the measurement of capital.

any rise in I/Y will raise P/Y. If the sensitiveness of v to P/Y is great, P/Y can no longer be regarded as being determined by the equations of the model; the *technical* relation between v and P/Y will then govern P/Y whereas the savings equation (equation (2) above) will determine I/Y and thus (given G) the value of v.[1] To exclude this we have to assume that v is invariant to P/Y,[2] i.e.:

$$v = \bar{v} \qquad \ldots \ (7)$$

If equation (4) is unsatisfied, we are back at the Ricardian (or Marxian) model. I/Y will suffer a shrinkage, and will no longer correspond to Gv, but to, say, γv where $\gamma < G$. Hence the system will not produce full employment; output will be limited by the available capital, and not by labour; at the same time the classical, and not the Keynesian, reaction-mechanism will be in operation: the size of the "surplus" available for investment determining investment, not investment savings. It is possible however that owing to technical inventions, etc., and starting from a position of excess labour and underemployment (i.e. an elastic total supply of labour) the size of the surplus will grow; hence I/Y and γ will grow; and hence γ might rise above G' (the rate of growth of the "full employment ceiling", given the technical progress and the growth of population) so that in time the excess labour becomes absorbed and full employment is reached. When this happens (which we may call the stage of *developed* capitalism) wages will rise above the subsistence level, and the properties of the system will then follow our model.

If equations (5) and (6) are unsatisfied, the full employment assumption breaks down, and so will the process of growth; the economy will relapse into a state of stagnation. The interesting conclusion which emerges from these equations is that this may be the result of several distinct causes. "Investment opportunities"

[1] This is where the "marginal productivity" principle would come in but it should be emphasised that under the conditions of our model where savings are treated, not as a constant, but as a function of income distribution, the sensitiveness of v to changes in P/Y would have to be very large to overshadow the influence of G, of s_p and of s_w on P/Y. Assuming that it is large, it is further necessary to suppose that the value of P/Y as dictated by this technical relationship falls within the maximum and minimum values indicated by equations (4)-(6).

[2] This assumption does not necessarily mean that there are "fixed coefficients" as between capital equipment and labour—only that technical innovations (which are also assumed to be "neutral" in their effects) are far more influential on the chosen v than price relationships.

may be low because G is low relatively to G', i.e. the entrepreneurs' expectations are involatile, and/or they are pessimistic; hence they expect a lower level of demand for the future than corresponds to potential demand, governed by G'. On the other hand, "liquidity preference" may be too high, or the risks associated with investment too great, leading to an excessive r. (This is perhaps the factor on which Keynes himself set greatest store as a cause of unemployment and stagnation.) Finally, lack of competition may cause "over-saving" through excessive profit margins; this again will cause stagnation, unless there is sufficient compensating increase in v (through the generation of "excess capacity" under conditions of rigid profit margins but relatively free entry) to push up Gv, and hence I/T.

If, however, equations (2)-(6) are all satisfied there will be an inherent tendency to growth and an inherent tendency to full employment. Indeed the two are closely linked to each other. Apart from the case of a developing economy in the immature stage of capitalism (where equation (4) does not hold, but where $\gamma < G$), a tendency to continued economic growth will only exist when the system is only stable at full employment equilibrium—i.e. when $G \geqslant G'$.

This is a possible interpretation of the long-term situation in the "successful" capitalist economies of Western Europe and North America. If G exceeds G', the investment/output ratio I/T will not be steady in time, even if the *trend* level of this ratio is constant. There will be periodic breakdowns in the investment process, due to the growth in output capacity outrunning the possible growth in output; when that happens, not only investment, but total output will fall, and output will be (temporarily) limited by effective demand, and not by the scarcity of resources. This is contrary to the mechanics of our model, but several reasons can be adduced to show why the system will not be flexible enough to ensure full employment in the short period.

(1) First, even if profit margins are assumed to be fully flexible in a downward, as well as an upward, direction the very fact that investment goods and consumer goods are produced by different industries, with limited mobility between them, will mean that profit margins in the consumption goods industries will not fall

below the level that ensures full utilisation of resources in the consumption goods industries. A *compensating* increase in consumption goods production (following upon a fall in the production of investment goods) can only occur as a result of a transfer of resources from the other industries, lured by the profit opportunities there.

(2) Second, and more important, profit-margins are likely to be inflexible in a downward direction in the short period (Marshall's "fear of spoiling the market") even if they are flexible in the long period, or even if they possess short period flexibility in an upward direction.[1]

This applies of course not only to profit margins but to real wages as well, which in the short period may be equally inflexible in a downward direction at the *attained* level,[2] thus compressing I/Y, or rather preventing an *increase* in I/Y following upon a rise in the entrepreneurs' desired rate of expansion. Hence in the short period the shares of profits and wages tend to be inflexible for two different reasons—the downward inflexibility of P/Y and the downward inflexibility of W/L—which thus tend to reinforce the long-period stability of these shares, due to constancy of I/Y, resulting from the long period constancy of Gv and $G'v$.

We have seen how the various "models" of distribution, the Ricardian-Marxian, the Keynesian and the Kaleckian are related to each other. I am not sure where "marginal productivity" comes in, in all this—except that in so far as it has any importance it does through an extreme sensitivity of v to changes in P/Y.

---

[1] Cf. the quotation from Marshall, note 2, page 226 above.

[2] This operates through the wage-price spiral that would follow on a reduction in real wages; the prevention of such a wage-price spiral by means of investment rationing of some kind, or a "credit squeeze", is thus a manifestation of downward inflexibility of W/L.

INDEX TO AUTHORS